Discerning God's Will

Discerning God's Will:
Ignatius of Loyola's Teaching on Christian Decision Making

Jules J. Toner, S.J.

St. Louis
Institute of Jesuit Sources

Number 8 in Series III: Original Studies Composed in English

Library of Congress Catalog Card Number 91-75156
ISBN 0-912422-82-3 clothbound
ISBN 0-912422-83-1 sewn paperbound

FOR THE COMPANY OF JESUS

Fellow workers for the Kingdom of God
Companions on the way
Friends in the Lord

Contents

Preface

There are two distinct but overlapping parts of Saint Ignatius' teaching on spiritual discernment, that on discernment of spirits and that on discernment of God's will. The first of these was studied in a previous volume by the present author, *A Commentary on Saint Ignatius' Rules for the Discernment of Spirits*. His teaching on discernment of God's will includes both individual and group discernment. The present volume takes up the former, individual discernment of God's will.

Although the reader can understand a great part of this book without having studied the book on Ignatian discernment of spirits, there are nevertheless large portions where the meaning of what is said or the force of it cannot be as clearly and accurately grasped as it could be by one familiar with the analysis and the interpretation given in the earlier work.

The method followed in this study will parallel that used in the former, choosing a central text for detailed analysis and interpreting it in the light of Ignatius' other writings. In this present work, *Spiritual Exercises* [175–189] is the central text. It is interpreted within its immediate context, within the larger context of the whole *Spiritual Exercises*, and within the full context of Ignatius' other writings, including his *Autograph Directory*, his *Spiritual Diary*, his letters, the *Constitutions of the Society of Jesus*. Along with these I have used other writings which deserve careful attention as more or less authoritative secondary sources of his thought, especially the *Deliberatio Primorum Patrum* and the *Directoria* written by Jesuits.

Although there has been a considerable amount of writing in recent times on Ignatian discernment of God's will, there is still a great need for the kind of work attempted in this book. Why this is so, I will show in Chapter 1.

Ignatius' teaching on spiritual discernment does not deal with what is peculiar to Jesuit spirituality, but with matters that are essential to any Christian spirituality. From the time of Ignatius until now, the Spiritual Exercises and the teaching on discernment which is essential to them have been used with profit, not only by Jesuits and lay persons uncommitted to any particular spiritual tradition, but also by religious communities in order to help them convert more deeply to their own spirituality and to grow in it. So also these Spiritual Exercises have been used by bishops and diocesan clergy and by ministers and laity of the Protestant faith to help them in their Christian life. Therefore, in writing these studies of Ignatian teaching, I have hoped to meet not only the needs of my brother Jesuits but also those of a much wider readership, even perhaps of some who are not Christians but believe in God and strive to follow the light as they see it.

Acknowledgements

I want to take this opportunity to acknowledge a debt to John Futrell, S.J. No one to my knowledge has done more in our time to spread interest in Ignatian discernment. For his truly outstanding work we are all in his debt. However, I owe him a special debt for what I learned not only from his writings but also from an apprenticeship to him during a period of conducting workshops on group discernment and for the impetus he gave to all my subsequent work in the area of Ignatian discernment.

I also owe warm thanks to Terri Larocque and Marjorie Costello for their generous work in typing the manuscript for this book. Along with them I wish to thank the students in the course on Ignatian discernment whom I taught in the theology program at Creighton University for many summers and those with whom I have worked in seminars and workshops on Ignatian discernment over a period of twenty years. Their encouragement, questions, suggestions, and criticisms have been invaluable. Finally, I am indebted to the patient editor of this book, John Padberg, S.J., and (once again) George Ganss, S.J., for all he taught me while editing my previous book on discernment of spirits.

Chapter 1
Introduction

The Christian Vocation to Seek and Find God's Will

*J*esus said, "I do as the Father has commanded me, so that the world may know that I love the Father."[1] For this "I have come down from Heaven, not to do my own will but the will of him who sent me."[2] To do this is his "food."[3] To do always what pleases the Father,[4] this is the aim and meaning of Jesus' life.

The one who truly loves Jesus, so he himself tells us, is the one who does his will as he does the Father's will.[5] Only by doing so can we be his friends.[6] Doing his will is doing the Father's will, and the one who does the Father's will is to Jesus his brother and sister and mother.[7] To do God's will is the vocation of every Christian, of every person.

The true disciples of Jesus will not be satisfied with just doing good works; they will always be seeking to find among the good works to be done which works God wills for them to do. Like Jesus himself, who confined his mission to "the lost sheep of the tribe of Israel" because that is what his Father willed for him. Like St. Paul,

---

[1] *Jo.* 14:31.
[2] *Jo.* 6:38.
[3] *Jo.* 4:34.
[4] *Jo.* 8:29.
[5] *Jo.* 14:21–24, 15:12–14.
[6] *Jo.* 15:14.
[7] *Mt.* 12:15.

1

who turned back from preaching the Gospel in Asia or Bithynia and went rather to Macedonia because the Holy Spirit told him that that was God's will for him. Like St. Ignatius of Loyola, who gave up his pilgrim way of life and his plan to preach the Gospel to infidels in order to go to school with little boys so that he could finally be able to study theology because that was God's will for him.

In order to do God's will, we must find out what he wills. Our vocation to love God and express that love in doing his will includes a vocation to seek and find what he wills, to give him the service of our intelligence as well as of our will. Sincerity, honesty, and generosity in seeking to find God's will and to do it in every situation where we think he may have a will for our free choice of action is the fundamental and most certain test of Christian love. So it is that Holy Scripture is constantly urging us to think before doing;[8] to look carefully and try to discover what is pleasing to the Lord, what he wants us to do;[9] to abound more and more in knowledge and discernment;[10] to come to the fullest knowledge of God's will and be able to live the life he wants of us "in all its aspects."[11]

A Special Need in Our Times for Learning Discernment of God's Will

The call to seek and find God's will, which is central to the Christian vocation at all times, has been brought to the forefront of Christian consciousness with special force and urgency in our present times by the widening exercise of free choice which is offered to us and even imposed on us. In our time we find a growing recognition of the dignity of every human person and of the truth that we grow as persons by the exercise of responsible freedom. As a consequence we find a growing recognition that we ought to respect the freedom of every person, observe subsidiarity in government, and allow for coresponsibility in making decisions for communities and societies. Add to all this the ever-widening range of choice opening up for persons in our culture and the bewildering rate of change which continually calls for new decisions.

---

[8] 1 *Thess.* 5:21.
[9] *Eph.* 5:10, 15–17.
[10] *Phil.* 1:9–10.
[11] *Col.* 1:9–12.

2

As in every experience of human growth, especially in the perilous beginnings of it, we see deplorably extreme responses to the new situation that calls for growth. The suddenness with which unprecedented freedom and reponsibility have been thrust on many unprepared for it has given rise in some to an adolescent euphoria of freedom asserting itself irrationally; in others it has given rise to an irrational fear of responsibility to search for answers and make decisions. Even those who have been able to hold emotional balance are harried by the continual demands for deliberation and choice to which they are unaccustomed and not ready to handle with grace and confidence.

We see all this happening in every area of human life. As strikingly as anywhere, we see it in the Church. Under the inspiration and guidance of the Holy Spirit, a new era in the life of the Church has begun. Individuals and groups now find themselves having to make decisions about their own moral and spiritual lives and also to share in making decisions for communities to which they belong, the kinds of decisions which before were made by those in authority and passed on to them without any consultative process in the community.

A Providential Response to Our Need

With this swelling wave of freedom and responsibility for decision making and with the rapid changes in the Church, very many have felt an urgent need for enlightenment on how to go about their decisions in a truly Christian way, how to go about seeking God's will regarding the choices they have to make. It is very interesting to look back and see how divine providence appears to have been preparing a help to meet this need.

In the history of teaching on Christian discernment of God's will, Ignatius of Loyola is the central figure. It was to help others in their efforts to find and do God's will that Ignatius wrote his little book entitled *Spiritual Exercises*. In it we find a presentation of a "formal, systematical method" for seeking God's will for the individual's choice among alternatives when all of them appear to be for God's service and glory.[12] "We should even like to risk the

---

[12] See below, pp. 28–30.

3

assertion that they (the *Spiritual Exercises* of St. Ignatius) are actually the first and so far the only detailed attempt at such a systematic method''—so says Karl Rahner; and he adds that "viewing the matter broadly, they have not encountered very much understanding for their astonishing originality.''[13] Nevertheless, it is true that their fruitful use by Christians, Protestants as well as Catholics, in all states of life—bishops; priests and ministers; religious of every kind; the laity—has increased rather than diminished in the centuries since Ignatius died. They have never been more widely known and used than they are at present.

For a long time before the middle years of this century, there is reason to think, the genuine tradition of Ignatius' *Spiritual Exercises* and the discernment method embedded in them were in some measure lost. Then some years before Vatican II, there was a rediscovery and revival of interest in the genuine tradition and, consequently, a revival of interest in Ignatian teaching on discernment of spirits and discernment of God's will.[14] This renewal swelled to a powerful wave concurrently with the changes after Vatican II. At first, there was some fanfare and, along with it, some talk of the movement being a passing fad. Now, however, the enthusiasm continues to grow quietly and steadily. The reason is that, while the Ignatian method meets a need of any time in Christian history, it very especially meets the need of our own time, for reasons indicated above. It is the Ignatian teaching which has principally shaped the recent movement in the Church to emphasize individual and community discernment of God's will.

What has just been said suggests the response to a difficulty that occurs to some. They think that the Ignatian method of discerning God's will may be excellent for Jesuits and for those whose spirituality is in the Ignatian tradition, but not for others. The experience of those in every spiritual tradition among Christians (and

---

[13] Karl Rahner, S.J., *The Dynamic Element in the Church* (New York: Herder and Herder, 1964), pp. 115, 116. Hereafter referred to as *Dynamic Element*.

[14] Although discernment of spirits is an instrument in discerning God's will, the two are not one and the same thing. Each can be done without the other. See John C. Futrell, S.J., "Ignatian Discernment," *Studies in the Spirituality of Jesuits*, vol. 2, no. 2 (April, 1970), p. 48 (hereafter referred to as "Ignatian Discernment") and Jules Toner, S.J., *A Commentary on St. Ignatius' Rules for the Discernment of Spirits* (St. Louis: The Institute of Jesuit Sources, 1982), pp. xii, 12, 235, 249–250, 289. Hereafter referred to as *A Commentary*.

even among some non-Christians) has shown that the *Spiritual Exercises* of Ignatius and, in particular, his teaching on seeking and finding God's will are valuable for every Christian.[15]

Present Confusion in Writing on Ignatian Discernment of God's Will

As might be expected, the new need for Ignatian teaching on how to discern God's will and the resurgent interest in returning to his genuine teaching have brought with them plentiful literature on the subject. The many popular articles that have appeared could convey the impression that the fundamental concepts involved in such discernment are clearly understood and that there is a generally accepted interpretation, at least of the essentials. The real situation is surprisingly different. Any critical study of more serious writing uncovers areas where important concepts remain insufficiently analyzed and, therefore, leave areas of confusion. It also uncovers sharp disagreements about fundamentals. If one listens to the many who never write on discernment but do read others' opinions, and who, above all, direct others in discerning God's will—if one listens to them, the same unclarity and disagreements can be heard. In short, there is no well-developed and more or less fully agreed-upon understanding of what Ignatius was saying on which one could base a set of practical directives and expect them to be generally acceptable to the serious students of Ignatius.

The most significant opinions will be documented, classified, and critically evaluated in the course of this book. But for the sake of a general background and for the sake of showing the reader that what I am trying to do needs doing, I shall right now merely note the many basic questions on which there are disagreement and often head-on conflicts.

Two correlative concepts that especially are still in need of conceptual analysis are God's will as the object of discernment and the limits of discernment. There does not seem to be any notable controversy about these concepts, for the reason that they have not been investigated deeply enough to make them matters of serious controversy. As will be shown, however, much misunderstanding

---

[15] Jules Toner, *A Commentary*, pp. 15–16.

5

of, and skepticism about, discernment of God's will have been the result of a lack of precision regarding these concepts.

Although the necessity of indifference to all but God's will as a condition for sound discernment is admirably stressed and its nature well explained, there are still questions of practical importance which have not been dealt with or, if they have, the results have not become widely known.

The most diverse and most sharply opposed interpretations are found regarding the three Ignatian times for, and modes of, seeking God's will. There are clashing views on what Ignatius means by each of his three times or occasions for reaching a good decision, on how each of the three corresponding modes of discernment is to be carried out, on their relationship and their comparative value for finding God's will.

Regarding the first time for discernment, there are different, even contradictory, answers to such questions as these. Is it a miraculous event? Is it a mystical phenomenon? Does it necessarily involve consolation without previous cause? Is it altogether unusual, a rare experience, or is it more or less common?

Most of all, when we turn to the second time for, and mode of, finding God's will by spiritual consolation and desolation and by discernment of spirits, we find many differences of interpretation regarding the following: the nature of spiritual consolation and desolation; the differences between spiritual consolation with and without previous cause; the value of each of these kinds of consolation for second-time discernment of God's will; the way of going about this mode of discernment. In all these matters, the differences are neither merely nuances nor notable differences which have little or no practical consequences. The views are substantively different and logically entail very different ways of practicing discernment of God's will—so much so that one view sometimes implies an outright denial of the other as giving a valid mode of discernment.

Even if there were a common understanding of how to carry out the second Ignatian mode of discernment, we would still have to face other questions of practical importance on which there is wide disagreement. One of these centers on the third mode of discernment, which is carried on by weighing the foreseen advantages and disadvantages of opposing alternatives for God's service and glory. Does this mode have any value for finding God's will independently of the second? Some say it does; some say it does not; some even go so far as to say that it is merely a defective form of the second mode and has no use except as a preliminary exercise leading to the second mode. Some grudgingly grant it to be of some independent value for lesser decisions when it is not possible to reach a decision by the first or second modes. Ignatius, they say, did not allow for a decision about one's state of life to be made with the help of the third mode. But others say it is a distinct and independent mode and that in the mind of Ignatius it is of equal practical value with the first and the second, a less noble but a more secure mode. Even when all that is settled, there is still dispute regarding the function of the second way in the third-time election.

The relationship of the three modes in practice involves the preceding issues, but can also raise more issues to which there are opposing answers even for those who could agree on how to do second-time discernment and on the value of the third-time discernment. This is true even more so for those who disagree. Are the modes really fully distinct or do they merely form one complete mode of discernment? If they are distinct, is each autonomous? If we do use more than one mode and if the conclusions from the two modes conflict, what is the discerner to do?

From reading what the literature says about "seeking confirmation" for a decision, one might believe that at least here no problem exists. The fact is, as I think I show, that the common understanding of this step in one way goes beyond anything Ignatius says about it and in another way falls far short of what is shown in his own practice.

Finally, there is the crucially important question: Can the conclusion of a sound discernment of God's will justifiably be held to as certain or only as highly probable or merely the best decision one can reach but without even sound probability? Opinions clash, but little is done to establish any of them; and the more common opinion seems to ignore Ignatius' own statements.

Two things are surprising about what has happened. The first is that there should be so many and such fundamental disagreements among Ignatian scholars on discernment of God's will. That there should be disagreements we expect, but not so many touching on what is so basic to practice. The second surprising aspect of recent developments is that, despite all the confusing disagreements and uncertainty, Ignatian discernment has continued to be fruitfully used. It would be a grave misunderstanding if what I have been saying were taken to imply that I think the discernment which has been going on has not been effective in finding God's will. Why I believe that, despite all, it has been effective and why, nevertheless, I think it is imperative that we do all we can to improve our understanding and practice of discerning God's will—to answer these questions will take most of the chapters on our relationship with God in discernment, on the necessary conditions for sound discernment, and on the reason for trusting the conclusion of a sound discernment.

The Purpose of This Book

Is it possible to point out the radical cause or causes of the deplorable confusion among Ignatian interpreters? What my own reading has led me to suspect is that the root of our trouble is the large proportion of writing, even sometimes brilliant speculation, which is not founded on any exacting exegesis of the Ignatian text. (It may be well to point out that copious references to the works of Ignatius and copious quotations are not signs of such exegesis.) Karl Rahner finds that theologians have not really taken the *Spiritual Exercises* with theological seriousness[16] and that the work of the commentators is characterized by "meagreness and lack of precision."[17] John Futrell, making some exceptions, seems to incline toward a similar judgment.[18] Ironically, Daniel Gil thinks that Rahner's own essay at understanding consolation without previous cause and its role fails because the Ignatian text is bereft of exegesis.[19] It is with hope of making some helpful contribution to the needed exegesis and, as a consequence, to a more sound and generally agreed-upon understanding of Ignatian discernment that I have undertaken this book.

In accord with that aim, I shall try to analyze the relevant texts

---

[16] *Dynamic Element*, pp. 84–89, 94–109.

[17] Ibid., p. 116.

[18] "Ignatian Discernment," pp. 86–87, note 3.

[19] *Daniel Gil*, S.J., *La Consolación Sin Causa Precedente* (Rome: Centrum Ignatianum Spiritualitatis, 1971), p. 90, note 11.

with as much precision as I can, even if it becomes wearisome. For what I am principally striving to achieve in this work is not to move the reader to seek God's will or even to interest those who are not already interested in Ignatian discernment; rather, I am striving to reach as accurate an understanding as I possibly can of what Ignatius said. Given the state of Ignatian scholarship that calls for writing with this aim, I cannot allow any desire for reaching and pleasing a wide audience to interfere with it.

While my purpose is to give a greater accuracy and precision to Ignatius' practical directives on discerning God's will, it is not to produce a new directory, that is, a more or less complete, step-by-step set of directives for carrying out the search for God's will. Any work in that direction should be based on the results of a prior task—an undertaking to which I hope this book will be some contribution. At present, we would have to draw up a number of diverse directories according to a number of diverse interpretations of Ignatius' teaching.[20]

Ignatius' Own Theology of Discerning God's Will

To say that my aim is to reach an accurate understanding of Ignatius' practical directives is not an adequate statement. Implied in that aim is my effort to explicitate Ignatius' theology of discerning God's will. By the latter I mean the theology which was working in his own mind, shaping his attitudes toward discernment, shaping his own practice and his practical directions to others, and justifying to him his trust in the conclusion of discernment soundly carried out. Ignatius never presented a theology of discernment in any developed or systematic form. It has to be gathered from indications here and there in his writing. It is of utmost importance to be alert to these indications and to draw out their meaning if we are to interpret his directives intelligently and answer the questions which

---

[20] There is still nothing better to replace the Official Directory of 1599. Some commentaries may be more accurate or more enlightening on this or that particular point; but, all in all, the 1599 directory is still far and away the best available: more inclusive, orderly, clear, and accurate. The text may be found in *Directoria Exercitiorum Spiritualium* (1540–1599), MHSJ (Rome, 1955), pp. 562–751, hereafter referred to as *DirSpEx* MHSJ. An authorized English translation was published under the title *Directory of the Spiritual Exercises of Our Holy Father Ignatius* (London: The Manresa Press, 1925).

are at issue among Ignatian scholars. Doing so is an essential part of sound exegesis.

In his theology of discernment, we shall find no heady speculations, not even very sober ones which have no clear bearing on the practice of discernment. As we shall see, Ignatius' special theology of discernment is sometimes subtly nuanced and demands a keen power of distinguishing similar concepts; but always it has direct practical significance. What we may look for, and I hope to show we can find, is the theology of a devout and practical spiritual person with keen insight, a theology issuing directly in a method for seeking to find God's will in concrete situations for choice and justifying the method and its results by the truths of Christian faith.

If it would not sound pretentious, I could say that Ignatius' theology of discernment is a special theological epistemology. For it is concerned with a series of epistemological issues such as the limits within which we can find God's will; the necessary conditions for sound discernment; the several possible kinds of evidence for God's will; the way to evaluate these and draw a conclusion; the firmness of assent which can justifiably be given to a conclusion. When the indications of Ignatius' thought on these matters are put together, they yield a surprisingly coherent and subtle body of thought which constitutes an unarticulated theological epistemology—theological, because his Christian faith governs all his thinking in these matters.

It would be a bad misunderstanding if what I am trying to do were confused with an effort to develop a theology of Ignatian discernment by bringing to bear on what Ignatius says my own or another's developed and systematized theological or philosophical insights in ways that never occurred to him.[21] Such a speculative enterprise should be done on the basis of sound, well-established exegesis of the Ignatian text; but, as already indicated, there is reason

---

[21] As is done, e.g., by Gaston Fessard, S.J., *La Dialectique des Exercices de Saint Ignace de Loyola* (Paris, 1956 and 1966); Edouard Pousset, S.J., *Life in Faith and Freedom: An Essay Presenting Gaston Fessard's Analysis of the Dialectic of the Spiritual Exercises of St. Ignatius.* Translated and edited by Eugene L. Donahue, S.J. (St. Louis: The Institute of Jesuit Sources, 1980); Karl Rahner, "The Logic of the Concrete Individual Knowledge in Ignatius Loyola," *Dynamic Element,* pp. 84–170; Harvey D. Egan, S.J., *The Spiritual Exercises and the Ignatian Mystical Horizon* (St. Louis: The Institute of Jesuit Sources, 1976), hereafter referred to as *Mystical Horizon.*

to think that as yet we lack an exegesis which is adequate for that purpose. Much work already done may need considerable revision when we do achieve a credible exegesis.

Chapter 2
God's Fundamental Will for Human Life

F or those not familiar with Ignatian teaching on discernment
of God's will, the limited meaning of the term "God's will" in the
context of such discernment must be clearly distinguished from the
many meanings it may have in other contexts. Before making the
necessary distinctions, however, it is necessary first of all to understand what Ignatius believed is God's basic or fundamental will[1]
regarding human life. For it is in the light of this fundamental will
that Ignatius sees God's will regarding every detail of human life
in every situation and, in particular, regarding every human's free
choice.

---

[1] In this context, "will" is to be understood in the conative sense, that is, willing an end
to be achieved and the acts to be performed as means to that end.

Ignatius was a theologian, even a great one, in the sense of having through mystical experience an experiential knowledge of God and of the Christian mysteries.[2] In the realm of teachable truth, Ignatius was also a great theologian, but not a speculative one. His theology is purely practical; it revolves around how to find and respond to God in all things and, especially, how to find God's will and do it for the glory of God. His theology of seeking and finding God's will is found embedded in his immediately practical instructions and counsels on how to prepare for and go about discerning it and in his descriptions of his own efforts to do so.[3]

Although interesting to note, it is not, therefore, surprising to see that what Ignatius has to say about the will of God regarding human life is not to be found so much in what he says directly about it but rather in his remarks about what we should will. For, in accord with the Christian Gospel, Ignatius thinks that we ought always to strive to conform our will to God's will. Therefore, we can find what Ignatius sees God's basic will to be regarding our human lives by seeing what he says our own basic will ought to be.

Leaving aside all questions about what our will ought to be in any individual situation or even in any particular kind of situation, let us ask what Ignatius thought our basic will should be; the will, that is, which should inform and ground our every act of willing, of which our every act of willing should be a modification or a development. Ignatius leaves no room for uncertainty about his answer to this question. In every act of willing we should explicitly

[2] See Ignatius' *Autobiografía* and *Diario Espiritual (1544–1545)* in *Obras Completas de San Ignacio de Loyola* (Madrid: Biblioteca de Autores Cristianos, 1977), pp. 89–159, 318–386. Hereafter referred to as *Obras Completas*. There are several English translations of the *Autobiografía*. The most widely used is that by William J. Young, S.J., *St. Ignatius' Own Story* (Chicago, 1956, now obtainable from Loyola University Press). To my knowledge, there is only one English translation of the *Diario Espiritual*, that by William J. Young, *The Spiritual Journal of St. Ignatius Loyola* (Woodstock, MD.: Woodstock College Press, 1958). Hereafter referred to as *Spiritual Journal*.
Ignatius the Theologian by Hugo Rahner, S.J., trans. Michael Barry (New York: Herder and Herder, 1968) provides an excellent overall treatment. There are a number of very interesting studies of Ignatius' mystical illuminations and mystical life: Adolf Haas, S.J., "The Mysticism of St. Ignatius according to His *Spiritual Diary*," *Ignatius Loyola, His Personality and Spiritual Heritage, 1556–1596*, ed. Friedrich Wulf, S.J. (St. Louis: the Institute of Jesuit Sources, 1977); Elmer O'Brien, *Varieties of Mystical Experience* (New York: Holt, Rinehart and Winston), pp. 244–254; Hugo Rahner, *The Vision of St. Ignatius in the Chapel of La Storta*, 2nd ed. (Rome: Centrum Ignatianum Spiritualitatis, 1979).

[3] See all references in note 2.

or at least implicitly be willing the glory of God. All his writings are filled with the phrase "for the glory of God our Lord" or with variations on it, such as "for the divine glory," "for God's glory and praise," "for the glory and service," or "for the glory and honor of God our Lord." These phrases occur in almost every page of his writings and sometimes in almost every paragraph.[4] God's glory expresses the meaning of Ignatius' life; the highest, deepest, and constant aspiration of his heart; the motive and guiding principle of all his thoughts, choices, and actions. He thinks it should be so for everyone.

Characteristic of Ignatius' spirit and necessary for a more precise expression of what he thinks our basic will should be is the addition of the words "more" and "greater." We should always will what is *more* for the glory of God, what is for his *greater* glory, for his greater praise, honor, or service.[5] This shift to the greater, the more, is not to be passed off as a mere idiosyncrasy of Ignatius' fiery and aspiring temperament but of no great significance either for understanding his belief regarding God's basic will or for a theology (both speculative and practical) of discerning God's will. As we shall see, it is of central, even essential, significance for an understanding and justification of Ignatius' teaching on discerning God's will.[6]

If we put this matter in terms of ends and means, as Ignatius does, God's greater glory (honor, praise) is the ultimate end of human action and is to be sought in every action; every choice among actions is a choice among means to that end. As we shall see,

---

[4] See *The Constitutions of the Society of Jesus*, translated with an Introduction and a Commentary by George E. Ganss, S.J. (St. Louis: The Institute of Jesuit Sources, 1970), p. 8. Hereafter referred to as *ConsSJComm*.

[5] See e.g. *Cons*MHSJ, [138, 161, 230, 258, 266, 305, 308, 343, 349, 437, 510, 603], etc.

[6] An indication of how thoroughly this understanding of God's fundamental will regarding human life—always for the better, for the greater glory—penetrated all Ignatius' thought can be found in Rule 5 of his second set of rules for discernment of spirits (Sp. Ex., [333]). There he asserts that any mental process which begins with holy thoughts and affections and, therefore, seems to be from the Holy Spirit, but which ends in a desire for what is less good than what was previously intended, is not from the Holy Spirit but from the evil spirit. Never, in Ignatius' thought, does God, in any concrete situation for human action, positively will or lead us to will what is, in that situation, less good, less for his glory in us.

therefore, his criterion or norm for choice among actions is greater conduciveness to that end.[7]

The Glory of God: Ignatius' Meaning

If clarity about what is God's basic will according to Ignatius is best reached through what he says our fundamental will ought to be, so also understanding of the latter depends on understanding what he means by the glory of God.

When Ignatius uses this phrase, "the glory of God," he sometimes has in mind the meaning of glory as our cognitive and affective response to what we perceive as praiseworthy; in the scholastic definition *clara cum laude notitia*, "clear knowledge with praise." He certainly understood that praising God in the sense of recognizing and declaring his greatness is to give him glory and that praising him in this way is itself a gift of God to us, a constitutive element of the happiness for which God made us.[8] But such a notion of glory is altogether inadequate for understanding Ignatius' ordinary meaning of such phrases as the "glory of God" or "praise of God" or "honor of God" as the end of human actions. (All these are commonly synonymous in his writings.)[9] For in its deepest Ignatian meaning, glory means participation in God, transformation of created life by its union with God in Christ, in which God is present and revealed to his creatures. This glory of God in creation is for Ignatius praise of God, honor to God, declaration of his beauty and goodness and wisdom and power in a more fundamental sense than any human thoughts and words and affections about God.

Most of all, for him the glory of God refers to the kingdom of God in its eschatological fullness; the goal of human history, when all in the kingdom are filled with divine splendor and totally divinized in Christ, the refulgence of God. It includes also every partial beginning of that life in human history, all that we are and

---

[7] *SpEx*, [23]. See George E. Ganss, ed., *Jesuit Religious Life Today* (St. Louis: The Institute of Jesuit Sources, 1977), pp. 17–20.

[8] See Thomas Aquinas, *Summa Theologica*, II–IIæ, q. 132, a.1, ad 1. For an interesting and reasonable speculation on what in the thought of Peter Lombard and Thomas Aquinas might have influenced Ignatius' thought on the glory and praise of God and have saved him, if he needed saving, from thinking that God created the universe in order to get honor, praise, or glory for himself rather than for us, see Ganss, *ConsSJComm*, pp. 10–11, 18–19.

[9] George Ganss, *ConsSJComm*, p. 8.

do and become inasmuch as these make God's life and loving kindness in Jesus Christ present and manifest in human life. It includes our lives of prayer and contemplation, our courageous and magnanimous deeds of practical charity to those in any spiritual or material need, our endurance of pain or humiliation in the service of God and neighbor—all that is involved in being one with Christ and carrying on his mission of revealing the Father in his person and deeds and in bringing about the fullness of the kingdom of God.

Nowhere does Ignatius in one text give such a description of what he means by the glory of God. However, when we read him carefully, we find that he uses a variety of other phrases which in context are equivalents of, or express facets of, what he means; and these phrases refer to the elements in the foregoing description. Thus, to will always the glory of God is to seek always the "salvation and perfection" of our own selves and of our neighbor. It is to grow and to help others to grow spiritually.[10] Our spiritual growth is "for his (God's) honor and praise,"[11] "for the divine glory."[12] Our will should be that in everything "God our Lord may be glorified through our bodies and souls."[13] The glory is what God works in us and through us in other persons. It is "the salvation and perfection of persons,"[14] "the knowledge and love of God and the salvation of their [our neighbors'] souls,"[15] "the ultimate end for which they were created."[16] Praise and honor to God; progress in knowledge and love of God and neighbor; knowing, loving and following Christ Jesus; salvation; the ultimate supernatural end—these phrases are scattered through Ignatius' writings and express inseparable and mutually overlapping aspects of what he means when he speaks of the glory of God.[17] He very largely uses them interchangeably.

It is clear, then, that for Ignatius the glory of God which we should will in every act of willing is God's glory *in us* and, as we

---

[10] *Cons* MHSJ, [3].
[11] Ibid., [135].
[12] Ibid., [136].
[13] Ibid., [300].
[14] Ibid., [4].
[15] Ibid., [446].
[16] Ibid., [307]; and see [156, 813].
[17] Ibid., [258, 360, 508, 547, 605, 622a, 803].

shall see, *for us*. We are "an image of the most holy Trinity and able to hold its glory;[18] we are vessels of divine glory. The glory of God is the kingdom of God in us and among us. In truth, it is human persons insofar as they are alive with God's life in Christ and are manifesting that life in the world.

The Greater Glory: Ignatius' Meaning

The glory that human persons are now is obviously a very limited glory, not only received by finite beings in a world of time and history but also in a wounded world, where "all have sinnned and fall short of the glory of God."[19] Destined as we are to "an eternal weight of glory,"[20] the glory we reach in this world is always unfinished; and our call in Christ is always to the greater glory, as by God's power we, "beholding the glory of the Lord, are being changed into his likeness from one degree of glory to another."[21]

That Ignatius' attention should fasten on the imperfection of God's present glory in us and its endless perfectibility is readily understandable in terms of his aspiring temperament and driving energy. However, as said above, his emphasis on the greater glory, greater praise and service, and so on, is not merely an expression of his temperament. It is rather of decisive importance for expressing with theological accuracy what he thinks our basic will ought to be. It also involves another key idea in Ignatian spirituality, one which illuminates his teaching on our fundamental will, on God's fundamental will, and on the importance of discerning God's particular will in concrete situations for choice.

This key idea concerns the way God brings his glory to be. Not only is God's glory coming to be in human persons; it is achieved by God through the free decisions and actions of human persons. They are persons called not only to be recipients and vessels of divine glory but also to be intelligent and free co-workers with God in achieving it and in preparing the world finally to receive fully the gift of uncreated glory, God himself.[22] The "divine majesty"

---

[18] . . . *uno imagen de la santísima Trinidad y capaz de su gloria* (*Obras Completas*, p. 684)
[19] *Rom.* 3:23.
[20] *2 Cor.* 4:17, *Col.* 3:3–4.
[21] *2 Cor.* 3:18.
[22] *SpEx*, [234].

17

is a phrase that appears over and over in the writing of Ignatius; he is always in joyful awe of the transcendent God. But he is always finding the majestic, transcendent God immanent in all things, not only present in and living in them, but also working in and through them, and giving himself, especially in and through human persons, to other human persons.[23]

Implicit in this insight of faith is the idea that only by calling into being an incomplete universe, an unfinished created glory, is it possible for God to create the great glory of persons who have the amazing destiny and dignity of being his intelligent, loving, and free co-workers.

In fact, it would not at all conflict with Ignatius' cast of mind to think not only of this life but even of heavenly life as dynamic, as a continuing growth of divine glory in us, glory given to us through each other in Christ, an endless seeking and finding and sharing of the endless depths of divine beauty and its expression in creation.[24]

The Glory of God in Sacred Scripture

The better we understand the meaning of God's glory, the better we will be able to understand how Ignatius conceives of God's basic will regarding creation and what our basic will should be, and so be able to understand his theology of discerning God's will and the crucial significance for human life of such discerning. For this reason it seems justifiable, even called for, to reflect on the meaning of the glory of God in Sacred Scripture, which directly or indirectly formed Ignatius' thinking. Such a reflection offers many advantages for our purpose. The words of Sacred Scripture about God's glory, especially in the Johannine and Pauline writings, are richer in explicit theological content and more moving rhetorically than those of Ignatius. Growth in faith, hope, and charity, knowledge and love of God, the salvation and perfection of souls, praise and honor to God, the ultimate supernatural end—such phrases as these in Ignatius' writing point to the same reality as the words of Scripture but do not touch us with the same power or convey to us the flame and splendor of glory that we experience in the words of Paul or John.

---

[23] Ibid., [235–236]. See also Jules Toner, *A Commentary*, pp. 157–160.

[24] See Edmund J. Fortman, S.J., *Everlasting Life after Death* (New York: Alba House, 1976), pp. 206–212, 313–316.

Reflection on the glory of God in Sacred Scripture will uncover to us some of the riches contained in, but hidden by, Ignatius' concise but rather pedestrian formulas.

There is no need for a thorough study of "glory" in Holy Scripture, its nuances in various contexts, and its growth of meaning through salvation history;[25] nor is there need for a fully developed theology of glory based on Holy Scripture. All we need is a brief recall and synthesis of some principal ways in which it speaks of God's glory.

The basic scriptural meaning of God's glory as a created phenomenon in this world is the finite manifestation of his presence and of his uncreated glory. These finite manifestations of God's presence, power, splendor, goodness, and wisdom shade the uncreated glory that is too much for us to endure.[26] In some way and measure, all the goodness of creation is God's glory. He is present in all things, revealing himself, his love and power and wisdom, surrounding and penetrating us with his glory.[27] "Heaven and earth are full of your glory."

But within creation there are special glories, special signs of God's special presence. In the Old Testament there is the cloud by day and the pillar of fire by night during the exodus;[28] the cloud and the fire, thunder and lightning and earthquake on Mt. Sinai;[29] the splendor on the face of Moses after speaking with God, which he had to cover with a veil;[30] the cloud that filled the temple of Solomon.[31]

The created glory in which the uncreated splendor of God is made present and revealed beyond all expectation or understanding but is also hidden and subdued to our human capacity is Jesus. He is the glory of all divine glories in this world, the one to whom all the other glories of God in the world lead, in whom they find their

---

[25] For an account of the development of the meaning of "glory" in the Bible, see John L. McKenzie, S.J., *Dictionary of the Bible* (Milwaukee: Bruce, 1965), pp. 313–315.

[26] *Exod.* 33:18–33.

[27] *Rom.* 1:18–23.

[28] *Exod.* 13:22; 40:34–38.

[29] *Exod.* 19:16–18; 24:16.

[30] *Exod.* 34:29–35.

[31] 1 *Kings* 8:10–11.

ultimate meaning. For he is the eternal Son of God become man: "We beheld his glory, the glory as of the only Son of the Father."[32] To him, before the world was, God gave the fullness of his own eternal life and glory.[33] He is God's Word,[34] in whom God expresses his whole life and glory. "He reflects the glory of God and bears the very stamp of his nature."[35] In the Word made flesh the Godhead dwells fully in a human body.[36] He is "God with us," revealing himself to us: "No one has seen God, the only Son has made him known."[37] He is light from light, eternal light come into the world to be light for us.[38] He alone has looked on the face of God and lived;[39] but now whoever sees him sees the Father,[40] and "God has shone into our heart to give the light of the knowledge of the glory of God in the face of Christ."[41]

Not only is Jesus the glory of the Father *for* us, the sign of the Father's presence to us, the revelation of his love, power, and wisdom; he is also God's glory *in* us who accept him with living faith. We are "full of glory,"[42] filled with "the riches of the glory of this mystery, which is Christ in you."[43] He, the light from light become the light of the world, by living in us who believe, makes us "children of light"[44] and "the light of the world."[45] The glory we are as creatures made to God's image is transformed into the glory Christ is as the Incarnate Son of God, whose fullness we are.[46] Inasmuch as we open ourselves to receive Christ by faith, the glory of God who is love is poured into us: "We rejoice in our hope of sharing the glory of God . . . and hope does not disappoint us,

---

[32] *Jo.* 1:14.
[33] *Jo.* 17:5, 24.
[34] *Jo.* 1:1.
[35] *Heb.* 1:3.
[36] *Col.* 2:9.
[37] *Jo.* 1:18.
[38] *Jo.* 1:4, 9.
[39] *Jo.* 1:18, 6:46; 1 *Jo.* 4:12; 1 *Cor.* 13:12.
[40] *Jo.* 14:7–9.
[41] 2 *Cor.* 4:6.
[42] *Eph.* 2:27.
[43] *Col.* 1:27.
[44] *Eph.* 5:8.
[45] *Mt.* 5:14.
[6] *Eph.* 1:22–23; *Col.* 2:9–10.

because God's love has been poured into our hearts through the Holy Spirit which has been given to us."[47] Our union of mutual love in Christ makes present and reveals the union of Christ with his Father and the Father's love for us. Our union is God's glory: "The glory which thou hast given me I have given to them, that they may be one even as we are one, I in them and thou in me, that they may become perfectly one, so that the world may know that thou hast sent me and hast loved them even as thou hast loved me."[48]

Jesus, then, is the Father's glory, and we are called to be the glory of Jesus[49] and in him, with him, and through him to be the Father's glory. When Jesus is glorified, the Father is glorified in him: "Now is the Son of Man glorified, and in him God is glorified."[50] When we are glorified, Jesus is glorified in us.[51] Jesus prayed for his own glorification that in him the Father might be glorified: "Father . . . glorify thy Son that the Son may glorify thee."[52] So too, we are called to pray and to seek in all that we do or endure that God may glorify all of us, the Mystical Christ, so that in us Christ the head may be glorified. "In all of you God is to be glorified through Jesus Christ."[53]

The absolute reign of God through the Holy Spirit in each human life and all human lives together; the fullest sharing in God's life of loving communion and joy; oneness with Christ, with the Father in Christ, with each other in Christ, as he and the Father are one; Christ all in all, the whole Christ come to maturity—this is the kingdom, this is the glory. The kingdom is begun and is yet to come more fully. The glory is, but is unfinished. It is glory in the making.

Consequent Ignatian Understanding of God's Basic Will

With a richer understanding of what Ignatius means by glory, we can now return to our main line of thought. Ignatius, we said, speaks more about what our basic will should be than he does about

---

[47] *Rom.* 5:2, 5.
[48] *Jo.* 17:22–23.
[49] 2 *Cor.* 8:23; 1 *Thess.* 2:12; 2 *Thess.* 1–10,12 and 2:14; *Eph.* 1:18.
[50] *Jo.* 13:31. See also 12:23–28; 17:1, 4–5.
[51] *Jo.* 17:10.
[52] *Jo.* 17:1.
[53] 1 *Peter* 4:11.

what God's basic will is regarding human life. But, since he believes our basic will should conform to God's, whatever he says about the former enables us to see how he understands the latter. If, then, Ignatius believes our basic will should be always for the glory of God, even for the greater glory of God, that is, his glory *in us*, then it should come as no surprise to find him declaring that "we ought always to take for granted that what the Lord of the whole world works in persons [*las animas racionales*][54] is either for the sake of giving us greater glory or for the sake of lessening our evil" when we are not disposed to receive the greater glory.[55] There are two things regarding this declaration of faith on which some brief reflection is called for. The first is the phrase "to give us greater glory." The second is a reflection on the absolute faith involved in this declaration.

To speak of God's basic will, as Ignatius does here, is a shift from his ordinary expression "for the greater glory of God," but should not be surprising if we have understood what he, in accord with Sacred Scripture, means by the glory of God. To say that God always wills to give us greater glory (or to lessen harm to us if we do not have good dispositions) expresses in a condensed statement what Ignatius is leading the exercitant in the Spiritual Exercises to see and feel in the climactic exercise of the whole Spiritual Exercises, the "Contemplation for Love." In this exercise we can see Ignatius' intense faith in a love beyond all our imagining, the love of God who gives me (each one) being in his own image; who for me creates all the universe; who lives in me and for me lives in all things; who works in me and for me in all things; who saves me from sin and death through the life and death and resurrection of his Son incarnate; who through his Spirit draws and guides me; from whom all creation descends as a fountain of shining gifts from the sun of his uncreated glory.[56]

In Ignatius' thought, therefore, to will God's greater glory is to will our own greater glory, or greater fullness of godlike life; and to will our greater glory is to will the greater glory of God, the

---

[54] For justification of this translation, see Ganss, *ConsSJComm*, p. 77, note 10.

[55] *Obras Completas*, p. 622.

[56] *SpEx*, [234–237]. See also *Letters of St. Ignatius of Loyola*, trans. William J. Young (Chicago: Loyola University Press, 1959), p. 125. Hereafter referred to as *LettersIgn*.

created manifestation of his uncreated glory, of his infinite life. What we have said so far about this great mystery of God's glory is altogether inadequate until we insert it into the mystery of Christ. The Father wills all the glory for his Christ. Since we are the members of Christ, his fullness, with him forming the whole of Christ, and the Father loves us with the very love with which he loves Jesus, all the glory is ours. And since all the glory in the whole Christ is of the Father and directed to the Father, all the glory is the Father's glory. So God's basic will regarding the universe is his greater glory in Christ, the whole Christ. It is all for us, all for Jesus, all for the Father. "For all things are yours . . . and you are Christ's; and Christ is God's."[57]

The understanding we have reached of what Ignatius means by "the greater glory of God" enables us to avoid two main errors about God's basic will regarding our lives. On the one hand, we escape the danger of losing a theocentric and Christocentric focus on life and of slipping into an egocentric focus or at least a focus centered on humanity. On the other hand, we avoid thinking that God is out to gain something for himself by willing his greater glory and calling us to do so—as if he were not infinite fullness of being, infinitely beyond all need in himself, having need only in us because of his infinite love for us.[58] The greater glory that God wills for us is our greater participation in his eternal and infinite glory. It is *from* God its giver and *to* God who is glorified in us. It is *in* us as our fullness of life and *for* us whose happiness is in being glory to God and giving his glory to each other. In us in Christ, God, who is all in all, is present and living and revealing himself. In order that we do not let slip this inclusive meaning of the term "God's glory," the terms "our glory" or simply "the glory," both God's and ours, will from here on be used interchangeably with it.

The second reflection on Ignatius' declaration of faith in God's basic will regarding human life is to note how enormous is the faith that is involved in really believing it if we also believe that God is infinitely wise and powerful. Despite its foundation in Sacred Scripture and Christian tradition, Ignatius' stark declaration of belief

[57] 1 *Cor*. 3:21–23.
[58] See Jules Toner, *The Experience of Love*, pp. 75–76.

seems naively unrealistic in face of the ugly reality of human history. On the other hand, if we really believe that God is not only infinitely wise and powerful but also infinitely loving, how can we back away from believing that he wills always what is *ultimately*, even if not immediately, what will bring us greater glory?[59] To say this does not do away with the mystery of evil and pain in a world created by the God of love. Rather, it intensifies the mystery by holding clearly and firmly to the opposing terms that constitute it.

Few men or women in history could be thought to have greater faith in God's love or have experienced it more intimately and intensely than Ignatius did. It is, then, not surprising that, despite all the pain and evil of life with which he was so broadly and deeply familiar, his faith in what he declares to be God's basic will for us never wavered. It was the foundation stone of his own life and of his *Spiritual Exercises*. Without awareness of his belief in this fundamental will of God, no one can understand his teaching on how to find God's will in concrete situations for choice. Without such belief, no one can fully carry through his way of discerning God's will regarding these situations or, as we shall see, have solid ground for trusting the conclusions reached by such discernment.

---

[59] See below, chapter 16.

Chapter 3
God's Will as Object of Discernment

*T*he principle that whatever God wills in regard to our lives is to give us greater glory applies to his will in all its many different modes: his imperative or appealing or exhortative will, his positive or permissive will, and his necessitating or non-necessitating will. It applies to his will regarding what we do and what is done to us, to what each individual ought to do and what everyone ought to do. And so on.

Limiting God's Basic Will to God's Will as the Goal of Discernment

But it is not God's will in its basic meaning or in all its modes that is to be sought through Ignatian discernment. God's will as the object of discernment has very severe limits; it is only a fraction of

25

all that God wills concretely regarding our lives. These limits must be made clear if we are to avoid serious, even ludicrous distortions of Ignatius' teaching. After we have set down these limits, unless the context clearly indicates otherwise, any reference to God's will is to be understood as referring to his will in the limited meaning which it has as object of Ignatian discernment.

It is obvious that whatever limits are set for God's will in this meaning are also limits for the meaning of Ignatian discernment of God's will, and the other way around. Some of these limits are, however, more readily seen from the side of God's will and some from the side of discernment. For the present, our focus will remain on the former limits; further on, we will focus on the latter.[1]

God's Will Limited to an Act to Be Done in a Concrete Situation

We can immediately and without delay put aside any idea that Ignatian discernment pertains to God's permissive or positive will that something be done *to* the person discerning. It pertains, rather, to God's positive will regarding something to be done *by* that person.[2]

Further, in his way of finding God's will, Ignatius is not proposing a way of finding any universal moral principle or rule applicable to all persons or to some class of persons or to some class of situations or cases. Whether the Ignatian discernment method or some adaptation of it can be used for such purposes is another question. What is certain is that Ignatius never presented it for that purpose. Ignatius is rather proposing a way of finding God's will for this particular person with this temperament and character, with these gifts or limitations of nature and grace, at this certain stage of development (physical, intellectual, emotional, moral, religious).[3] God's will thus understood involves this person's relationship with God and with other humans in this present situation with all its

---

[1] See below, chapter 5.

[2] In this study, attention is focused on individual discernment of God's will. With some necessary changes and additions, what is found will apply also to group discernment.

[3] *SpEx*, [4, 9, 10, 14, 16, 18–20, 89, 12, 162, 205].

circumstances of place, time, culture, social structures, customs, and so on.[4]

How greatly Ignatius was concerned about the individual person when seeking God's will shows up most clearly in many of his directives in the Constitutions of the Society of Jesus, especially in his counsels for superiors when discerning God's will with regard to their government. As we shall see, the superior is, properly speaking, directly discerning God's will regarding his own act of directing another.[5] But, since his own act is directive of another's act, the concrete situation for the superior's act involves the other's personal condition and concrete situation for acting. Over and over again Ignatius adds to his general directives or counsels such phrases as these: "according to the persons, times, places, and their contingencies"; "adapted to the times, places, and persons in different houses, colleges, and employments"; "observe the measure and proportion of what each one can bear, as discretion will dictate"; "to the extent that nature, usage, office and other circumstances of the persons permit"; "whose [the superiors'] duty it will be to consider whether for certain reasons with particular persons, something different is more expedient"; "according to the subjects, places, conditions, times, in the way that seems best to them [superiors] for the greater divine glory"; "according to the age, ability inclination, and basic knowledge which a particular person has."[6]

The same concern for differences among persons and concrete circumstances shows also in Ignatius' understanding of the Consti-

---

[4] John Futrell speaks of Ignatian discernment of God's will as "prophetically" interpreting the concrete situation as the "existential word of God" in light of the revealed word of God. See "Ignatian Discernment," pp. 49–50. This article and his book *Making an Apostolic Community of Love* (St. Louis: The Institute of Jesuit Sources, 1970) (hereafter referred to as MACL), chapters 5–6, are Futrell's principal writings on discernment. The latter is primarily concerned with discernment by a Jesuit superior regarding God's will in the community and for each individual in it, insofar as he (the superior) has responsibility to do so. Nevertheless, as his treatment touches on what is essential to any Ignatian discernment, it has value for anyone interested in this matter.

[5] See below, pp. 51–53.

[6] For the phrases quoted, see *Cons.*, [64, 136, 285, 297, 343, 354]. For other illustrations see [66, 70, 71, 211, 228, 238, 285, 287, 290, 297, 301, 395, 462, 471, 581, 671, 746]. John Futrell gives an excellent account of the demands Ignatius put on superiors when discerning God's will to understand the individuals governed (MACL, pp. 131–142) and to understand other factors in the concrete situation (MACL, pp. 149–150).

An interesting application is found in Ignatius' humane instructions on how the subject should deal with his superior (*LettersIgn.*, p. 391).

tutions themselves as subject to change with changing times, with different persons in different situations having new needs, in order always to seek the greater glory in new situations.[7]

God's Will Is Limited to the Discerner's Free Choice of an Act to Be Done

It is not every act which God wills to be done by an individual person in a concrete situation that can be the object of Ignatian discernment. It is only an act which is to be freely chosen by the person or, more precisely, an act of freely choosing among proposed alternative acts.[8] God's will which is sought through discernment is not an element in God's complete and irrevocable plan prior to our exercise of freedom and independent of it. What his will may be at the next step depends on what is freely chosen now.[9]

This limitation involves a number of things about God's will as object of discernment. That will is personally addressed to the human person as a free agent and is calling for a free personal response. The divine call expresses God's preference, without necessitating that the person do what God prefers. It is a call not merely to do some act but to choose freely that act rather than some other real alternative and to choose it because it is what God prefers.[10]

Limitation to Free Choice among Alternatives Which Are All for God's Glory

Further, even God's will regarding a person's free choice to be made in a concrete situation is not in every case the object of Ignatian discernment. Further limitation is required. Ignatius sees two distinct kinds of situations where discernment of God's will regarding alternatives for choice is called for. In one I have to discern whether or not the alternatives for choice are "either indifferent or

---

[7] John Futrell also has some valuable pages on this topic in MACL, pp. 150–155.

[8] *SpEx*, [15, 23, 169–189].

[9] How God, in eternity, taking account of free choices which are future to us, wills all history at once without doing away with our freedom of choice or its influence on history is a theological question which cannot and need not be treated in this study.

[10] By a "real alternative" I mean one of which the person is aware, which appears to him or her as a possible and, under some aspect, desirable way of responding in this concrete situation. What is in fact objectively possible but does not appear to be so to this person or what appears as possible but in no way whatever as desirable (not even because less undesirable than the other alternatives)—neither of these is a real alternative for this person's choice.

good in themselves[11] and such that they are lawful within the Holy Mother, the hierarchical Church, and not evil or repugnant to her''[12]—or, as he puts it elsewhere, they are "permitted to the liberty of our free will and not forbidden.''[13] In the other kind of situation for choice, I have already judged that both alternatives are permitted and I need to discern which alternative God wills me to choose, which one is more for his glory in us.[14] Ignatius is concerned only with discernment in this second kind of situation for choice.

Some clarifications are to be kept in mind if this limited meaning of God's will as object of discernment is to be correctly understood and used in practice. First, when we see that one alternative must be more for the glory of God, it is necessary to remember what was said above: the better, or what is for the greater glory, must be understood in relation to this individual agent in this concrete situation, with his or her strength or weaknesses, maturity or immaturity in certain respects. What appears in the abstract to be more for the glory may not at all be so in the concrete. The better choice for one person in the concrete may be very different for another in that same kind of situation or for the same person at an earlier or later stage of growth.

Second, the greater glory is not to be thought of merely in terms of the immediate consequences of a choice or even in terms of the clearly envisioned long-range consequences, but in terms of the consequences for the ultimate glory to be achieved through the whole of history. However, any judgment about consequences of an act for the whole of future history is impossible for us; only God can know about that. Is Ignatius' criterion, therefore, useless? The answer to that question involves all the rest of this book: our rela-

---

[11] By alternatives "in themselves" Ignatius might mean "apart from concrete circumstances, in the abstract"; or he might mean "apart from any elective tension between them as alternatives for choice in this concrete situation," that is, apart from any *comparative* value for the glory of God. In context, the latter meaning seems to me the only acceptable one.

[12] *SpEx*, [170].

[13] Ibid., [23].

[14] When no alternative for a choice is forbidden, does Ignatius see any moral obligation to find and choose the alternative which is more for the glory of God? A case could be made that he does not. If that answer is correct, then he fits into a long tradition in moral thought which denies any obligation to do the better so long as one does what is not forbidden by a material precept, and which sees doing the better as beyond the call of duty. A strong case can be made for asserting such an obligation, once the necessary explanations and qualifications are given. This issue, however, lies outside the scope of this study.

tionship with God in discernment, the several Ignatian modes of
seeking God's will, and Ignatius' answer to the question whether
we can reach any justifiable conviction regarding God's will.

What of the situation for choice in which the discerner might
know that each alternative is equally for the glory of God, none for
the greater glory? If such a situation were possible in the concrete,
Ignatius could not consistently think that God had any preferential
will regarding the person's free choice among those alternatives.
Then Ignatian discernment would be impossible, because the choice
of one alternative over the other would have no bearing on love for
God or attainment of the ultimate end of human life. Some might
want to urge that God would will that the person exercise his or her
freedom and take responsibility for the consequences—none of
which, bear in mind, are of any greater moment for the glory of
God than the others. That might well be so; but it would still be
true that God would not care which alternative was chosen. There
would be no will of God to discern.

Summary Statement

To sum up what we have been saying about God's will as
object of discernment, we can say that it is a call that springs from
divine love, which wills always his greater glory for us; a call that
is personally addressed to the individual person in a concrete situation for choice; a call for a personal response of love to be expressed
by finding and choosing whatever in this situation is for God's
greater glory in all of us.

The Range and Frequency of Situations for Ignatian Discernment of God's Will

The concept of God's will as object of Ignatian discernment
has been reached by limitation after limitation on the general concept
of God's will. Does this imply that the occasions for Ignatian discernment are infrequent? The common, but not universal, opinion
is that such occasions are very frequent, even daily. To my knowledge, Ignatius made no direct and explicit declaration on the matter,
but the implications of what he has written strongly supports the
common opinion.

Thus, in the "Principle and Foundation" of the *Spiritual Ex-*

ercises, he says that, in order to strive as fully as we can for the ultimate goal of life for which God created us, we need to become electively "indifferent to *all* created things" in "*all* that is left to the liberty of our free will."[15] Whether our choice has to do with riches or poverty, receiving honor or being dishonored, living a long or short life, and likewise "in *all* the rest," we should be ready to choose only what is more conducive to the end for which God created us.[16]

Further on in the *Spiritual Exercises*, there are many and diverse illustrations of matters about which Ignatius thinks God has a will to be discerned, in which the greater or lesser glory is at stake.[17] In one place, after enumerating several such matters, he adds "or *anything else* which has not been decided by an immutable decision."[18]

To anyone already settled in a state of life but wishing to bring his or her way of living it out more in accord with the Gospel, for the glory of God, he gives this counsel. Such a person should discern God's will about many details; for example, how large a house and household should be maintained; how the household is to be governed and instructed and edified by example; how much of his or her income should be spent on domestic needs and how much given to the poor or to other charities—"neither desiring nor seeking anything other than the greater praise and glory of God our Lord *in all and through all* [*en todo y por todo*]."[19] This last phrase in the autograph text could be interpreted to mean that the greater praise and glory of God should be sought in all decisions about all matters whatsoever. The Latin of the *versio prima* decisively indicates this interpretation as the right one. There, instead of "in all and through all," it reads "in all things and everywhere" (*in omnibus et ubique*).[20]

---

[15] See below, pp. 79–87 (emphasis mine).

[16] *SpEx*, [23]. Emphasis mine.

[17] He mentions such things as one's vocation to a state of life [172], in particular to marriage [169, 171–172] and to the priesthood [172]; accepting a source of income, an office or benefice [16, 169, 171, 178, 181], or to some other temporal benefit [171]; the distribution of alms, to whom and how much [338–342]; details of running a household [189].

[18] *SpEx*, [178]. Emphasis mine.

[19] Ibid., [189]. Emphasis mine.

[20] *SpEx*, MHSJ, p. 279.

31

The Constitutions of the Society of Jesus give some illustration of what is implied by the word "all" in the several phrases given above. There Ignatius makes clear that he thinks God has a will to be discerned regarding all kinds of things in a Jesuit's life.[21]

The idea that God cares only about a few important decisions is foreign to the Ignatian perspective and even in direct conflict with its fundamental shaping principle. For Ignatius, it seems that every choice is important precisely because God does care which way it goes, and he cares because in every choice the human person more or less helps or hinders the coming of God's kingdom among all persons. Everywhere we look in Ignatius' writing, we find that, when he speaks of making decisions, he assumes God has a will regarding which way the decision goes. Nowhere to my knowledge does Ignatius ever speak of a decision which is neither between good and evil alternatives nor between good and better. In every decision he seeks God's will. No choice to be made is so unimportant as to lie outside the scope of God's will and, therefore, outside the need for us to seek and find it.[22] If Ignatius did envisage the possibility of a choice among alternatives all of which are precisely equal for the glory of God in us, or of a choice in which one alternative is more for the glory but God has no will regarding it, we have no record of his saying anything even to hint at it—unless it be where he speaks of the third mode of humility. This seeming exception will be considered further on.[23]

What I have been saying can be summed up in a fine passage

---

[21] For example, God's will is to be sought regarding admitting candidates to the Society [161], dismissing members [211, 219–220], the renunciation of money and other temporal goods in favor of the poor or of relatives [55, 258–259], vigils, other austerities and penances, times set for prayer, and so on [582–583], the means to be used in apostolic work [414], details of academic protocol in the colleges [508], the choice of missions and assignments of men to the missions by the superior, whom to send and how many [618–624, 596], traveling within the region to which one is sent [633], all the decisions to be made by the general congregation [711,715]. See Brian O'Leary, "The Discernment of Spirits in the *Memoriale* of Blessed Peter Favre," *The Way*, Supplement no. 35 (Spring, 1939), p. 132. Note the continual discernment carried on by Peter, covering all details of his life.

[22] See the fine pages on seeking God in all things as including seeking God's will at every hour of the day, in Josef Stierli, S.J., "Ignatian Prayer: Seeking God in All Things," *Ignatius of Loyola, His Personality and Spiritual Heritage, 1556–1956*, ed. Friedrich Wulf (St. Louis: The Institute of Jesuit Sources, 1977), pp. 152–156.

[23] See below, pp. 87–93

from Edouard Pousset, who asserts that Ignatius saw his ways of making an election as having a "universal bearing."

> They are valid not merely for the macro-decision that involves an entire life, nor even merely for the decision of a moderate magnitude that plans a reform. They are also suited for directing the multitude of choices implied in the running of a household, the carrying out of a profession, and all our relationships with others, even if it is only a question of saying or not saying a *word*. In short, there is no micro-decision in our daily life, however tiny it may be, that does not fall within their competence.[24]

Some practical difficulties that appear to be involved with this view hinder some people from seeing the evidence for Ignatius' understanding of God's preferential will or prevent them from agreeing with it if the evidence is seen. What bothers some is the danger of a person's being exaggeratedly introspective or being under excessive tension about finding God's will, perhaps becoming scrupulous and on a continual guilt trip. For others the problem merely regards the unreasonable amount of time and energy that would be expended on continual discernment. Even if valid, neither of these difficulties can change our interpretation of what Ignatius taught, which is our immediate concern. To see the full force of these difficulties and how they can be resolved within the Ignatian perspective would require much of what is yet to be worked out. Treatment of them will be put off to a later chapter.[25]

---

[24] Edouard Pousset, *Life in Faith and Freedom*, p. 130.
[25] See below, chapter 16.

Chapter 4
Our Relationship with God in Discerning His Will

*E*verything we now have to take up regarding discernment of God's will, its limits, conditions, modes, and the firmness of assent which can be given to its conclusion—all these depend in one way or another for their intelligibility on an understanding of how Ignatius sees our relationship with God in the discernment process. Ignatius' main teaching on discernment of God's will is found within the *Spiritual Exercises* and must be understood within the context of that book. It is there that we shall best see what the relationship is between God and the human person during a process of discernment.

A Relationship of Personal Communion[1]

"Just as one friend communes with another" is the way Ignatius says we should relate with God in prayer during the Spiritual Exercises, even when we come to God with deeply felt shame and sorrow for sin.[2] When he presents Christ's call, it is a call first and foremost to be "with him," sharing, as a friend shares, everything in his life: his toil and suffering, his poverty and humiliation, his final victory and glory.[3] In the contemplations on the risen life of Christ, Ignatius tells us to understand what Christ does in light of "the way in which friends are accustomed to console one another";[4] and in the "Contemplation for Love" it is the relationship between lover and beloved sharing with each other all they have and are that serves as his symbol of our relationship with God.[5]

Ignatius' primary emphasis is on God's love, but with the intention of thereby inspiring the exercitant to a greater return of love for God. He begins by calling attention to the truth that God created the whole universe to help me reach the goal of sharing his life.[6] The love that does this is also an endlessly forgiving love, which despite my sins continues to make all creation work in my favor: the angels and the saints loving me and interceding for me, the sun and moon and stars, the birds and beasts and plants, all serving my needs.[7] His love gives me Jesus Christ, who does and suffers all he does and suffers "for me."[8] He wants to share with me all that he has and, as much as I can receive the gift, wants to give me himself.[9]

Through the Exercises Ignatius intends to lead me to an "intimate knowledge"[10] of this divine love and its gifts, above all to an intimate knowledge of God's supreme gift, Jesus Christ. By an

---

[1] For a descriptive analysis of the essential structure of personal communion, see Jules Toner, *The Experience of Love*, chapter 9.

[2] *SpEx*, [54].

[3] Ibid., [93, 95, 98].

[4] Ibid., [224].

[5] Ibid., [231–237].

[6] Ibid., [23].

[7] Ibid., [60].

[8] Ibid., [116, 197].

[9] Ibid., [234].

[10] Ibid., [233].

intimate knowledge, Ignatius means a knowledge that penetrates the inner reality of these gifts, and especially the knowledge that experiences the love which is in them as only one can experience it who is in personal loving communion with the giver. He wants me to reach a knowledge that draws from me "a cry of wonder,"[11] a question, "What will I do for Christ?"[12] and a love that inspires me to "more love and follow Him."[13] Such knowledge will, he hopes, issue in a love for God in Christ so great as to free me from the undue influence of any desire that is not in accord with God's will for the greater glory, or even from the desire itself.[14]

In the measure that I have reached such a knowledge of God's love and such a response of love to him, I have entered into the relationship Ignatius requires as a condition for beginning discernment of God's will. To what extent this loving communion must take possession of the discerner's affective life and what is the main test of its genuinity will be discussed at length when we take up the essential conditions for sound discernment of God's will.[15]

Divine Influence on Human Discernment

Within that relationship of personal communion, Ignatius believes, we are open to receive the divine influence, mediate or immediate, on our discernment. By influencing our contemplation of Jesus in the Gospels and our meditation on his teaching, God's Spirit forms in us a certain vision of life common to every Christian but also colored by each one's individual personality and experience. He calls forth certain memories, draws our attention to certain aspects of a present concrete situation more than to others, enables us to feel the force of some reasons or motives for choice more powerfully than others, enlightens us to experience more keenly certain needs in self and in others, and to see certain values as greater than others. He may give us volitional impulses toward ways of acting or touch our sensibilities with feelings of delight, peace, warmth, sweetness, and so on. In all these ways, the Holy Spirit can lead

---

[11] Ibid., [50].

[12] Ibid., [53].

[13] Ibid., [104].

[14] Ibid., [1, 104, 155, 179, 184].

[15] See below, chapter 6, especially 87–90.

our discernment to the conclusion he knows is in conformity with the Father's will for his greater glory in us.

Thus, Ignatius says in the *Spiritual Exercises* that God moves or attracts us when we are seeking his will,[16] gives love from above to motivate choice,[17] guides and counsels us,[18] gives us light,[19] and confirms or disconfirms our judgment.[20] In the Constitutions Ignatius speaks of God inspiring us,[21] efficaciously bringing our discernment to a right conclusion about his will,[22] enlightening us,[23] teaching what that will is by the unction of the Holy Spirit,[24] indicating it,[25] and communicating prudence to us.[26]

It is to this influence of the Holy Spirit on the human mind and affections that Ignatius wishes the discerner to be open during discernment. In order to remove obstacles to that influence, Ignatius urges the exercitant to remain as much as possible in seclusion and solitude,[27] urges him insistently to beg for God's direct loving action "to put his desires in right order,"[28] and holds before him the ideal of indifference to all motives for choice other than pure love of God and desire for the greater glory.[29]

Further, in order to prevent even the director of the Exercises from interfering with the divine influence, Ignatius gives two strong warnings. First, the director should be very sparing in proposing subject matter for meditation for the reason that what the exercitant finds by his own reasoning means more to him than what he is told by another.[30] An even more important reason is that the person should be left open to receive enlightenment from God himself; although

---

[16] *SpEx*, [175,189].
[17] Ibid., [184].
[18] Ibid., [318].
[19] Ibid., [176].
[20] Ibid., [183].
[21] *Cons*MHSJ, [700].
[22] Ibid., [624a].
[23] Ibid., [711].
[24] Ibid, [161, 414].
[25] Ibid., [219].
[26] Ibid., [414].
[27] *SpEx*, [20].
[28] Ibid., [16, 180].
[29] Ibid., [1, 5, 16, 23, 166, 169, 179, 184, 189].
[30] Ibid., [2].

at another time it may be altogether fitting to urge what seems to be the wiser decision, during the Spiritual Exercises such urging is altogether out of place. Rather, by guiding the exercitant through the Exercises, the director should help him to become open to the Spirit and, for the rest, allow the Creator to influence him without mediation by the director.[31]

Human Effort in Discernment under Divine Influence

When saying that within a relationship of intimate personal communion God guides our discernment by influencing our thoughts and affections, Ignatius in no way means to de-emphasize the essential role of our own efforts if we are to find God's will. A relationship between God and the human person in discernment is essentially collaborative.[32] Divine influence supplies for what no human efforts could possibly achieve, but it does not replace those efforts.[33] God guides our seeking; but, if we do not seek, there is nothing for God to guide. If without seeking we should passively receive infused knowledge of God's will, we could not be said to "find" his will; no active discernment would have taken place. Therefore, we see throughout Ignatius' writings on discernment of God's will an emphasis both on God's influence and on our own efforts. In fact, these two are joined, even fused, in all Ignatian teaching on spiritual life.[34]

This teaching on our entire dependence on God and at the same time our collaborative relationship with him in discernment, which is found in the *Spiritual Exercises*, is seen even more clearly and strikingly in a document to which we will turn time and again. It

---

[31] Ibid., [15], and see [16].

[32] Thomas A. Dunne, S.J., "Models of Discernment," *The Way*, Supplement no. 23 (Autumn, 1974), pp. 18–26. Dunne shows that Ignatian discernment of God's will is truly but inadequately conceived in the models of discovery and decision. A more adequate model is that of collaboration in love with Jesus, of making a joint decision with him to collaborate with him in a definite course of action.

[33] See *DirSpEx*MHSJ: Polanco, nos. 5–8, on pp. 277–279; Miró, nos. 86–87, on pp. 401–402; Dávila, [110–111, 140] on pp. 514, 521.

[34] See Jules Toner, *A Commentary*, pp. 157–160.

is entitled *Deliberation of the First Fathers*.[35] In it we have an account of how Ignatius and his first companions sought and found God's will for them as a group, as a community. When they began their search together to find God's will, they agreed that they would all pray and meditate, make the best effort they could in seeking his will and, for the rest, cast all their concerns on the Lord.[36] How they went about their first discernment shows what their best efforts involved.

> We began therefore to expend every human effort. We proposed to ourselves some questions worthy of careful consideration and forethought at this opportune time. Throughout the day, we were accustomed to ponder and meditate on these and prayerfully search into them. At night each one shared with the group what he judged to be more appropriate and helpful, with the intention that all with one mind would embrace the truer way of thinking, tested and commended by the more powerful reasons and by majority vote.[37]

Despite all their output of mental energy for some days in drawing up, discussing, and weighing reasons, when they reached their unanimously agreed-on conclusion, they made a very surprising statement about it.

> We want it understood that nothing at all that has been or will be spoken of originated from our own spirit or our own thought; rather, whatever it was, it was solely what our Lord inspired and the Apostolic See confirmed and approved.[38]

If their conclusion did not originate from their own spirit or

---

[35] The document can be found in *Cons*MHSJ, I, vol. 1, pp. 1–7. For an English translation with a commentary, see Jules Toner, S.J., "The Deliberation That Started the Jesuits," *Studies in the Spirituality of Jesuits*, vol. 6, no. 4 (June, 1974). Hereafter referred to as "The Deliberation." Although this document was not written by Ignatius, there can be no reasonable doubt that the method of discernment which it describes is an application of the election method in the *Spiritual Exercises* and authentically expresses Ignatius' thought.

[36] Jules Toner, "The Deliberation," p. 186 [1, c].

[37] Ibid., p. 187 [2,d].

[38] Ibid., p. 193 [3,g].

their own thought, what part did all their work play, all their reasoning and discussing? And what becomes of the earlier statement in the document that they rested their decisions on what seemed to them the stronger reasons?[39] The only way to make sense of what they say is to understand that their conclusion did not originate *only* or *primarily* from their own spirit or their own thought but from the Holy Spirit inspiring their thoughts and leading them through their own thinking to the conclusion. The conclusion is truly based on what appears to them as the strong reasons; but it is not those reasons alone or mainly which founded their sure assent to it as expressing God's will. The principal foundation for their trusting assent is belief in the Spirit inspiring and leading them through their own efforts.[40]

After this first success, the group undertook its most important and most difficult discernment. This time the members at first failed utterly to reach a conclusion, even after many days of trying. They finally drew back and reflected on possible ways of trying again.[41] One of the ways they considered was that all or a delegated few would go to some hermitage for thirty or forty days and give themselves to meditation, fasting, and prayer, with the hope "that God might listen to our desires and mercifully impress on our minds the answer to our question."[42] Read out of context, this passage could easily be understood to mean they were hoping to be told God's will as the answer to prayer and fasting without any effort at gathering and weighing evidence.

Even if such an interpretation proved to be the true one, it would in no way change anything that has been said about Ignatian discernment. It would merely mean that Ignatius and his companions were considering withdrawal from the active search involved in discernment in the hope of receiving knowledge of God's will by some direct revelation or infused knowledge from the Holy Spirit. This is outside the realm of discernment understood as seeking and finding God's will.

---

[39] Ibid., p. 187 [2,d].

[40] In the relationship between their stronger reasons and the Holy Spirit's guidance, as well as between their conclusion based on those reasons and their motive for assenting so firmly to it, is found the deepest insight into Ignatian discernment of God's will as a faith enterprise. It will be considered at length in chapters 15 and 16.

[41] Jules Toner, "The Deliberation," p. 195 [5,i].

[42] Ibid., p. 196 [5,j].

However, if we attend to what went before and, even more, what comes after in the account, such an interpretation does not seem to fit. They rejected this proposal because it would withdraw them entirely from their priestly ministry in the city.[43] They still hoped God would impress on their minds the answer to their question. But what that means to them is evident from the preparations for discernment they now worked out and from the process of discernment to be followed once they were prepared. As preparation, they worked out several ways of opening themselves more freely to the influence of the Holy Spirit.[44] But they expected the Holy Spirit to influence their own efforts of reflection and deliberation individually and together, and through their efforts finally to lead them to a true judgment of what would be for the greater praise and glory. A reading of how they carried on their discernment through many days of arduous work leaves no room for reasonable doubt that this is so.[45]

The understanding of our relationship with God in discerning his will which appears in the *Spiritual Exercises* and in the *Deliberation of the First Fathers* shows up over and over again in the Constitutions of the Society of Jesus, especially where Ignatius gives counsel on how superiors should discern where to send men on apostolic missions, how many to send, what men, and so on. Thus, in one passage, after several pages of considerations on which superiors may reasonably base their decisions about these matters,[46] Ignatius says:

> Although it is the supreme providence and direction of the Holy Spirit that must efficaciously guide us to bring deliberations to a right conclusion in everything, and in sending to each place those who are more suitable and who will fit in better with the men and work to which they are sent, still this can be said in general. First, that for a matter of greater importance and one in which more depends on avoidance of error, as far as this depends on

---

[43] Ibid., p. 197 [6,k].
[44] Ibid., pp. 197–198 [6,1].
[45] Ibid., pp. 201–208 [7m–9,r].
[46] *Cons*, [622–623].

41

the part of the one who with God's grace must provide, subjects ought to be sent who are more select and in whom greater confidence is had.[47]

Even read by itself, the import of this statement is plain enough. Read in context, its import comes out more strongly and clearly. For it is not only preceded by many rational norms to guide the superior's reasoning, but it is also followed by many illustrations to help him see how to apply what has just been said.[48]

Many similar passages can be found elsewhere in the Constitutions.[49]

A Difficulty: Does the Holy Spirit "Manipulate" Us?

Some find difficulty in accepting the idea of the Holy Spirit's lead in finding a will of God which is prior to our discernment and choice. To them it sounds as if the Spirit were a puppeteer pulling the strings of our minds and hearts in order to carry out a preconceived plan ("blueprint" is the word they like to use), without regard for our dignity as images of God, gifted with godlike freedom and creativity.

The response to this difficulty is an *a fortiori* argument. Even human agents can influence us as we make decisions about our personal lives or strive to win support for some proposal, and they can do so honestly, reverently, and with respect for our dignity. They do so by leading us to see some truths, to reason honestly, to use our imagination effectively, or to become aware of and understand our emotions, while leaving us free to make our own judgments and choices. Not everyone is manipulating us who calls attention to certain facts judged important for us to consider or leads us along a line of thought or evokes our emotions in order to help us to realize some truth. He or she may well be freeing us from the blinding power of irrational emotions, of rigid mind-sets, of ignorance; in short, they are bringing alive what is best in us. Truly great teachers, great religious leaders, great writers or artists do not lessen our human personhood by their powerful influence. We can all distin-

---

[47] *ConsSJComm*, [624a].

[48] *Cons*, [622a–626].

[49] Ibid., [134, 161, 219, 414, 583, 700, 711, 814].

guish between demagogues and behavioristic social engineers on the one hand and true leaders on the other. The former degrade us; the latter vitalize and ennoble us by their influence and enable us to actualize our truest selves with freedom, initiative, and creative imagination.

Infinitely more so does the Holy Spirit of God when he acts upon us with infinite love, with infinitely delicate power, working not from without (as any human agent has to work) but from within, more intimate to us than we are to ourselves, creating and cherishing our freedom and dignity at every instant, with perfect, limitless understanding. The Holy Spirit touches us totally in accord with all that is peculiar to our real individual selves (our temperament, character, whole psychological personality as shaped by heredity, environment, past experiences, and memories), in accord with our individual ways of apprehending things, of reasoning, of responding emotionally. The Spirit's power is infinitely, exquisitely delicate, such as no created person could possibly exercise on another or even imagine. So, far from merely moving us like puppets or automatons, when the Holy Spirit moves us through discernment to choice and action, he calls us to actualize our most real selves under control of the freedom which he creates in us.

What is more, as we have noted and shall establish further on,[50] Ignatius thinks we can have no justifiable certainty of being led by him in our discernment unless we freely choose to be led, freely opening ourselves to his guidance and freely exerting our abilities and energies to the reasonable limit in actively seeking. Because of our dignity, the Spirit leaves us with a corresponding sweet but sometimes-heavy burden of responsibility. Under his influence our intelligence, creative imagination, and freedom are not only respected and preserved, but are greatly enhanced.

What easily misleads us when we speak of God's power influencing our minds and hearts is an image of a kind of power that acts from without and against resistance, the power of a hammer shaping metal, the power of exploding atoms, the power of mighty military forces or the power to break down a psychological personality through brainwashing techniques, or the subtle, even subcon-

---

[50] See below, chapter 6.

sciously functioning, power of advertising or peer-group pressure. A much greater kind of power is the power to influence others from within and in accord with their truest selves so that they act from their own deepest reality, freely doing what at their inmost center they most want to do. The Holy Spirit does not hammer or squeeze our minds into a mold imposed from outside or shrewdly manipulate us in violation of our dignity. Rather, from within, at the very springs of our being, he touches us lovingly and reverently. Precisely because the influence of the Spirit is attuned to our reality with infinite sensitivity and reverence for the Father's creation, redeemed by the Son and entrusted to his love, he himself a gift to us from the Father and Son—precisely because of all this, we must understand that his influence on us is for the sake of helping us to take the initiative in seeking the most loving, personal response to him, and enabling us to find it. (What ''finding'' means in the thought of Ignatius will be studied in Chapter 15.)

Chapter 5
The Limits of Discerning God's Will

*T*he limits we have already found to the meaning of God's will as object of discernment are also limits of discernment. They narrow the range of questions about God's will which can reasonably be brought to discernment. All questions are excluded except those which inquire about God's will regarding a humanly free choice among proposed acts in a concrete situation for choice when every alternative is in itself for God's glory in us, and we want to find which one is more for the glory than the others. Conversely, any limits we find Ignatius setting to the range of discernment will also be limits to the meaning of God's will as object of discernment. This chapter on the limits of discerning God's will, therefore, is a further inquiry into the limited meaning of God's will as object of discernment, just as the earlier one was an initial inquiry into the

45

limits of discerning God's will. The reason for separating the two topics is that the limits to be shown now are better understood after clarifying our relationship with God in discernment.

If we are to understand the theory and practice of discerning God's will, we can hardly exaggerate the importance of noting and understanding these limits. Without such understanding we may try to find and even think we have found God's will on matters which are beyond our knowing through discernment. Some consequences, as will be shown, are unwarranted and painful tensions, confusions, recriminations, loss of confidence in one's capacity to discern. Another very important consequence is that Ignatian discernment appears vulnerable to negative theological criticism.

To my knowledge, no developed thematic treatment of the limits of discerning God's will is to be found either in Ignatius' writings or in his commentators. However, considerable indications of what Ignatius thought on this matter are given in his accounts of his own discernment.

The Fundamental Principle for Limiting Discernment of God's Will

Even before searching out evidence for Ignatius' thought on this matter, it is possible to show at work in his thinking the principle for establishing these limits. For it is implied by what we have already seen regarding his teaching on our call to choose in every concrete situation for choice what God wills, and to choose it just because it is God's will. This call to choose presupposes a call to discern God's will; for we cannot fulfill our vocation freely and responsibly to choose God's will and do so because it is God's will unless we can find—before we choose—what he wills. If God calls us to find his will and to choose to do it, we may reasonably hope that he will enable us to find it insofar as is necessary in order for us to choose it. But our vocation to do his will gives us no ground for hoping that, through Ignatian discernment, we can find anything about God's will which is not necessary in order to freely choose it.

Beginning from Ignatius' understanding of our relationship with God in discernment, we can reach the same conclusion. For, as was shown above and will be shown more fully further on, our hope of reaching a trustworthy decision about God's will through discernment rests entirely on having sound reasons for believing in the Holy Spirit's guidance. But there are no good grounds for any firm belief that the Holy Spirit will lead or has led us to find what it is not necessary for us to find in order freely to choose in accord with God's will.

The fundamental principle governing the limits of discerning God's will may, then, be stated in this way: A question about God's will can rightly be brought to discernment when and only when knowing the answer to it is necessary for the discerner in order to answer the call from God in this concrete situation freely to choose what is for the greater glory and to choose it precisely because it is God's will.

The Main Source of Light on the Limits of Discernment: Ignatius' Letter to Borgia

With the help of this principle we could ourselves deduce some limits and say that Ignatius ought to hold them if he is to be consistent. There is no need to proceed in such an *a priori* way. For we have a document which gives us concrete evidence on the point from Ignatius' own experience and his comments on it. It is a letter which he wrote to Francis Borgia.[1] This letter is unusually valuable for understanding a number of important aspects of Ignatian discernment of God's will; there will be occasion time and again to return to it when we take up other questions. At present our only interest is the light it casts on the question of limits.

This letter contains an account by Ignatius of one of his own discernments. In his account he shows an awareness of certain limits to discerning God's will which to my knowledge he never declared explicitly in a general way. His account cannot be understood without some background on the situation which occasioned it.

For manifold reasons Ignatius did not want Jesuits to hold positions of ecclesiastical dignity and power,[2] so much so that all professed Jesuits were to promise God never to seek any such ap-

---

[1] *Obras Completas*, pp. 784–785.

[2] The main reasons are put together in a letter from Ignatius to Ferdinand I, King of the Romans (*LettersIgn.*, pp. 111–113) and in a letter to Father Michael de Torres (ibid., pp. 115–120).

pointment.[3] Ignatius had to oppose kings and the emperor when they wanted to appoint some of the early Jesuits to bishoprics.[4] Among those Jesuits, some of the best known were Jay, Canisius, Laínez, Bobadilla, and the one we are now interested in, Francis Borgia.[5]

In the year 1552, Emperor Charles V requested Pope Julius III to make Francis Borgia a cardinal. Ignatius, in his letter to Francis, tells of his immediate, spontaneous, negative response to the idea and of his search to find whether or not God willed for him to follow that initial response. So illuminating is this account that I shall give it in full now and frequently refer back to it.

> With regard to the cardinal's hat, I thought that to God's greater glory I should give you some account of what has gone on in me, speaking to you as to my own soul. It was as if I had been informed of the certain fact that the emperor had nominated you and that the pope was pleased to make you a cardinal. Immediately, I had this idea or inclination to prevent it in any way I could. However, I was not certain of the divine will; for many reasons on one side and the other occurred to me. So, I gave orders that all the priests in the house should celebrate Mass and those who are not priests should offer prayers for three days that I would be guided in the whole matter to the greater divine glory. Pondering on the matter and discussing it from time to time during this three day span, I perceived that certain fears came on me or at least that there was no liberty of spirit to speak against and prevent the project. I asked myself, "How do I know what God our Lord wishes to do?" Consequently, I did not feel entirely secure in [the thought of] obstructing it [the emperor's project]. At other times, during my customary prayers, I perceived that these fears had departed

---

[3] *Cons*, [817].

[4] For a full and very interesting account of Ignatius' tenacity in opposing such attempts to have Jesuits appointed as bishops and the political maneuvering by both sides, see the letter to Michael de Torres (note 2, above).

[5] *ConsSJComm*, p. 335, note 13.

48

from me.[6] Going on with prayer at various times, some-times with this fear and sometimes with the contrary, I finally found myself during my customary prayer on the third day, and always ever since, with a fully settled judgment that, as much as I could, I should turn the pope and the cardinals from their purpose. My judgment was so conclusive and my will so tranquil that I held and still hold for a certainty that if I did not act in this way, I would not give a good account of myself to God, but rather an entirely bad one.

Consequently, I held and now hold that it is the divine will for me to oppose this [appointment], even though others might think otherwise and bestow this dignity on you. There would be no contradiction at all involved; for the same Divine Spirit is able to move me to that action for certain reasons, and for other reasons to move others to the contrary action and to bring about the result to which the emperor was pointing. May God our Lord always in everything do what will be to his greater praise and glory. I believe it would be appropriate for you to respond to the letter which Master Polanco is writing at my order and to declare the intention and purpose with which God our Lord has inspired you and may now inspire you. It would in this way appear in writing, which could be shown whenever it might be necessary, leaving the whole matter to our Lord, so that in all our affairs his holy will may be done.[7]

Several things in this account had better be highlighted immediately. Note that Ignatius' discernment led him to answer a different question about God's will than the question which occasioned his beginning to discern. Since he could see that there were many reasons for the project as well as against it, he had to admit

---

[6] The following three sentences translate one sentence in Ignatius' letter, an extremely long and very complex one, in which every phrase is significant for accurately understanding his thought on the limits of discerning God's will and other matters to be taken up in this study. In order to preserve all that is in his sentence, I have had to restructure it, while adhering as closely as possible to a literal translation.

[7] For the Spanish text, see *Obras Completas*, pp. 784–785.

to himself that the appointment might be what God willed. "How do I know," he asked himself, "what God wishes to do?" Hence the need for spiritual discernment. However, as he describes the discernment, it becomes very clear that the question he is concerned with is not what God wills to do, not whether God wills for Borgia actually to be made a cardinal. Neither was the question what God wills for the pope and emperor to do. One gets the impression that he considered these questions to be unanswerable by his discernment. All he thought he could find and needed to find was what *he* had to know in order freely to choose what God willed for *him* to do in this situation. At the end of his discernment, he was confident that he had the answer to that question. The answer, however, provided not the least clue to what God willed the emperor and pope to do or what he willed the eventual outcome to be. What is more, even if Ignatius had been able to know the answers to these questions, the answers would in no way disclose God's will for his own choice of action in this situation. God might be moving the emperor and pope to intend what he willed Ignatius to try to prevent. He might will for Ignatius successfully to oppose the emperor's plan or to oppose it and fail.

Implications for All Discernment of God's Will

This account of Ignatius' discernment on a particular question indicates several limits which hold for every discernment of God's will. (1) Discernment is limited to finding God's will regarding the discerner's *own* free and responsible choice. (2) Among the discerner's own free choices, discernment is limited to finding God's will regarding those choices which the discerner has a *right* to make. (3) Discernment is limited to finding God's will at the moment of decision and choice.[8]

The meaning of these assertions may be better understood if we also put them negatively. (1) No one can discern God's will for another person's free choice (when every alternative is in itself for

---

[8] God's will regarding this choice will, however, ordinarily continue into the future (see below, p. 66), even though the discernment by which the judgment about the choice to be made cannot justify any judgment that God will so continue to will.

the glory of God).[9] (2) No one can discern God's will for his or her own choice when he or she does not have a right or present responsibility to make that choice. (3) No one can through discernment reach a justifiable conclusion regarding God's will for what will follow as a consequence of choice.

To my knowledge, Ignatius never explicitly stated any of these limits as holding for every discernment of God's will. On the other hand, I can find no reason, apparent or hidden, for thinking that what he says about the limits of his actual discernment regarding this particular question should be peculiar to it.[10] Further, as will be shown, when understood as applying generally, these limits closely cohere with the rest of Ignatius' teaching on seeking God's will; in fact, they appear to be implied by them. There is, then, sound reason for thinking that in Ignatius' own mind such limitations on discernment apply in every case.

The following pages will, I hope, strengthen this opinion. If not, I am still confident that reflection on experience leads us to find these limits and requires that we accept them if we are to avoid confusion and possible cynicism about discernment of God's will; for in their absence Ignatian teaching on discernment of God's will cannot withstand intelligent criticism. Let us now consider in detail each of the three limits to discerning God's will.

1. Discernment Is Limited to Finding God's Will regarding the Discerner's Own Free and Responsible Choices[11]

Recall Ignatius' statement that he did not know after his discernment what God willed for anyone else to do, including the pope and the emperor; all he was sure of was what God wanted *him* to do. Does this statement of fact have any implications regarding

---

[9] This qualification has to be kept in mind or we are no longer talking about Ignatian discernment of God's will. See above, p. 28.

[10] There are, in fact, other instances to be found in Ignatius' discernments. For example, see his discernment about resigning from his office as general of the Society of Jesus. (For a translation of his proffered resignation, see below, pp. 263–265.) In urging the general congregation to free him, he first says that after discernment, he "simply and absolutely" renounces the office for reasons that seem to him altogether convincing. But it is clear that he knows he cannot, and has not discerned what God wills for the congregation to do, to accept or refuse his resignation. It is up to them to find God's will for their own decision; his own discernment in no way settles that.

[11] A free choice and a responsible choice are materially identical. I only wish to stress both aspects or formalities of the act.

discernment in general? What God willed regarding the pope's and emperor's choices would surely have been a question for Ignatius. Why could he not find the answer through discernment?

To answer this question, recall the fundamental principle for limiting discernment of God's will: We can find nothing through discernment which we do not need to know in order freely and responsibly to choose to do God's will in a concrete situation for choice. Now, in order to find and choose to do God's will in a concrete situation, I have no need to know what God wills someone else to choose to do (that may be, as Ignatius points out, the contrary of what he wills for me), and no one else needs to know what God wills for me to choose in order to know God's will for himself or herself. Therefore, in Ignatian discernment each of us may be confident of the Holy Spirit's guidance to what each has to find in order to choose God's will; but no one can be confident of that guidance for finding what God wills for anyone else to choose. Limiting discernment to God's will for me does not eliminate my having an opinion about what God wills for another. It only excludes my thinking that this opinion has the force of a justifiable conclusion from a sound discernment under the guidance of the Holy Spirit.

Further, to say that I cannot discern what God wills for another freely and responsibly to choose does not exclude finding by my discernment that God wills me to choose a way of acting or speaking intended to sway another's judgment and choice. If I discern whether God wills for me to advise or persuade or exhort another, my conclusion is concerned only with *my* choice of *my* act toward the other, not with what God wills for the other to choose to do. God may will that the one whom I try to persuade will make a decision to do something quite different from what I urge. Ignatius found that God willed for him to try to persuade the pope away from the emperor's project, but he understood that God might at the same time be willing for the pope to choose to support the project.

Does this mean that I cannot rightfully petition the Holy Spirit to guide me so that I may advise another to choose what really is God's will for that person? No, I may commendably pray in this way. But, like all prayer, my petition should have a condition, expressed or unexpressed: if it should be God's will and, therefore, for the greater glory. The Holy Spirit might for the greater glory

52

lead each of us to a decision that accords with his will, but results in a conflict situation. At first hearing, this statement is at least puzzling. It sounds altogether at variance with the way Christians think of the Holy Spirit. Are not peace and union of minds and hearts his work in human life? Deeper reflection, however, in light of Christian teaching and experience clears up the puzzle.

Remember that every alternative to which the Spirit may lead us in spiritual discernment should be for God's glory and be desired by the discerner only because it is judged to be for the greater glory of God in all. Conflicting judgments about the proposed good acts or even conflicts of good projects in the order of action can often lead to what is spiritually and apostolically more fruitful than agreement on one or another course of action. Further, when the Holy Spirit moves us to disagree, he moves us to do so in a Christian way; that is, with humility, mutual respect and love, and openness to each other; with peaceful trust in each other's good will and in God's providence to make all come out for the greater glory. From disagreement in this way may come not only a better understanding of the course of action to follow but also a deeper mutual respect, love, and trust, deeper than we would have had without the disagreement.

I have seen this happen over and over, especially in group discernment. Persons who were quite antagonistic before striving to reach the attitudes required for discernment have during the discernment, to their great surprise, been drawn together in the Spirit with peace and harmony of hearts. This happened, not despite their disagreement, but precisely because of it and the way they carried on their search for agreement. Besides being an occasion for deeper union of hearts, these tensions from conflicting divine movements in different persons or groups can, in God's wise and kind providence, be fruitful of ideas and achievements which are more for his glory in us than either person or group could have foreseen. The essential thing for all is openness both to the Holy Spirit acting within their own minds and hearts, and to his influence on them through the others, with honesty, simplicity of heart, and peaceful trust in God.

The First Apparent Exception to This Limit: Consultative Discernment

Hopefully, what has been said so far clarifies what is being asserted and not asserted about limiting discernment of God's will to his will for the person discerning; and why this limit must be asserted. However, there are some cases which come to mind as possible exceptions to this limitation. First, what about consultative discernment? This apparent exception is relatively easy to explain, once what has already been said is understood; it is, nevertheless, worth some extended discussion because in practice it is frequently not understood—with very disturbing consequences.

Consultative discernment of God's will is directed to finding what choice is to be recommended to another who has a decision and choice to make, especially when the latter is himself intending to discern God's will and has requested the help of a consultative discernment. It might seem that in some sense the consultative discerner is seeking God's will for another. Suppose, for example, that the pope had called Ignatius to make a discernment about what he, the pope, should choose to do regarding Borgia and to give him the results of it to help him in his own search to find God's will. Could Ignatius then rightly think he had found what God willed for the pope to do? What has been said above would not allow such a conclusion, for a consultative discerner (in this case, Ignatius) is really seeking only what God wills for him to recommend to the other (in this case, the pope). The decision reached by consultative discernment of God's will concerns the discerner's own act of counseling one way or another. What God wills this discerner to recommend may not be what God wills the other to choose.

It follows, therefore, that the results of a consultative discernment of God's will are not overthrown if by a sound discernment the one counseled arrives at a different decision. Neither, therefore, are the results confirmed as sound when they agree with what is counseled. God may not have had such agreement in mind, and one or the other discerner may have failed to discern soundly.

An illustration of a consultative discernment actually made by Ignatius shows his thinking. It is found in his *Spiritual Diary*. Ignatius had been commissioned by the companions with whom he founded the Society of Jesus to compose constitutions. His diary covers a period during which he was trying to find God's will on a matter of religious poverty which he considered to be of greatest importance for the Society of Jesus. An extraordinary series of spiritual movements all pointed to the same decision.[12] So also did the carefully worked-out set of reasons which Ignatius considered frequently and for long periods of time.[13] All this evidence led him to a firm conviction about what God willed for him to write into his draft of the Constitutions which he was composing, and to urge it on his companions. But he was well aware that his discernment was only consultative, providing material for that which was to be done by all of them together. In the entry for February 23 of his diary, after expressing his conviction, he wrote (awkwardly but in the context clearly enough), ''For my part, I added, doing as much as I could, and this last step was directed to the companions who had given their signatures [to a previous document with which Ignatius' thought did not now agree].''[14] He was under no illusion that all the extraordinary evidence he had regarding God's will for his action provided any assurance of what God might will for the whole group to decide. He knew, as indicated above, that God might move the group to reject what he now moved Ignatius to write into the draft of the Constitutions. If they did so, that fact would say nothing about the validity either of his or their earlier discernment.[15]

A Second Apparent Exception: Entrusted Discernment

A second seeming exception to the general limitation of discernment to what God wills for the discerner himself to choose is considerably more difficult to eliminate as a real exception. Entrusted (delegated, commissioned) discernment of God's will superficially resembles consultative discernment; but it is in reality sharply differentiated from it. An exact statement of the difference and the conditions under which entrusted discernment is valid can

---

[12] *Diario Espiritual*. See, for example, entries for Feb. 6, 8–11, 16.

[13] *Deliberación sobre la Pobreza*, in *Obras Completas*, pp. 297–299. See below, pp. 179–180.

[14] See *Cons*MHSJ I, vol. 1, p. cxvii; *Obras Completas*, p. 338, note 129; W. Young, *Spiritual Journal*, p. 16, note 19.

[15] For a conflicting interpretation, which seems valid if my account of the limits Ignatius saw for his discernment is not correct, see J. Futrell, MACL, pp. 145–146.

be given more clearly after seeing Ignatius' own practice of it and his directives on it.

In his autobiography he relates an experience of entrusting a discernment to his confessor. He was about to embark for his pilgrimage to the Holy Land. Since he had no money, a kind shipmaster agreed to give him free passage, but only on condition that he brought on board enough biscuits—or hardtack—for his need. When arranging to acquire the biscuits, Ignatius became troubled, wondering whether bringing such a supply accorded with absolute faith and hope in God's care for him. He saw "probable reasons" on both sides of the question and could not reach a decision either way. As a final resort he decided "to put himself in the hands of his confessor," to whom he explained the whole problem and his desire for whatever would give more glory to God. His confessor decided that he should beg for what was necessary and take it on board. That settled the matter; for, when Ignatius decided to put himself in the hands of his confessor, he was not merely looking for advice. He was deciding to commit himself beforehand to whatever the confessor would see as God's will.[16]

Later on, when he and his companions were deliberating whether God called them to try to begin a new religious order in the Church, they earnestly tried for several days to reach a conclusion, but without success. At that point they considered what to do next. One proposal was for a few to go out to a hermitage to pray and fast with the hope of finding God's will "in the name of all."[17] They finally rejected this proposal, but there is not the slightest hint that they did so because they thought that entrusting the discernment to a few in the name of all was not a sound mode of finding God's will for all of them.

When papal approval had been given to their forming a religious community, the companions set about electing a superior general. Not surprisingly, Ignatius was elected. He experienced a great reluctance to accept the office; and, when he could not come to any

---

[16] *Autobiog.*, [35–36].
[17] Jules Toner, "The Deliberation," p. 196, [5,j].

conviction about God's will himself, he again entrusted discernment to his confessor and followed his decision.[18]

When he was general, Ignatius wrote a letter to the local community at the college of Gandía in which he entrusted to the members of the community the decision about who would be the local superior. He gave instructions on how to arrive at the decision, clearly by a discernment process very like the one by which he had been elected general.[19] The man they would elect in this way, he says, "I already approve until you shall have heard otherwise from me."[20]

In the Constitutions Ignatius drew up instructions for the general congregation, the supreme legislative body, on how to go about making decisions. According to his view, the congregation is entrusted by the whole Society of Jesus to find God's will for it. In turn, the whole congregation in certain cases is to entrust that work to a group of three or five members. The first case can occur in the process of electing a superior general. That this election is to be done after the manner of Ignatian discernment of God's will[21] is clear from the directions which Ignatius gives for preparing to vote, for voting, and for acceptance by the entire congregation.[22] If, after purification of heart, prayer, reflection on the candidates, and voting, no one receives a simple majority, three or five "electors" should be chosen by majority to elect the superior general in the name of all.[23] The second case concerns matters other than this election. When, after adequate discussion, one view is not favored by all or nearly all, four "definitors" are to be elected. These, along with the superior general, have authority to settle the matter, either by unanimous or majority vote; "and the whole congregation will accept it [their decision] as from the hand of God our Lord."[24]

---

[18] For a full account, including Ignatius' painful struggle, see Javier Osuna, S.J., *Friends in the Lord*, trans. Nicholas King, S.J., *The Way*, series 3 (1974), pp. 137–138. See also John Futrell's interesting comments on this event and on Ignatius' attitude toward the confessor's role in discerning God's will, in MACL, pp. 32–33, note 50.

[19] Javier Osuna, *Friends in the Lord*, p. 137.

[20] *LettersIgn.*, p. 145.

[21] Not exactly the same, however, as the method found in *The Deliberation of the First Fathers*.

[22] *Cons*, [694–705].

[23] Ibid., [707].

[24] Ibid., [715].

How do these discernments just described differ from consultative discernments? Two primary differences appear.

First, the person entrusting discernment to another freely accepts in advance as his or her own decision regarding God's will whatever decision the other arrives at through a sound discernment process. If another makes a consultative discernment, even at my request, I reserve the right and the responsibility to make my own discernment, taking account of the consultative decision, of course, but only as data for my discernment. The discernments described above as entrusted call for prior commitment by the person entrusting them to the conclusions reached by those to whom they are entrusted.

The second difference between entrusted and consultative discernments lies in the occasion for them. Consultative discernment may be requested at any time when it would be helpful to have another's advice, on the principle that many heads are better than one. Even in case of disagreement, some light will likely be thrown on the subject by the different views or some new way of thinking about the question may be suggested. Entrusted discernment, however, is the last resort after the one entrusting has made every reasonable effort on his own without success and the decision brooks no delay. Entrusting discernment to another before having made all reasonable efforts or when a decision could reasonably be delayed would be shirking responsibility, and there would be no reason for believing that the Holy Spirit would guide the discerner to find God's will for the one who entrusted the discernment.

Ignatius, in both the cases which we considered, turned to his confessor only when he found that despite his own best efforts he could get nowhere, and a decision had to be made with some promptitude. In the *Deliberation of the First Fathers*, Ignatius and his companions considered entrusting discernment to a few only when, after many days of trying, they were no nearer to a decision, and the demands for their ministry made it seem unwise for them all to go into seclusion. In the Constitutions Ignatius makes very clear that entrusting discernment to "electors" or "definitors" should be a last resort for the general congregation.

Is entrusted discernment really an exception to the limit for discernment which excludes finding God's will for another person's free and responsible choice? Certainly, at first glance it seems so.

Therefore, it seems, not every discernment of God's will concerns exclusively his will for the discerner.

A more careful analysis of what is going on calls into question this apparently clear conclusion. For, from the side of the one doing the entrusted discernment, nothing is really different from a consultative discernment. The discerner is seeking to find what God wills him or her to counsel the other. The discerner seeks for God's will regarding his or her own act of counseling. What makes the difference between this and a purely consultative discernment is wholly on the side of the one entrusting the discernment. This one has already made all reasonable efforts and is committed in advance to whatever the other recommends. This commitment in no way intrinsically alters what the trusted discerner does. Could not the latter even be unaware of that commitment and be thinking of making a purely consultative discernment? Should we not think of the one entrusting discernment to another as the principal discerner, to whom the other is related as subordinate, as instrumental? Is not the real situation to be understood this way: The one entrusting discernment to another has simply judged that, under the present circumstances when all else has been tried and failed and a decison must be made without delay, the decisive evidence is what the other will recommend. The principal discerner has already made his own discernment and in principle reached a decision to choose in accord with what the other recommends. When the awaited recommendation is in, his decision is *ipso facto* specified and actual.

Even though so subtle as to seem to be special pleading, this analysis seems entirely reasonable to me. If it is, entrusted discernment is no exception to the limitation set down for discernment in general. If not, then we have a special case which does constitute an exception.

2. Discernment Is Limited to Finding God's Will regarding Choices That the Discerner Has a Right to Make

Even to discernment of God's will for my own free choices, there is a futher limit, one so closely related to the foregoing limit as to be overlapping it, but one which needs explicit treatment. Questions for discernment of God's will are limited to those about free choices which the discerner has a right to make. If I have no

59

right to make the choice, I have no ground for believing that the Holy Spirit will guide my discernment. The conclusion I reach may be what God wills, but I have no grounds for believing it is so.

If this limit should seem too obvious to delay over, I think those who have had much experience in practicing discernment and helping others to do so will attest to the fact that in practice it is frequently not attended to. Questions for discernment are frequently formulated and conclusions frequently understood in such a way as to violate this limit. Such mistakes lead in turn to false expectations, disappointments, personal tensions, even bitterness, unfounded accusations of some other person overriding God's will, and so on.

Consider a common-enough case. A member of a religious community takes a vow of obedience which she and the community understand to mean that she has given over to the community the right to mission her to whatever work is chosen by the person or persons in whom the community vests authority. Suppose that such a person now seeks to discern whether or not God wills her to leave her present ministry and take up a different one for which she sees great need. By a sincere discernment, she concludes that God does so will. The person or group of persons in whom the community vests authority, however, thinks she is so badly needed in her present work and is accomplishing so much for God's people that change is out of the question. Does this turn of events indicate that this woman was not really open to God's will in her discernment or to the Spirit's leading? Or does it indicate that those in authority are overriding God's will? Not necessarily either of these.

The trouble may lie, rather, in the mistaken way the question for discernment and, consequently, the conclusion were understood. What this individual, as described above, has a right to decide is whether God wills for her to choose to propose and, perhaps, to urge a change of ministry. That, then, is the limit of what she can discern about, and trust the conclusion as that to which the Holy Spirit has guided her. In this situation there can be only consultative discernment unless, of course, the person in authority entrusts the discernment entirely to her. If those with the right and responsibility to make the decision do so, having taken into account her discernment, and find they must decide against her proposal, they too may be led by the Spirit. Neither the individual proposing the change nor the person in authority has reason to question the other's docility to the Spirit because of this situation. (Whether there are other reasons to do so is not relevant to this discussion.)

The conclusion of a consultative discernment is not, therefore, a conditional one. The conclusion is not that God wills this person to change her ministry if the person who has just authority over her in this matter approves her decision. It is simply that God wills her to choose freely to propose or recommend this change or, more precisely, as we shall see in the next limit, to *intend* to propose it.

Recall Ignatius' discernment about Borgia.[25] He did not conclude that God wanted him to forbid Borgia's elevation to the cardinalate if and only if the pope did not rule otherwise. Rather, he concluded unconditionally that God willed him to oppose the project in every way he could until the pope should finally rule on it. The pope's decision, therefore, would say nothing about whether Ignatius had found God's will in his discernment. The conclusion of Ignatius was not a tentative conclusion waiting for a confirmation or disconfirmation from God through just authority. No exercise of authority confirms or disconfirms any subject's legitimate and sound consultative discernment of God's will—for the reason that, when accurately formulated, the questions for the two discernments are simply different questions. Either the consultative discernment begins with the right understanding of what is to be discerned and ends with a finalized legitimate and unconditional conclusion, or it begins with an illegitimate question and ends with an illegitimate answer, both violating the proper limits of discerning God's will. This point will be of considerable significance when discussing what Ignatius means by "confirmation" of discernment.[26]

Even if one grants the accuracy of what has been said, a bothersome question may still remain. If God is guiding us in discernment, why does he not move to congruent conclusions those who, in all good will, want to exercise authority in accord with his will and those who want to obey authority only as he wills? The answer to this question could be: Who knows the mind of God? But I think we can say more than that. We have already noted that, by moving

---

[25] See above, pp. 48–50.
[26] See below, pp. 218–221.

61

different persons to decisions which create a conflict situation, God can providentially bring about fruitful results. In a similar way, God can achieve some good through a proposal coming from consultative discernment and made to one in authority, who subsequently turns it down. Thus, in the illustration used above, the request or proposal to the superior may call her attention ahead of time to an important but neglected ministry for which the Holy Spirit is preparing the way. As a result, she may be ready later on, at God's *kairos*, to send the one who proposed to undertake it or some other who is better equipped and/or better able to be withdrawn from other work. It may be also that the Holy Spirit is forming the subject in humility and abandonment to God's providence, or leading her to experience her great worth to the Church in the work she is already doing.

3. What God Wills Actually to Happen as Consequences of the Discerner's Decision and Free Choice Is beyond the Limits of Discernment

So far we have seen that discernment is limited to finding God's will regarding the discerner's own free choice among alternatives which are all for the glory of God, when the discerner has the right and responsibility to choose. What Ignatius says in his letter to Borgia points to a further stringent limitation. It is another one that, when once pointed out, seems too obvious to delay over, but which both in the theory and the practice of discernment is frequently ignored and violated.

In his letter Ignatius says that he could not find through discernment what God wished actually to effect regarding the project for making Borgia a cardinal. He does not explain why, but what he says implies and is an obvious application of the fundamental principle for limiting discernment of God's will. For to know what will actually happen in the future is prophetic knowledge and is not needed in order to find and do God's will now; therefore, Ignatius has no grounds for believing that the Holy Spirit has led or will lead him to such knowledge.[27] It is true that, in one mode of Ignatian discernment, projections into the future or intelligent guesses about what will follow from one choice or another are data for reaching

---

[27] See above, pp. 46–47.

a judgment of what God wills. But the concluding judgment to which discernment leads is not that God wills actually to happen that which is projected. It is only an assertion that God wills the discerner to choose the course of action to which the projections point as more for God's glory. What will actually follow is another matter altogether. Whether, therefore, the chosen action will succeed in attaining the concrete goal intended is beyond the reach of discernment. In fact, whether the discerner will ever actually even begin to execute the course of action which is chosen is beyond the limits of discernment.

No one, to my knowledge, explicitly asserts that discernment of God's will is a way of trying to reach predictions; but there is plentiful evidence of an assumption to this effect. Even some unusually knowledgeable and wise writers on Ignatian discernment seem at times to be working from such an assumption.[28] Others who have little theological understanding of discernment find themselves frustrated and confused, doubting the value of past discernment or of discernment in general when the actual events consequent on discernment are altogether at variance with what they intended and expected.

The ordinary way of stating questions for discernment, when taken at face value, strengthens the hidden assumption that discernment yields predictive judgments; for it implies that the discerner is asking not merely what act of choice God wills him or her to

---

[28] The assumption shows up, for example, in arguments proposed for demonstrating the uncertainty of any conclusion reached by discernment. Thus, the biblical story of Jonah's prediction of the fall of Nineveh is said to be "a salutary warning to all discerners"—as though discernment of God's will were concerned with what God wills actually to happen in the future (Ladislas Orsy, S.J., "Toward a Theological Evaluation of Communal Discernment," *Studies in the Spirituality of Jesuits*, vol. 5, no. 5 [1973], p. 177). Similarly, appeal is made to the case of a religious superior making a decision contrary to that reached by the discernment of a high school community under his authority and to the mistaken prediction of Vincent Ferrer, O.P., on the end of the world (Thomas H. Clancy, S.J., "Three Problems Concerning Obedience," *Review for Religious*, vol. 33 [1974] pp. 850–851). The conclusion and warning to be drawn from these cases is not that sound discernment can easily lead to mistaken judgments, but that it cannot lead to justifiable prediction. Orsy himself shows clear awareness of this limit in his later publication *Probing the Spirit* (Denville, New Jersey: Dimension Books, 1976), p. 44. Once this limit is clear, the main point made by Orsy and Clancy is even more firmly made, namely, that discerners should be aware of their limitations and that the need for religious obedience is in no way lessened by individual or group discernment of God's will. Whether Ignatius thought that sound discernment can or cannot reach justifiable certainty is a different question, one which will be taken up in chapters 15–16.

make but also what God intends should actually follow as a consequence of that choice. For example, it is asked: Does God will that I live a life of consecrated celibacy or that I get married? If the former, does he will that I join a religious community? If to get married, does he will that I marry this person or some other? Does he will that I become a doctor or a social worker? and so on. Not one of these questions or any like them, taken at face value, is within the limits of Ignatian discernment.

At first, such a denial must strike many or even most readers as very strange. Perhaps the best way to make clear what is at issue here is to construct a case, analyze it, and draw the full implications of it. Suppose I set out to discern whether or not God wills for me to organize a pressure group and through it to persuade Congress to pass a bill allocating a large sum of money to provide food for people in a famine area. A positive answer will lead to my taking most of my time and energy for many weeks and may mean letting go other work I am doing. I make what by all Ignatian criteria seems to be a sound discernment and conclude that God wills me to do this.

Suppose, however, that I do get the pressure group organized and it does everything possible to achieve the goal, but that it fails to sway Congress. Must I infer that my discernment was a failure? If I really understood the question for discernment as it was stated, then that inference is inescapable. For I was asking whether God willed for me to organize a pressure group and sway Congress. I concluded affirmatively and then did not sway Congress.

But let us suppose that I was really aware it might be God's will that I should work to achieve this goal even if not to achieve it. Suppose I was only expressing the question imprecisely and that the question I really sought to answer was this: Does God will for me to organize the group and bring pressure to bear on the members of Congress with the hope of swaying them? Suppose despite my best efforts I fail even to organize the pressure group and, therefore, never get around to working at influencing Congress. Was my discernment then a failure? If I mean the revised question exactly as stated, surely my discernment failed. But assume again that I was merely imprecise, that what I really meant to discern was only

64

whether God willed for me to try to organize a pressure group, even if I should not succeed.

Now suppose that after concluding this discernment in the affirmative, circumstances arise which make it impossible or unreasonable for me even to try to organize a pressure group. Suppose that I am incapacitated by a serious accident or a sudden illness or that someone with just authority tells me to do something else that leaves no time for such an undertaking. Am I to say again that the trouble lies in an imprecise statement of the question? If so, what is left for me really to mean by it? What can I ask about God's will and remain within the proper limits of discernment?

The answer to this question can be established more clearly and convincingly if we first ask and answer another question: What is it about the formulation of every one of the questions so far in this case which causes trouble, even the last one? It is the unnoticed assumption that the discernment of God's will can lead us to predictive knowledge. All the questions ask what God wills positively and permissively actually to happen at some time consequent to the decision which concludes the discernment. But no discernment of God's will can ever justify any such knowledge, not even regarding the future immediately following the conclusion of the discernment.[29] I may with good reason on the basis of past experience and the grace God gives me be confident that I will carry out my decision *if* forces beyond my control do not prevent me. But that is an "if" which cannot be removed by discernment. In any case, even my conditional confidence of what I will do is not at all based on dis-

---

[29] It is true that we are almost always right in foreseeing what we will do a few seconds after choice and, therefore, feel very certain about it. Our foresight turns out to be less and less reliable as the time span between choice and action increases. But essentially there is no difference between the problem of knowing with certainty what we will do ten seconds or ten years after choice.

cernment of God's will but on trust in God's grace and my resolute will as shown in past experiences.[30]

In the case presented above, then, the accurate formulation would be: Does God will that I choose to organize a pressure group in order to sway Congress? So also, in all other questions for discernment of God's will. When formulated with precision, they do not ask whether God wills me to do this or that, but whether he wills me to *choose* to do this or that—understanding that his willing my choice does not necessarily mean willing that I actually carry out the chosen course of action or, much less, achieve the goal intended through that action. On the other hand, it must be understood that choosing a course of action does necessarily involve genuinely intending to carry it out if and when the situation makes it possible and suitable to do so and, when it does, to continue carrying out the intended course of action as long as there is no clear sign that a new discernment is called for. Choosing an action is in every instance choosing really to intend the action as opposed to having a mere velleity. To think that this understanding of the limits of discerning God's will is less demanding of stubborn fidelity in carrying out a decision would be a total misunderstanding.

The Practical Value of the Third Limit to Discernment

When all has been said about this third limit, even if truly said, is such precision of thought and language practicable for most persons? If it is, does it have any practical value significant enough to warrant the bother of attending to the subtlety involved?

It is certainly not realistic to hope that discerners, including those who have a thorough grasp of this limit, will always or usually avoid the ordinary ways of formulating their questions for discernment, their evidence, and their conclusions. Ignatius did not do so. We will go on speaking imprecisely much as we all go on talking

---

[30] The point I have been trying to make clear and to establish in a general way is what I understand Paul Quay, S.J., to be declaring regarding a vocation decision in his article "God's Call and Man's Response" (*Review for Religious*, vol. 33 [1974], p. 1073): "Whether, then, God desires for someone the objective toward which he calls him (something he will not ordinarily know except by the fact of reaching it) or not, He does desire this first movement of free response, this particular, concrete engagement of this person's liberty, and indeed in an affirmative sense: by making his own God's manifested desire. . . . " It is, Quay goes on to say, "the first free response by which the person moves to embrace that call that is the only thing we can be wholly certain that God is willing when He calls someone."

about the sun coming up and going down, although we have more astronomical knowlege and can call on it when we have need for it. It would be much too bothersome to do otherwise; in fact, the effort to obtain full accuracy of expression in accord with this limit of discerning God's will, especially when formulating evidence, would be such a distraction as to ruin most discernment. Further, sound discernments have certainly been carried through without reflective awareness of this limit; to think otherwise would be foolish.

On the other hand, if not always necessary for every discerner, knowledge of this limit is always desirable and is sometimes necessary. There are at least three times when it is necessary. The first is when one is thinking about the question of confirmation or disconfirmation of a discernment by events after the discerner has reached a decision and choice. Much misunderstanding about confirmation and disconfirmation has resulted from overlooking this limit of discernment.[31] The second arises when one is considering whether we can, by discernment, reach any justifiable conviction of what God wills. Invalid reasons for denying that we can are based, among other things, on assumptions which conflict with this limit.[32] Third, it is sometimes necessary that spiritual directors and directors of the Spiritual Exercises have an accurate understanding of this limit and are able to apply their understanding in order to prevent or clear up confusions in the minds of those whom they direct. For, if my experience and reading are a sound indication, not a few persons, as a result of not understanding this limit, are led by inaccurate thought and language to false expectations of discernment, to unjust demands on, or false accusations of, those who stand in the way of carrying out their decisions, or to unjust evaluations of their own discernments, and eventually even to wondering whether the idea of discerning God's will is an illusion. A typical case or two will show how this happens.

Case 1: "I discerned God's will regarding my vocation and found he was calling me to be a priest. I had no doubt about it at the time of the discernment or afterwards. However, after trying as hard as I could for a year in the seminary, I was told to leave. Did

---

[31] See chapter 12.
[32] See below, pp. 293–294.

67

I fail God? Or are those who told me to leave failing to respect God's will? Or did I just make a bad discernment to begin with?"

Response to Case 1: There may be other factors that need to be investigated, but on the basis of the facts stated, there is no need to question your discernment or your fidelity to God's will or the discernment by the seminary authorities. The thing that caused your problem is an ignorance of the limits of discernment. There was no way your discernment could find whether God wanted you actually to become a priest. You could not even find beforehand whether God wanted you actually to go to the seminary and study for the priesthood. All you needed to know in order to do God's will and all that was within the limits of your discernment was whether God willed for you freely to intend to become a priest and, therefore, to continue intending until God should show you that he did not will for you actually to become a priest. If it now becomes clear that God planned for you to spend only a year in the seminary and experience the training in prayer which you received, the friendships you made, and so on, that is entirely compatible with what you could have really discerned, though not with what you mistakenly thought you could discern. Those who told you to leave may have made a good discernment or a bad one. In either case, once you understand what you can discern, there is no reason to think that their decision in any way questions the soundness of your earlier discernment or necessarily implies any lack of sincerity on your part in carrying out what you chose as God's will.

Now, you would do well to discern again whether God wants you to choose some other way of serving him or wants you to choose to apply to another seminary (after working out any problems that appeared during the last year before applying elsewhere). The reasons given by those who told you to leave the seminary should be seriously taken into account during this discernment.

Case 2: "I made what I thought was a good discernment, more prayerful than ever before, with the best dispositions I have ever had, with clearer and stronger evidence than ever before. The conclusion was that God wanted me to put aside for a few years my ambitions in life and to work with the Peace Corps somewhere in the Third World. It was a terribly painful decision, but I experienced such a desire for whatever God wills, so much greater than at any other time, that I had no difficulty whatever in making the decision. Immediately after saying yes to God, I found great joy and peace in God at the thought of doing this for him and my neighbor. All my fears vanished. My director said that this was a strong confirmation of my decision. But, while getting ready to go, I became ill, and the doctor says that there is no sense in thinking of ever going, that I would soon be dead or a burden to others. With that medical report I will not be accepted; and it wouldn't make any sense to go even if I could. Doesn't this experience show that discerning God's will is really beyond us or at least beyond me and that I had better let it alone?''

Response to Case 2: The events following your discernment give no reason at all for questioning its soundness. Your discernment could not justify a judgment whether God willed for you actually ever to go to the Third World. That would be predictive knowledge. What God wanted of you was the purification of your heart and the courageous choice of genuinely intending to go. You have grown spiritually by the experience and are now better prepared to do or suffer what God wills for you in the future. Perhaps, also, God in this way is leading you to pray more for the Third World, to see your illness as something to offer with Christ for the people there, and later on to do what you can in this country to help them.

Chapter 6
The Essential Conditions for Sound Discernment of God's Will

*S*eeking to find God's will outside the limits that have been shown is worse than useless. But even within those limits, Ignatius teaches that a discernment of God's will may still be sound or unsound, depending on whether two conditions are fulfilled. If the discerner does observe the limits of discernment and does fulfill those two conditions, then the discernment is a sound one. (Whether or not Ignatius thinks that in a sound discernment one actually does find God's will is a question to be dealt with later on.) As far as sound discernment is concerned, no absolutely sure answer to that further question is needed; the discernment is not said to be sound or unsound because it has or has not found God's will, although it may possibly turn out that it is said to have found God's will because it is sound.

What are the two conditions to be fulfilled? They follow from Ignatius' understanding of our relationship with God in discerning his will. That relationship has two aspects: We depend entirely on the guidance of the Holy Spirit to find God's will, and the Spirit will guide us only through our own activity of mind and heart in seeking to find his will. The conditions for sound discernment, therefore, concern our being sufficiently open to the Holy Spirit and adequately carrying out the discernment process through which the Holy Spirit guides us.

It is true that the Holy Spirit can lead us to a true judgment without these conditions being fulfilled; or, from a purely human point of view, we could by luck make the right judgment and choice. But unless the conditions are fulfilled and we are sure that they have been fulfilled, we have no sound reason for thinking that we have in fact been guided through discernment to God's will. Suppose, however, the Holy Spirit should give one who has not fulfilled the conditions an infused knowledge and certainty of his will. That is possible, but such an event would not be discernment in the sense of seeking and finding God's will; it would be merely a passive reception for which no directives are needed or possible.

The First Essential Condition for Sound Discernment of God's Will: Openness to the Holy Spirit

Openness to the Holy Spirit is, in general, fundamentally constituted by living faith, faith issuing in charity and hope. However, there are many different ways of acting and many different attitudes which are obstacles to the Spirit's influence in a variety of situations and activities of Christian life. There are various corresponding factors in faith life by which these obstacles are prevented or overcome.

For one who is seeking to find God's will regarding a free choice to be made, Ignatius sees three main obstacles to receiving the guidance of the Spirit: (1) a failure to acknowledge entire dependence on God's help or, in other words, trusting in human resources alone or mainly to reach the right decision; (2) a divided heart, a heart that wants God's will but also wants something without regard for whether it is or is not God's will; (3) laziness or impatience

71

that is not willing to pay the price in time and effort which may be needed for one to reach adequate openness to the Spirit and/or to wait on the Spirit for his time to bring the discernment process to its goals.

Opposed to these obstacles to the influence of the Holy Spirit, Ignatius sees certain qualities or attitudes which free the discerner to receive the Spirit's influence: (1) prayer for and trust in the Spirit's guidance; (2) Christian simplicity of heart; (3) generous readiness to pay whatever price is necessary in order to be led by the Spirit in his way and in his time. These three are essential constituents of openness to the Holy Spirit in the context of discerning God's will. Each one of them calls for some comment to make clear what importance they have in the thought of Ignatius and how he understands them.

1. The First Factor in Openness to the Holy Spirit: Trust and Prayer

The first factor, trustful prayer for the light of the Spirit, presupposes that the one praying desires to know and do God's will, is aware of his own helplessness to find it without God's guidance, and has faith that God will answer his prayer. Desire, humility, and trust are all openings for the Spirit's influence.

Thus, we find in the *Spiritual Exercises* that the one seeking to find God's will is counseled to beg God that he himself (presumably by his direct action[1]) would dispose the discerner's mind and heart toward what is more for the praise and glory of God.[2]

We find in the discernment made by Ignatius and his companions regarding their future life together that they were all in full agreement about the first thing to be done; namely, to "give ourselves to prayer, Masses, and meditations more fervently than usual" and to trust in the goodness of God who "never denies his good Spirit to anyone who petitions him in humility and simplicity of heart."[3] An echo of Luke's Gospel is evident here.[4]

In the Constitutions of the Society of Jesus, Ignatius counsels

---

[1] *SpEx*, [15].
[2] Ibid., [180].
[3] Jules Toner, "The Deliberation," p. 186 [1,c]. See also p. 195 [5,1] and p. 196 [5,j].
[4] *Lk*. 11:13.

the superior who has to make a difficult decision that ''the first thing'' to be done is to pray and get his community to pray that God would make known his will.[5]

The more difficult the decision, the more should he pray.[6] When setting down directions for the general congregation, the highest legislative authority in the Society of Jesus, Ignatius says:

> But first of all, since the light to perceive what can best be decided upon must come down from the First and Supreme Wisdom, Masses and prayer will be offered in the place where the congregation is held as well as in the other regions of the Society. This should be done throughout the time the congregation lasts and the matters which should be settled within that time are being discussed, to obtain grace to conclude them in a manner conducive to the greater glory of God, our Lord.[7]

That Ignatius in his own discernment as a superior was consistent with his direction for others shows up in the letter to Francis Borgia which we analyzed in the previous chapter. There he tells how he himself prayed for divine guidance and got his community to pray and offer Masses for that intention all during the days of his discernment.[8]

2. Second Factor in Openness to the Holy Spirit: Christian Simplicity of Heart

Among the essential factors in openness to the Holy Spirit, the one which Ignatius stresses above all others in the *Spiritual Exercises* is Christian simplicity of heart. The reasons for stressing this factor are that it is the most necessary, the most difficult to achieve, and also the central one which ensures fulfillment of the others.

How important Ignatius considered this condition for successful seeking of God's will is suggested by the fact that, in the *Spiritual Exercises,* its essential function is stated in the first paragraph of the book and is repeated over and over as if Ignatius thought we all

---

[5] *Cons.*, [220] and [618].

[6] Ibid., [211].

[7] *ConsSJComm*, [711] and see [701].

[8] See above, p. 48.

too easily forget it in our discernment (as indeed we do) but should not forget it on pain of failure.[9] When giving his directions for the actual discernment process, after all preparations are completed, he relentlessly and insistently recalls it.[10]

In the Ignatian tradition, Christian simplicity of heart is, with good reason as we shall see, most commonly referred to as "indifference to all but God's will" or simply (and misleadingly to those not familiar with Ignatian thought) as "indifference." Even the fuller formulation can be misleading; for indifference to all but God's will is only the obverse and negative side of simplicity of heart and is not intelligible apart from the positive side. Nevertheless, as will be shown, there is very good reason for bringing out and stressing the negative side.

Neither the positive nor the negative side can be satisfactorily explained without reference to the other. However, in order to understand simplicity of heart as a condition for discerning God's will in some depth and with as much precision as we can, we will describe it from both positive and negative sides. Since the positive side holds priority, the descriptive analysis will begin with it.

The Positive Side of Simplicity of Heart

Seen from the positive side, simplicity of heart is constituted by such an integration of affectivity that the person in some true sense has only one love, one desire, and one choice. This statement obviously cannot mean that the person has numerically only one act of love, one act of desire, or one act of choice. What it means is that there is one root love, desire, and choice which rule or inform all others and to which all others are related for their ultimate meaning. Desire presupposes love for someone, self or another, for whom something is desired.[11] However, in Ignatius' exposition of the requirements for spiritual discernment of God's will, he focuses first on desire and then on love as the motive for desire. This order is not surprising in a context centered on choice among alternative

---

[9] SpEx, [1, 5, 16, 23, 150, 153–155, 157, 166, 169, 172, 177, 179–180, 182, 184, 189, 234, 238, 242].

[10] Ibid., [177–189].

[11] Jules Toner, The Experience of Love, pp. 72–75.

74

desired acts to attain a goal. The desires come more into the foreground of awareness. Let us, then, look first at the one desire.

One Desire

In what he entitles a "Preamble to Making an Election," Ignatius says that "in every good election so far as it depends on us, the eye of our intention ought to be simple, looking only to that for which I was created."[12] Or, more precisely, "in all and through all, wishing and seeking for nothing other than the greater praise and glory of God our Lord."[13] Only one end is to be desired, and all else that can be desired is to be in relationship to that end, to be desired as a constitutive element in that end or as a means to it. Our ideal, then, is so to integrate all desires in relationship to the desire for God's greater glory that all other desires are reducible to that one. That one desire for the greater glory is, then, the motive for all other desires and is virtually all desires.[14] Anyone who can hold to that simplicity in desiring will not, Ignatius says, prefer long to short life, riches to poverty, health to sickness, honor to ignominy, "and so *in all the rest*," except insofar as one is more conducive to the end, to God's glory.[15]

To desire anything other than God's greater glory without reference to that glory is to make the means an end. Thus, Ignatius says, some (without first discerning God's will in the matter) choose to have some source of income and only then ask how to use the income for God's service; or they first choose to get married (without asking about God's will) and only afterwards ask how to serve God in married life. Marriage and financial resources are ways and means among others for serving God and seeking the greater glory; so also are celibacy and poverty. To desire and to choose any of them without first finding out whether it is what God wills for the greater glory is to make it an end independent of the greater glory and so to divide one's heart.[16]

Does this meaning of having one desire exclude the possibility

---

[12] *SpEx*, [16]. See also [23].

[13] Ibid., [189].

[14] Ibid., [76]. See also [155].

[15] Ibid., [23] (emphasis mine). See also [166].

[16] Ibid., [169].

of a truly indifferent person's having any spontaneous affective inclination which is not able to be integrated with the desire or which is even in elective conflict with it? This question belongs more properly to a discussion of the negative side of simplicity of heart and will be taken up later.[17]

One Love

If, in a simple heart, desire for the greater glory of God is the sole motive for choosing one alternative rather than another, more ultimately the source or motive for that desire itself is love for God.[18] As noted above, every desire is for something or someone loved; without the love, no desire is intelligible. The desire for God's glory is desire for that glory in human persons and springs from a love which is primarily love for God and secondarily love for human persons that is rooted in or assumed into love for God.[19] The peak of such love is experienced when, by a gift of grace, one is so inflamed with love for God that "he cannot love any created thing on the face of the earth in itself but only in the creator of them all."[20]

However, even the desire for the good of human persons which springs from merely human love can come nearer to the one desire and one love Ignatius speaks of than desire for God's will and God's glory which does not spring from genuine personal love for God *and for human persons in God*. Sometimes desire for God's will and God's glory can be a mere obsession which not only falls short of Christian love but even comes into conflict with it and violates that love in the name of God's will or God's glory.[21]

---

[17] See below, pp. 79–87.

[18] *SpEx*, [184]. All desire presupposes radical care, which in turn presupposes radical love (Jules Toner, *The Experience of Love*, pp. 72–80).

[19] *SpEx*, [184] and [338]. Such love, according to Juan Polanco, no. 91 (*DirSpEx*MHSJ, pp. 317–318) allows for secondary motives which are in accord with and ultimately rooted in love for God.

[20] *SpEx*, [316]. Such love cannot be reached except by an extraordinary grace of God. It is rare and transient and not what Ignatius sees as required for discerning God's will (Jules Toner, *A Commentary*, pp. 95–99).

[21] Enlightening comparison can be made with the desire for God's kingdom as understood by Judas and by Barabbas in Nikos Kazantzakis' novel *The Last Temptation of Christ* or with Javert's neurotic obsession with (juridical) justice in Victor Hugo's *Les Miserables*. Like these, even a desire to do God's will can be sick and destructive if it is not rooted in Christlike love and practical wisdom.

It is, Ignatius sees, egoistic self-love which ultimately roots all selfish desire and mainly divides the hearts of those who are striving to integrate their loves into one love for God.[22] Therefore, he urges us to consider that "the measure of growth in the whole spiritual realm will be exactly the measure in which one has grown out of disordered self-love, self-seeking, and self-interest."[23] Since Ignatius sees that freedom from disordered self-love to be achieved by intensifying our love for God, the whole aim of the Spiritual Exercises up to the time of decision making and after is to grow in knowledge and love of God as revealed in Jesus Christ.

One Choice

To choose in any concrete situation what I judge to be less for the glory of God and, therefore, not what God prefers would be at least for that moment, in relation to that situation, to let go my one love and desire. It would be to divide my heart in some measure, whether great or slight. Inasmuch as I choose what is for the glory of God because it is for his glory, love for God and neighbor and desire for the glory motivate me. But insofar as I knowingly choose what is for the lesser glory, I am motivated by something other than love for God and neighbor and desire for the greater glory—usually, if not always, by some egoistic love and desire.

It is evident, then, that just as the one love (which integrates all loves into one for God) motivates the one desire (which integrates all other desires into one desire for God's greater glory in persons), so also this love and desire motivate (without necessitating) one choice which, in principle, integrates all other choices. That one choice is a choice to efficaciously intend to do[24] what is judged to be God's will in any and every concrete situation, what appears to be more conducive to the glory of God.[25] It is therefore, in principle, a choice of whatever the agent through discernment will find to be God's will.

So long as the freely chosen intention holds actually or virtually, no new act of choice is needed when the discernment process

---

[22] *SpEx*, [169, 189].
[23] Ibid., [189].
[24] See above, p. 66.
[25] *SpEx*, [23].

77

reaches decision. For that decision simply specifies what is already generically intended. The actual free choice of the intention to do whatever will be discerned to be God's will in this concrete situation for choice must, in Ignatius' view, precede discernment and render the person open to the guidance of the Holy Spirit. To try to find God's will for a particular choice without having already freely and resolutely chosen it in principle, to enter on discernment of what is for the greater glory with the intention of choosing whether or not to do it after finding it, this way of proceeding is not only futile, it is dangerous. For the discerner is in peril of his own will fathering the judgment that what he wills is God's will. So the discerner has no grounds for trusting the decision he reaches. Before entering on discernment of God's will, the only problem facing the person should be that of reaching a judgment. The problem of making a free choice should be firmly settled, so that reaching a judgment of what God wills is *eo ipso* making a choice of it.

If, in the process of discernment, the discerner begins to have any doubt whether he efficaciously intends to choose a very difficult course of action which might be God's will, Ignatius would have him stop the discernment process and go back to contemplation and prayer until he experiences the grace to have one love, one desire, one choice.

When the meaning of having one choice with one love and desire motivating it is understood, it is easy to see what Ignatius means when he leads the person making the Spiritual Exercises to the final offering and prayer, "Take and receive, O Lord, all my liberty."[26] For anyone to make this one choice is "with magnanimity and liberality" to give over to God all his power of love, desire, and free choice "so that his divine majesty may dispose of his person and of all he has in accord with his most holy will."[27] To intend by an act of free choice to choose what God wills in every consequent act of free choice is, at the moment of that act, to make a total gift of one's freedom to God. Freedom of choice must, of course, remain; otherwise it is not given over as a gift of love but, given up, re-pressed, destroyed. Therefore, the gift must be renewed in every

---

[26] Ibid., [234].
[27] Ibid., [5] and see [234].

choice thereafter; and, for weak and sinful persons like ourselves, it is a total gift for all time only in present resolution and hope.

Although the one choice in the present act does not eliminate the possibility of rejecting it in the future, even in the next moment, no other choice can be made in opposition to it as long as the freely chosen intention is actual. When a choice is made in discord with the choice that derives from the one love and desire, the person choosing, whether reflectively aware of it or not, has, at least for the moment and in regard to this act, renounced the one choice together with the one love and the one desire which grounds it. He or she may still love God, even very much, but no longer has only one love.

The Negative Side of Christian Simplicity of Heart

In the *Spiritual Exercises*, attainment of the negative side of simplicity of heart is mainly spoken of as ridding self of inordinate affections,[28] that is, affections not ordered to the ultimate goal of God's greater glory. Very rarely is it spoken of as becoming "indifferent," that is, indifferent to all but what God wills.[29] It is, therefore, surprising to see how, in the Ignatian tradition, the term "indifference" has largely displaced all other terms in referring to the negative side of Christian simplicity of heart. It is also, at first consideration, somewhat surprising to see the emphasis put on this negative side.

However, I do not think the tradition has erred in stressing as it has done the term and the concept of indifference to everything but God's will. Rightly understood, the concept serves better than any other to express the negative side of affective simplicity as a condition for discernment of God's will; and, as will be shown, it is of greatest value for testing the reality of the positive side. If there

---

[28] Ibid., [1, 16, 157, 172, 179]. See also [150, 153–155].

[29] The term "indifferent" (*indiferente*) to describe the requisite subjective condition for discerning God's will occurs only three times in *Spiritual Exercises*, [23, 157, 179]. It appears one other time where it has nothing to do with simplicity of heart [170]. It does not appear more prominently elsewhere in the writings of Ignatius. In the Constitutions, for example, the word is hardly ever used except in those passages dealing with men who are accepted into the Society of Jesus as *indifferentes*, that is, without any determination as yet whether they will become scholastics, brothers, or priests [15, 33, 72, 130, 132]; see also [111, 116, 117, 542]. Apart from this context, the only instance I have found in the Constitutions of Ignatius using the term in referring to discernment of God's will is [633].

79

has been in the Ignatian tradition of discerning God's will any falling away from Ignatius' own emphasis, it would be in not stressing and clarifying more than it has the one love, one desire, and one choice that constitute the positive side of simplicity—without diminishing at all the stress on indifference.

Since the term "indifference" or even the full phrase "indifference to all but God's will" can be understood in a number of ways that do not fit with Ignatius' thought or with Christian experience, there is call for a serious effort at clarification.[30] After that, the reason for stressing "indifference" along with the positive side of simplicity will be shown.

First of all, for the sake of focusing attention correctly, it will help to state what is a truism to anyone familiar with Ignatian thought on indifference. While there is often a problem of being indifferent to the roles persons are to play in my, or their own, life, there is no question of indifference to God or to created persons precisely as persons. Love for them is presupposed by the indifference of Christian simplicity. Neither is there any question of indifference toward the end which is the object of the one desire, the greater glory of God in created persons. Indifference is concerned only with what is relative to that end.

It is the affective response toward an act proposed for choice when that act is for the glory of God but not yet judged as more or less for God's glory than some other in the concrete situation. If the positive side of Christian simplicity of heart integrates all desires by relationship to desire for the greater glory, then it does not allow for choosing one alternative over another until the agent discerns which one is more for the glory.[31] Until then the person should be "like a balance at equilibrium,"[32] ready to be weighed down on either side by the greater evidence for what God wills.

It is essential for a correct and truly Christian understanding of indifference in the Ignatian usage that it be kept in the context of seeking, finding, and choosing God's will. Ignatius' indifference

---

[30] For an interesting and beautiful statement of what is involved in the negative side of purity of heart, see William J. Bryon, S.J., "Discernment and Poverty" in *The Way*, Supplement no. 23 (Autumn 1974), pp. 37–42.

[31] *SpEx*, [16, 23, 166, 169, 179].

[32] Ibid., [179] and see [15].

is *elective* indifference. What this means and the reason for insisting on it will appear immediately.

Elective Indifference Distinguished from Affective Apathy

Elective indifference is not constituted by affective apathy toward all the alternatives for choice prior to discerning God's will or to all but one after finding which one God wills to be chosen. Some of Ignatius' not-altogether-precise ways of speaking could lead the unwary to think that that is what he means. But such affective apathy is not at all requisite to or even compatible with the elective indifference which is the necessary condition for discernment of God's will. In fact, the character of elective indifference can be brought out in no better way than by contrast with affective apathy. At least three main contrasts readily come to mind. (1) Elective indifference presupposes and is the obverse side of a powerful love and a powerful desire flowing from that love—a love and a desire so powerful as readily to overrule the power of any opposing love and desire to sway choice. (2) Elective indifference is itself an active affective response. (3) This active response of indifference allows for other opposing spontaneous responses before and after discernment and choice of God's will; in fact, as the obverse side of dominant love, it sometimes implies such responses, which inevitably flow from love. A word about each of these points of contrast is called for.

1. The first of these contrasts is clear from everything said in this chapter, but an analogy with some other experiences of indifference may help to clarify it further. A person can become so intensely concerned with artistic creation, with philosophical or scientific discovery, with achievement in politics or business as to become relatively indifferent to things that, at other times, he or she finds important or intensely attractive. Family life, the needs of other people, social events, entertainments, eating and drinking may be seen as mere distraction from what is truly important. Some of these other activities may be seen as necessary if one is to continue with the all-consuming enterprise, but in themselves they are comparatively insignificant. Something similar happens to one who falls in love: everything is seen in relation to the happiness of the loved one and the lover's union with him or her. The lover's whole way of

seeing and valuing is affected; many things which were previously valued and held the lover's attention are now of slight concern except insofar as they relate to the lover's consuming interest. In none of these experiences would we say the person is apathetic. Rather, the person's affectivity has become more intensely alive and powerfully centered. There is a likeness here to what happens in a person who reaches one overruling Christian love, desire, and choice. All else is valued and chosen principally or solely for the sake of God's greater glory in created persons who are loved in union with God. It is the centering or integrating of affectivity by intensifying the integrating affection that renders a person electively indifferent.

2. Although Christian elective indifference is the opposite of apathy inasmuch as it presupposes an intense dominant love and desire, nevertheless one might still think that, in itself, the indifference is a sort of apathy, an absence of affective response to any alternative for choice not known to be God's will. For several reasons this way of thinking is a mistake.

Elective indifference is itself an affective act. It is not merely the absence of love or hate, desire or aversion, and so on. By elective indifference, I respond to each alternative for choice not yet known to be what God wills. I actively take a stand and adopt an affective attitude toward it as not worthy of being chosen except insofar as it is more for the glory of God than the other alternatives—something I do not yet know. But I do have an attraction to each alternative under whatever aspect it appears as more conducive to God's glory; and each alternative does have such an aspect or it would not be a real alternative.

3. But does not adopting such an attitude make me apathetic, at least in the sense that I cannot affectively respond to alternatives in ways which would be in tension with my one desire and choice? Would not elective indifference, in the measure that it is actualized, exclude *all* spontaneous desire for, or aversion to, delight in, or sorrow over alternatives for choice except insofar as they are conducive to the greater service and glory of God? Not at all. To see Christian elective indifference in this way would be a serious mistake. It would make such indifference impossible for a psychologically healthy person. It would imply that intense Christian love and desire, of which elective indifference is the obverse side, renders

one less fully human. This is a point that must be understood and emphasized.

Elective indifference does not imply insensitivity to the beauty and goodness which persons and things have in themselves and by which they can appeal to us in a way contrary to a dominant Christian desire and choice. Paradoxically, desire for that which is truly very beautiful and good (even though not for the greater glory in a particular situation for choice) may arise more powerfully in persons the more they love God and neighbor. For such persons become more, rather than less, sensitive to the beauty and goodness of persons than they would otherwise be, more capable of experiencing the joy and sorrow, the pain and delight of love and friendship. Growing in genuine Christian love enlarges, rather than stunts, our humanity and, consequently, makes us responsive to every good that has to be sacrificed for the sake of the kingdom of God.

At the time when Jesus had to say yes to death out of love for his Father and us, he still loved human life intensely. Did anyone ever love life in the world his Father made more than Jesus did or more willingly let it go in order to do his Father's will? Could Ignatius of Loyola and Francis Xavier have been such friends as they were save "in the Lord"? And could Ignatius, without bitter pain and profound sorrow, suddenly choose to send Francis to the other end of the earth for God's greater service? Or could Francis, who carried over his heart the signatures of Ignatius and other first "friends in the Lord" and read Ignatius' letters with profoundest emotion, without a terrible wrenching suddenly choose to say farewell with no hope of ever again seeing Ignatius and the others in this world? And yet Ignatius and Francis made their decision without hesitation, as if it were easy, when the greater glory suddenly called for it.[33] That is what elective indifference means. Those who have been through, or have helped others through, an Ignatian discernment to decide whether God called them to marriage or consecrated celibacy, no matter which way the decision went, know that, in becoming electively indifferent to the attraction of romantic love and marriage, they did not become less sensitive to the beauty of these human experiences, did not feel less attraction to them or less

---

[33] See Mary Purcell, *The First Jesuit* (Westminster, MD: Newman, 1957), pp. 299–300.

pain in the thought of sacrificing them. What they did experience was a desire for the greater glory of God rooted in love for God and neighbor, so much deeper and stronger than any other desire, that they were free from any undue influence on their judgment about the matter and, perhaps, could even make the decision and choice readily despite the pain.

Here, I think, is the most precise and accurate way of understanding Christian elective indifference as it shows up in experience: In any situation for choice I am able to be electively indifferent in the measure that my desire for the greater glory of God, flowing from love of God and neighbor, exceeds in its power to influence my deliberation and choice the power of any desire for one of the alternatives. The greater the gap between my desire for God's glory and any other lesser desire, the greater is my indifference. When the gap is closed or even notably narrowed, I will not have an attitude of elective indifference sufficiently strong to assure me that no motive other than love for God and desire for his glory will decisively influence my deliberation and choice.

Briefly put then, indifference in the Ignatian meaning does not mean total freedom from spontaneous desires and fears which conflict with desire for the greater glory in some concrete situation. It does mean, in the measure that indifference is achieved, freedom from confusion and struggle caused by opposing desires and fears, freedom from the danger of being misled by these. At times, struggles may still remain because of the difficulty of getting evidence or because of conflicting evidence, but that is another matter.

Ignatius' Stress on Indifference and the Reason for It

Unquestionably, Ignatius puts great stress on the negative as well as the positive side of Christian simplicity of heart. In the very first paragraph of the *Spiritual Exercises*, Ignatius describes spiritual exercises as "every way of preparing and disposing the person to rid self of all disordered affections and, after getting rid of them, to seek and find the divine will."[34] In the Principle and Foundation of the *Spiritual Exercises*, the point to which all leads is the need to make ourselves indifferent in regard to all that is left to our free

---

[34] *SpEx*, [1].

choices, that is, not morally commanded or forbidden.[35] At the time of immediate preparation for the "election" (the time for decision making), Ignatius has the exercitant consider what he calls the "three modes of humility." The second of these is constituted by indifference;[36] without this mode of humility, the director of the Spiritual Exercises is not to allow the exercitant to begin the election.[37] Finally, in the step-by-step instructions on how to carry out the election, after telling the exercitant to recall the question for decision but before any further step, Ignatius writes:

> It is necessary to have as goal the end for which I am created, which is to praise God our Lord, and to save my soul. Along with that, it is necessary that I have become indifferent, without any disordered affections, so as not to be more inclined or affected toward taking than leaving what is proposed for election or to leaving rather than taking it. Rather, it is necessary that I hold myself like a balance at midpoint, in order to pursue whatever I perceive to be more for the glory and praise of God our Lord and the salvation of my soul.[38]

All this emphasis on indifference, even when it is understood, bothers some people. After all, Christian perfection is summed up in Christian love with its inevitable expression in seeking and choosing what is more for the kingdom of God. Inasmuch as we so love and desire and choose, we will, whether we reflect on it or not, also be indifferent to all but God's will and greater glory. Thoughts of love and desire for heavenly glory are much more appealing, inspiring, and more powerfully motivating than thoughts of detachment or indifference. Why then so much emphasis on this negative concept? Why not keep our attention only on the positive side, on one love, one desire, one choice and say no more about the negative than is needed for explaining the positive side?

This question does not seem to occur to Ignatius. If it were

---

[35] Ibid., [23].

[36] Ibid., [166].

[37] *Directoria Ignatiana Autographa*, [17], in *DirSpEx*MHSJ, p. 74. Hereafter referred to as *DirAutog*.

[38] *SpEx*, [179].

put to him, he could respond with another question or series of questions. Why did Jesus say that those who want to be his followers must renounce themselves and be ready to renounce all they hold most dear, must take up the cross every day and lose their lives?[39] Why did Jesus not just leave it at what he says on other occasions, that they must believe in him, love God and neighbor, and seek always the kingdom of God? Why did Paul think the best way to convince us of Christ's love for us and to show us what it means to have the mind of Christ was through a lyrical proclamation of Christ's self-emptying to take on the form of a slave, to become poor that we might become rich, to die for us?[40] Why does Paul, when trying to express his own love for Christ, focus on all he let go and counts as rubbish in comparison to knowing Him?[41]

The answer to all these questions about the Gospel or about Ignatian stress on indifference lies in a common experience. We are all easily carried away by powerful feelings of love and desire into thinking we have a great, courageous, unselfish, faithful love. We feel so generous and courageous. But when face-to-face with demands for renunciation of what we desire or acceptance of what we fear, it often happens that all our feelings fade and our illusion of courageous love collapses. We back away from what genuine love calls for. What we take to be great love in ourselves for God and neighbor and the great desire for the glory of God can often turn out to be specious, inefficacious, a self-deception. Elective indifference is the one reliable test of genuinely unselfish love. Christian love and desire is genuine precisely in the measure that it issues in elective indifference to the alternatives for choice. In the measure that one falls short of such indifference, one may be sure that his or her love and desire fall short of being the one love and the one desire which are required for openness to the Spirit. On the other hand, one may *feel* little love or desire and be led to think he has little and yet be fully indifferent in the sense explained above. That indifference is the sure sign that he does have genuine unselfish love

---

[39] *Lk.*, 9:23–24, 14:25–27, 33.

[40] *Phil.*, 2:5–8; 2 *Cor.* 8:9; *Rom.* 5:8.

[41] *Phil.*, 3:7–9.

for God and neighbor and desire for God's greater glory, enough to fulfill the condition for discerning God's will.

Beyond Indifference: The Third Mode of Humility

Any account of Ignatius' thought on simplicity of heart as a condition for discernment of God's will would be incomplete without consideration of the attitude toward choice which he called the third mode or third degree of humility.[42] This attitude presupposes that indifference of the second mode has been reached. If in some sense the third mode surpasses the second, it in no way replaces it. Rather it includes and strengthens it.

Before seeing how that is, we had better see what constitutes the third mode of humility in contrast with the first and the second. All of them are attitudes concerned with choice of action. Not for anything, neither to avoid death nor to be lord of the whole world, would one who has the first mode of humility choose to act against God's will by a grave sin or even consider so doing.[43] To be firmly established in it is a very great gift of God and a great step in spiritual growth. The second mode is "more perfect humility."[44] It is the attitude we have been describing as the negative side of Christian simplicity of heart, which presupposes the positive side; that is, one love, desire, and choice. It is constituted by such elective indifference that, when faced with any choice of alternatives, such as riches or poverty, and honor or opprobrium, if the consequences for the service and glory of God are equal, the person has no preference for either alternative which could influence choice.[45] Insofar as the person has the third mode of humility, however, he or she does have a preference in such a situation for choice.

> The third is most perfect humility. That is to say, presupposing the first and second modes attained, when

---

[42] Because in the *Spiritual Exercises* St. Ignatius speaks only of three "modes," some object to calling them three "degrees" of humility, even asserting that they are not degrees but kinds. In his autograph directory of the *Spiritual Exercises*, [17], however, Ignatius himself speaks of the "second degree" and the "third degree" of humility in both the Spanish (*grado*) and the Latin (*gradum*) versions (*DirSpExMHSJ*, pp. 74–77).

[43] *SpEx*, [165].

[44] Ibid., [166].

[45] Ibid.

[in a situation for choice] the praise and glory of the divine majesty are equal, in order to imitate and become in actuality more like Christ our Lord, I desire and choose poverty with Christ poor rather than riches; humiliations with Christ filled with them rather than honors; and rather than be thought wise and judicious in this world, I desire to be put down as useless and a fool for the sake of Christ who before me was held as such.[46]

Illumination of the motive involved in the third mode of humility can be found in the contemplation which Ignatius entitles "The Call of the Temporal King."[47] The heart of this contemplation is Christ's call to be "with him." It is a call first of all to be with him in his struggle to establish the kingdom of God and to share his labor and watching, his hardships, and finally his victory and glory.[48] The call is to a life of friendship with Christ in the fullest meaning of the word, to mutual love and mutual sharing of lives. Anyone who has sound judgment, says Ignatius, will respond by offering his whole self with a willing heart for laboring with Christ. But those who desire to show greater affection for Christ and want to enter more fully into a life of friendship with him will do even more. Going against self-love (of the ignoble and un-Christian sort), they will offer themselves with deliberate and resolute determination to follow him "in enduring all injuries, all reproaches, and all poverty, actual as well as spiritual."[49] They will beg for this as a great gift from God. However, this desire to imitate and share in Christ's life by enduring humiliation and poverty with him is conditional; namely, "if only it is for your [God's] greater service and praise."[50] Nothing must supersede the greater glory! If riches and honors should be more for the glory of God, then that is what ought to be preferred and chosen, for that motive alone. But if the glory should be equal, then for the one who has the third mode of humility or

---

[46] Ibid., [167].
[47] Ibid., [91–98].
[48] Ibid., [93–95].
[49] Ibid., [98].
[50] Ibid.

love, the desire to be with Jesus in all ways, even in actual poverty and opprobrium, will determine his or her preferences.

Some clarifications or emphases are needed to prevent watering down the ideal presented by Ignatius. The poverty Ignatius is speaking of is not just poverty of spirit or, as he sometimes calls it, "spiritual poverty." The latter is a disposition to which Christ calls all his followers in every situation, even when choosing riches would be for God's greater glory; the second mode of humility in its perfection is complete poverty of spirit. The poverty Ignatius is talking about in the third mode of humility is actual poverty, lack of material goods, of economic resources, and of the power that rests on these. Further, this mode of humility disposes one to prefer and choose poverty and humiliation with Christ poor and humiliated rather than riches and honors, even when doing so would not bring the slightest increase of glory to God. Some seem to blunt this point in order to make the third mode more easily understandable and acceptable. To do so is to lose the whole point of the third mode and slide back into the second mode.

On the other hand, some emphases are needed to prevent overlooking certain qualifications without which the third mode of humility could be seen as un-Christian and even as a symptom of psychological sickness. Humiliation or opprobrium, it must be understood, is desired only on two conditions: first, that there be no offense to God and no sin imputed to the persons who impose them on me and, second, that I give no just cause for their doing so. Further, the reason for desiring opprobrium and actual poverty is not that these are given any value in themselves. They are valued solely because by them one shares more fully with Jesus in his life of poverty and humiliation. It is being *with Jesus* that is valued.

All the necessary emphases and qualifications are stated by Ignatius more clearly than anywhere else in his writings in the following passage:

> It is likewise highly important to bring this to the mind of those who are being examined [as candidates for the Society of Jesus] . . . to how great a degree it helps and profits one in the spiritual life to abhor in its totality and not in part whatever the world loves and embraces,

and to accept and desire with all possible energy whatever Christ our Lord has loved and embraced. Just as men of the world who follow the world love and seek with such diligence honors, fame, and esteem for a great name on earth, as the world teaches them, so those who are progressing in the spiritual life and truly following Christ our Lord love and intensely desire everything opposite. That is to say, they desire to clothe themselves with the same clothing and uniform of their Lord because of the love and reverence which he deserves, to such an extent that where there would be no offense to his divine majesty and no imputation of sin to the neighbor, they would wish to suffer injuries, false accusations, and affronts, and to be held and esteemed as fools (but without their giving any occasions for this), because they desire to resemble and imitate in some manner our Creator and Lord Jesus Christ, by putting on his clothing and uniform, since it was for our spiritual profit that he clothed himself as he did. For he gave us an example that in all things possible to us we might seek, through the aid of his grace, to imitate and follow him since he is the true way which leads men to life.[51]

Even given the foregoing clarification, there are still several serious questions which must be answered: In what way can the third be more perfect than the second mode of humility? Is the third mode concerned with a really possible situation? If not, what value does it have?

Is the Third Mode of Humility More Perfect than the Second?

If the motive for choice in the second mode of humility has priority over what is peculiar to the third, why does Ignatius say that the latter is the ''most perfect humility''[52] and that it is ''greater and better'' than the second?[53] At least when we are considering these precisely as dispositions for discerning and choosing God's

---

[51] *ConsSJComm*, [101].
[52] *SpEx*, [167].
[53] Ibid., [168].

will, what could be better than the utter Christian simplicity of heart constituted by one love, one desire, and one choice—and, consequently, by indifference to all possible motives for choice except God's will, God's greater glory?

Perhaps the answer to this question is found by distinguishing the degree of simplicity of the one love from its degree of intensity. Even love which is utterly simple can have degrees of intensity. Is it not the greater intensity of love for Christ which finds expression in wanting to share with him the hardships of his life just in order to be with him more fully? There are two love-inspired drives which differ in intensity in accord with differing intensities of love. There is, first, a drive toward the beloved's fullness of being and, second, a drive toward union with the beloved in all ways appropriate and possible. The more intense the love, the more these drives appear in conscious experience. To desire union with the beloved in the latter's pain, sorrow, humiliation, poverty, and all such experiences, even though this would bring no greater glory to the beloved or to anyone else—such a desire is a clear sign of unusually intense love. It is this unusual intensity of love for Christ that alone marks the third mode as "greater and better." No greater simplicity of heart is possible than that of the second mode in its fullness. The greater intensity of love for God in Christ and the greater corresponding readiness to renounce so much of what the human heart ordinarily desires for the sake of greater union with Christ is lost from the concept of the third mode of humility if we do not hold firmly to the phrase "the praise and glory of God being equal." When there is even the slightest inequality for the praise and glory of God seen in the alternatives for choice, the third mode of humility cannot function as a motive for choice.

There are indications that this is the way Ignatius thought about the third mode of humility, that is, as a sure sign of more intense personal love for Jesus Christ and, therefore, a sign of the Holy Spirit's influence. This interpretation fits perfectly with what he says in the meditation on the kingdom.[54] It explains why Ignatius looked for this attitude toward insults, slanders, and so on in those who sought admission into the Society of Jesus and why, if they did not

---

[54] See especially *SpEx*, [96–97].

have this attitude, he inquired whether they at least desired to have it.[55]

That also explains why he saw the third mode of humility or at least an approach to it as the most desirable disposition in anyone discerning God's will.[56] Before showing several ways in which the third mode of humility has a special value for one discerning God's will, a difficulty against its having any value at all had better be cleared up.

The Third Mode of Humility Involves an Impossible Supposition

The difficulty concerns the very possibility of the situation in which choosing either one of contrary alternatives, such as riches or poverty, honor or opprobrium, is equally for God's glory. Did Ignatius think that in the real world, where every choice has endless consequences, there could be a situation for choice in which there is not the slightest difference of value for the ultimate glory? If so, he would be making an enormous assumption, which seems to conflict with all our human experience, and would be proposing a situation in which human free choice would have no relationship with the ultimate goal of human life.

Perhaps he was only envisaging a situation in which the person strives unsuccessfully to reach any confident conclusion about which alternative is more for the glory, one in which the advantages and disadvantages for God's service appear to balance out pretty evenly; or the signs from consolation and desolation give no clear indication of where God is drawing him. This is altogether different from asserting that the alternatives really are themselves equally for God's glory. But two difficulties arise. First, Ignatius' language gives no hint that this is what he had in mind. Second, even assuming that it is, we still face the difficulty of his saying the third mode is "greater and better" than the second and is "most perfect humility." We have seen above in what sense these assertions are to be understood. If the third mode of humility is greater than the second, then to choose and act in accord with it is surely more for God's glory. Its motive and its consequence are to be more like Jesus, who

---

[55] *Cons*, [101–102].

[56] *DirAutog*, [17] (*DirSpEx*MHSJ, pp. 74–75).

chose poverty and humiliation as the way to reveal God's love and to save the world. Is not such following of Christ, all else being equal, some added glory of God in the agent?

The only way of understanding Ignatius which easily makes sense of what he says and does so without any loss to the power of the ideal he is holding up to us is to understand him to be presenting a purely hypothetical, actually impossible situation for choice, in order to show us an actually possible mode of love for Christ. The love is such that, in the impossible supposition of a situation for choice between riches and poverty and so on, in which the alternatives are equally for God's glory, the lover is to prefer and choose to be with Jesus in his poverty or humiliation just because it is his, and the lover wants to be more with him in every way possible. Nothing but extremely intense love could move anyone to such a desire.[57] It was such love that moved Francis of Assisi to speak of humiliation and contempt borne with Jesus as "perfect bliss." Not quite the same but similar is Teresa's impossible desire to go to hell so that there might be someone there loving and praising God. Love at the peak of intensity seeks expression in extravagant ways that seem bizarre to those who love less.

The Uses of the Third Mode of Humility for Discerning God's Will

If the situation for choice between riches or poverty, honors or opprobrium, when both are equally for God's glory, is merely an impossible supposition in order to bring out an ideal of intense love, what value does the third mode of humility have for discerning God's will in real situations for choice, where we look for the alternative that is more for the glory of God? At least two values come to mind. The first value is that it safeguards the indifference to all but God's will and God's glory, which is essential for a trustworthy discernment. Being more inclined to poverty and humility with Christ poor and humiliated (on the condition that the contrary is not more for the glory of God) is a powerful counteractive to any selfish

---

[57] One might desire real poverty and humiliation out of self–centered spiritual ambition or because of emotional sickness; but such desire would be altogether different from the third mode of humility, which is motivated by unselfish love for Christ and is basically a desire to be with him in all things.

tendencies toward riches, honors, pleasures, or anything of the sort which might diminish or destroy indifference. It frees one to hear and follow God's call, even if that call should conflict with these tendencies.[58] Ignatius' advice to the director of the Spiritual Exercises points to this use.

> In order that he [the exercitant]may be more inclined and more resolute toward God's glory and his own perfection, let him be directed to lean more toward the counsels than toward the precepts [only] provided this be for the greater service of God in the future.[59]
>
> Moreover, let [the director] guide and dispose him [the exercitant] in such a way as to require much greater signs from God for following the precepts [only] than for following the counsels; for Christ urged the counsels and pointed out the difficulty involved in having the possessions which may licitly be had while following the precepts [only].[60]

The same idea is found at work in the deliberation of the first fathers. Here it is a question of counteracting the tendency to self-will and to power over others. Ignatius and his companions were seeking to find whether God willed for them to take a vow of obedience to someone of their group. One of the important preparations they made was to arrive through meditation and prayer at a "predilection for obeying rather than commanding, when the consequent glory of God and the praise of his majesty would be equal."[61]

The second value of the third of mode of humility for discerning God's will is seen at those times when, after all reasonable effort, the discerner still cannot come to a decision about which alternative is more for God's glory. For then, the fact that one alternative leads to greater likeness to Christ poor and humiliated can be the decisive reason.

---

[58] *SpEx*, [157]. See also [16].

[59] For a sometimes-needed clarification about the meaning of "counsels" as opposed to "precepts [only]" and for resolving the seeming contradiction between this passage and *SpEx*, [15], see Jules Toner, "The Deliberation," p. 211, note 12.

[60] *DirAutog*, [8–9]. On this matter see also the directories of Polanco, no. 78, Dávila, no. 108, and the Official Directory of 1599, [172] (*DirSpEx*MHSJ, pp. 309, 513, 691).

[61] Jules Toner, "The Deliberation," p. 197 [6,1]. See also pp. 198–199.

In fact, for Ignatius, it could function as a strong reason in his discernment even when he was able to find which alternative was more advantageous for the glory of God. An illustration can be found in the account of his discernment about poverty when writing the Constitutions of the Society of Jesus. He had already drawn up two series of reasons why ''complete poverty'' would be more for the glory of God and his service and why it would not be so. The reasons for complete poverty were clearly stronger. Then the following experience occurred.

> . . . the thought of Jesus occurring to me, I felt a movement to follow him, it seemed to me interiorly, since he was the head of the Society, a greater argument to proceed in complete poverty than all the other human reasons, although I thought all the reasons for the past elections tended toward the same decision.[62]

Other Factors in Openness to the Holy Spirit

Besides all that is involved in simplicity of heart, there are other factors which are needed in order to be fully open to the Spirit. One of these is the ability to discern spirits or, in lieu of such ability, docility to someone who has the ability. Failure to discern spirits correctly can impede awareness of the Holy Spirit's guidance or bring one to see his guidance where there is none. How this is so can be shown only by a study of Ignatian discernment of spirits in general and, in particular, of Ignatius' second mode of discerning God's will. The latter will be done in later chapters. The former has already been done in a previous volume which was meant to serve as a preliminary study to this one.[63]

Another requisite for openness to the Holy Spirit is readiness to seek counsel from others who have experience, learning, and practical wisdom. This is especially so when the discerner is himself deficient in these qualities, either in general or only in regard to the particular kind of question at issue in the discernment at hand. But on any weighty question Ignatius seems to think that everyone should

---

[62] Entry for Feb. 23 (W. J. Young, trans., *Spiritual Journal*, pp. 15–16).

[63] Jules Toner, *A Commentary*.

seek counsel. We find him telling superiors in the Society of Jesus to do so,[64] and he himself did so.[65] This way of thinking is in accord with the whole Christian tradition that God helps us and guides us through others. To say this does not mean that others will necessarily give us the right answer, but they will at least help us by throwing new light on the question, stimulating us to do our own thinking better, by proposing a different point of view or giving a conflicting opinion that challenges us to serious and honest thought and prayer.

Finally, there is a factor in openness to the Holy Spirit which Ignatius does not mention but which is closely related to readiness to seek counsel, namely, freedom from prejudgments held with unjustifiable and unquestioned conviction. Sometimes, even without our noticing it, one or other of these prejudgments can play a major role in blinding us to the evidence for the decision to which the Holy Spirit is leading us.[66] These unquestioned prejudgments show up very clearly and readily in communal discernment (that is one of its many benefits). There, opposing prejudgments are often clearly implied by the open clash of reasons, none of which makes any sense to the other person who is working from a different prejudgment. Both prejudgments are thus brought out in the open and can be subjected to questioning. Seeking counsel during individual discernment of God's will can serve the same purpose.

The unjustified mind-sets are present more or less in all of us, including those who have high intelligence and are well educated. They are present even in those who have reached such indifference to all but God's will that for them to know God's will is to choose it. Such persons may be ready to seek facts and to reason with sincerity and honesty, but everything they hear and think is under-

---

[64] E.g., *Cons*, [211, 219, 221, 618].

[65] See his letter to Francis Borgia, above, p. 48.

[66] See Laurence J. Murphy, S.J., "Psychological Problems of Christian Choice," *The Way*, Supplement 24 (Spring, 1975), especially pp. 28–29. Also William R. Callahan, S.J., "The Impact of Culture on Religious Values and Decision–Making," *Soundings*, (Washington, D.C.: Center of Concern, 1974), pp. 8–12.

stood and evaluated in light of certain rigid and unfounded assumptions.[67]

These firmly held, uncritical presuppositions may have been absorbed from authority figures, from one's cultural setting, or from the spirit of the times. In some cases, they began long ago and have been lived by for many years until they appear to be unquestionable. They may, in fact, have been entirely reasonable judgments at an earlier time. In other cases (and both cases are possible in the same person), the person is caught up enthusiastically in new ways of thinking, usually in strong reaction to older ways, and frequently with feelings of resentment or ridicule toward the old ways as destructive or foolish. Having seen a number of long-trusted traditions exploded, having suffered themselves from trying to live by these traditions or seeing others harmed, some persons now have a firm mind-set averse to whatever is traditional and uncritically open to whatever is new.

There are two aspects to any of these uncritically accepted attitudes which make them influential in shaping our decisions, yet hard to uncover. The first is that they are tightly and intricately bound up with emotions, conscious or unconscious, of hate, fear, love, loyalty, or piety. Questioning them may call into question the value of much in our past or the validity of some dearly held goals around which our emotions or work have been integrated. They can be so interwoven with our religious and moral ideals that opposing or even questioning them is felt as infidelity. The second characteristic of these presuppositions which can make them hard to uncover is that they may be so built into the groundwork of our perception and thinking as to be unobserved for what they really are. Hidden from attention, they can be so powerful as sometimes

---

[67] "It is possible for a child of God to have a new life and a new heart but be without a new head. With too many . . ., the mind, though the heart is new, is still quite old. Their heart is full of love whereas their head is totally lacking in perception. How often the intents of the heart are utterly pure and yet the thoughts in the head are confused. Having become saturated with a mishmash of everything, the mind lacks the most signal element of all, which is spiritual insight. . . . Quite a number of God's best and most faithful children are the most narrow–minded and prejudice–filled. Already they have decided what is the truth and what truth they shall accept. They reject every other truth because these do not blend in with their preconceived notions. Their head is not as expansive as their heart" (Watchman Nee, *The Spiritual Man* [New York: Christian Fellowship Publishers, Inc., 1968] vol. 3, p. 11).

to blind us to basic moral values, even if we are otherwise reasonable, kind, and striving to be morally good people. Only think of the way that for centuries well-meaning and otherwise highly reasonable people have thought and acted in regard to slavery, women, economic justice, freedom of religion. Persons with admirably simple hearts can also, in some ways, be simpleminded. Persons with broad minds and expansive hearts can in some particular ways be narrow-minded.

Because of these two characteristics of prejudgments, it is often far more difficult to acknowledge them and liberate ourselves from them than it is to purify our hearts of obviously selfish affections. Even after becoming aware of them, being free from them is, at first, often felt as a shaking of the foundations of meaning in our lives.

How to Reach Openness to the Holy Spirit

When we have some understanding of what constitutes the openness to the Holy Spirit which is essential for sound discernment of God's will, the urgent question presents itself: How does one go about striving to reach such openness? The analysis made above indicates the focal point for our striving. If that analysis is true, then reaching openness to the Holy Spirit is fundamentally a matter of intensifying our love for God in Christ to such a degree that it dominates all our loves and integrates them into one love, a love that issues in so intense a desire for God's greater glory in ourselves and in all persons as to dominate and integrate all our desires into this one desire and so enable us to have one choice which, in principle, settles all choices.

Such a great love is, of course, a gift of the Holy Spirit. But from our side, how do we cooperate with him? How do we strive to intensify our love for God in Christ? Ignatius offers the Spiritual Exercises for that purpose. Every step in them leading to the election is remotely or immediately directed to helping us grow in intimate knowledge and love of Jesus. What we find in these exercises can serve as a model of preparation for briefer discernments insofar as the person has need of preparation and insofar as circumstances of time, energy, and so on allow. This may vary from a matter of days to a matter of minutes or even seconds. The ideal to be aimed at is a life in which, by God's grace and human collaboration with grace, the person habitually has the one love, one desire, and one choice which is the goal of the Spiritual Exercises and, consequently, is free of egoistic desires and fears and ready to let go of unfounded prejudgments. Such a person is ready to be led by the Holy Spirit and to find God's will every day in every situation for choice.

The Second Condition for a Sound Discernment

Besides being open to the influence of the Holy Spirit, our relationship with God in discerning his will requires our actual human effort in seeking to find that will. For, while finding God's will depends on being led to it by the Holy Spirit, the Spirit leads us, as we saw, through our own acts. This second essential requisite for sound discernment of God's will is an application of the Ignatian "trust-and-act principle," spoken of above.[68] Ignatius believed that God, who created us with the powers we have, wishes us to use them in collaboration with him, not only in doing the work which is for his glory,[69] but also in finding the works which will be more for the glory. Use of whatever one has of imagination, learning, experience, memory, foresight, reasoning, and sound judgment, it is true, cannot substitute for openness to the Holy Spirit. On the other hand, it is equally true that in God's ordinary providence over our lives a pure and trusting heart cannot substitute for using whatever measure of these gifts we have. Rather, the good will of a pure heart should lead to studying what is involved in a sound discernment process and then to carrying it out to the best of our ability.

Consequently, besides prayer to gain God's help and besides meditation, contemplation, and self-examination to reach openness to the Holy Spirit, Ignatius in the *Spiritual Exercises* requires of the discerner as much human effort in the process of seeking for God's will as is needed and of which the discerner is capable. His attitude and that of those whom he formed in discernment is seen in the *Deliberation of the First Fathers*.

> In full agreement we settled on this, that we would give ourselves to prayer, Masses and meditations more

---

[68] Jules Toner, *A Commentary*, pp. 156–160.
[69] *Cons*, [813–814].

fervently than usual and, after *doing our very best* we would for the rest cast all our concerns on the Lord, hoping in him. . . .

We began therefore, to *expend every human effort*.[70]

All that will be said in the following chapters on the Ignatian ways of seeking to find God's will is a development of what is or can be involved in fulfilling this second condition for sound discernment. No more need be said at present.

The fact that many chapters will be devoted to the study of method in the Ignatian discernment process must not be taken as a sign of the greater importance of methodical process over openness to the Holy Spirit. Both conditions are essential; but, if we are to assign comparative value to them, the first condition, openness to the Holy Spirit, seems far and away more important. One sign that Ignatius thought so is that in the few pages of the *Spiritual Exercises* where he gives instructions on how to carry out the election process, he keeps repeating over and over again, almost to the point of tedium, reminders of the need for those dispositions we have put together under the heading of openness to the Holy Spirit;[71] and, as we shall see, the four so-called "rules" given in the second way of the third-time election are ways of rendering the discerner more open to the Spirit.[72]

On the other hand, stress on openness to the Spirit, when rightly understood, can in no way lessen the importance of learning and using sound method in discernment. Rather, such openness involves a disposition to learn all one can about the ways of discerning God's will and to carry out the process as carefully and perseveringly as possible, for to do otherwise would be presumptuous and an obstacle to the Spirit's guidance. All this will become clearer, I hope, in the final section of the book, where we look for the grounds of conviction regarding a conclusion reached by Ignatian modes of discernment.

A Problem concerning Degrees

Only one thing is to be noted now about doing our best in

---

[70] Jules Toner, "The Deliberation," pp. 186–187 (emphasis mine).

[71] *SpEx*, [169, 177, 179, 180; 184].

[72] Ibid., [184–187], and see below, pp. 184–189.

being open to the Holy Spirit and about doing our best in the search for God's will. Inevitably, these two conditions will be fulfilled in varying degrees by different persons with different gifts and opportunities and by the same person under varying circumstances and with alternatives for choice of different degrees of importance. Is there any norm for judging when these conditions are fulfilled in a degree sufficient for a sound and trustworthy discernment?

Some seem ready to refer to any decision as a "discernment" even though made without any understanding or serious, well-informed effort to reach indifference to all but God's will by sound method. Such so-called discernment appears to others as, at best, the consequence of ignorance and, at worst, a camouflage for laziness and/or self-will. In reaction, they set up such high standards that very few individuals (or communities) could ever begin to discern God's will.

Neither of these extreme views has any place in Ignatius' teaching. What he thought on this question, however, can be understood much more clearly after seeing his teaching on the ways of seeking to find God's will, especially his teaching on the ground for putting faith in the conclusion of a sound discernment. Therefore, his resolution of our problem had better wait until we have seen his teaching on these other matters.[73]

---

[73] See below, pp. 299–312.

Chapter 7
Meaning of "Times for" and "Modes of" Ignatian "Election"

*T*he process which is requisite for fulfilling the second essential condition of sound discernment is constituted by one or more of what Ignatius calls the three "modes of election."[1]

Corresponding to these modes are three "times" or "occasions" for making a sound election.[2] Before taking up each of these

---

[1] *DirAutog*, [18–20] (*DirSpEx*MHSJ, pp. 76–77). Ignatius does make one passing mention of "four times" for an election (*DirAutog*, [6]). By parallel, there would be four modes of election. Ignatius does not speak of four modes, but Dávila does in his directory, [132] (*DirSpEx*MHSJ, p. 519). As we shall see, however, the so–called fourth mode is not fully distinct from or independent of the third; it is merely a development of the latter. See below, pp. 182–190.

[2] *SpEx*, [175].

times for and modes of election, it is necessary to be clear about what Ignatius meant by "election," by "time for" and a "mode of" election.

Meaning of "Election"

The Spanish term *elección* in the *Spiritual Exercises* and the term *hacer elección* are usually translated into English as "election" and "to make an election." Some object to this translation. The correct translation, they say, is simply "choice" and "to make a choice" or "to choose."[3] The latter translations certainly sound more idiomatic and may, perhaps, serve satisfactorily for a popular version of the *Spiritual Exercises*, in which precision may be sacrificed for the sake of readability.[4] But, for a precise understanding of Ignatius' teaching on discernment of God's will, they will not serve; for they do not take account of the complex structure of an election in its comprehensive meaning or of the various, more limited meanings in which Ignatius uses it.

The total complex experience to which Ignatius refers by the word in the *Spiritual Exercises* involves at least the following main factors: (1) the process by which a person seeks to find God's will; (2) the judgment or decision to which the process leads, in which it terminates, and which informs the act of choice; (3) the act of choice itself.[5] In the first two factors, the term "election" coincides with what Ignatius speaks of as "seeking and finding God's will,"[6]

---

[3] See Louis J. Puhl, S.J., *The Spiritual Exercises of St. Ignatius* (Westminster, MD., 1951; reprint, Chicago: Loyola University Press, 1968), pp. 183–184, notes 169–186, especially 169. See also pp. 185–186, notes 182, 183, 186, 187.

[4] David L. Fleming, S.J., adopts this translation throughout in his "contemporary reading" of the *Spiritual Exercises* in his book, *The Spiritual Exercises of St. Ignatius: A Literal Translation and a Contemporary Reading* (St. Louis: The Institute of Jesuit Sources, 1978).

[5] Like many others, Puhl is careless about the distinction between decision (an act of judgment) and the act of choice. See his note on *SpEx*, [21], p. 167 in his translation (note 3 above), and also his notes on [186] and [187], pp. 185–186.

[6] *SpEx*, [189] can cause some confusion here. After describing the three times for a sound election, Ignatius, in this paragraph, says that one who has "no opportunity or very prompt will to make an election" should use the methods for election and decide on ways of reforming his life. What constitutes the distinction between making an election and coming by the election methods to decisions about ways of reforming one's life is not clear. That Ignatius thought an election may be made about matters of less importance than a state of life is clear from many preceding passages in the *Spiritual Exercises*, [169, 171, 173, 178, 181] (and see above, pp. 30–32). The distinction which Ignatius had in mind, it seems, could have been only that between an election in a more proper sense and in a broader sense—the more proper being an election of a state in life.

and with ''discernment of God's will'' in current common but not universal usage.[7] In different contexts of the *Spiritual Exercises* and in Ignatius' own autograph directory, the term "election" refers primarily now to one and now to another of these factors in the total experience.[8]

The plural form, "elections," sometimes refers to the three modes described in the *Spiritual Exercises*, [175–188], but sometimes refers to a larger process in which a person takes up a logically ordered series of questions regarding God's will. Thus, Ignatius in his autograph directory advises one who is seeking to find God's will regarding his or her way of life to ask first whether God's call is to live the life of the evangelical counsels;[9] if so, whether in or outside of a religious community; if in a religious community, in what kind, when to begin, and what steps to take toward that end; if not called to the life of the evangelical counsels, in what other state of living.[10]

Meaning of a "Time for" and "Mode of" Election

In different contexts, the phrase "time for a sound election" can be understood in different ways. (1) It can mean a time when a person is faced with a necessity of finding and choosing God's will in some situation. (2) The phrase can also refer to the time when a person who already intends to seek God's will and is pre-

---

[7] For an example of the less common usage, see Thomas Green's very restricted understanding of this term in *Weeds Among the Wheat*, pp. 83–84, 87, 91, 98; and see below, Appendix B, pp. 324–327.

[8] When in the autograph directory Ignatius talks about modes of making an election, what he says about the second and third indicates different processes by which a decision can be reached. So also when in *SpEx*, [164] he uses the phrase "to enter on the elections." One does not enter on a judgment or an act of choice; one does enter on a *process*. On the other hand, when in *SpEx*, [171–174] he discusses "mutable" and "immutable" elections, he is surely referring to acts of choice or to what has been chosen. There could be no point in calling a process of seeking to find God's will mutable or immutable. In *SpEx*, [182–183] and [188], "election" seems to refer to the tentative judgment or decision which is to be offered to God for confirmation. But in *SpEx*, [169–170] "election" could refer to the process of seeking or to the concluding judgment, or to the choice, or to all these—though choice seems to be predominant. The same flexibility of meaning appears in Ignatius' *Spiritual Diary*; see the entries for Feb. 8, 9, 10, 11, 16.

[9] For the meaning of life according to the evangelical counsels as distinct from life according to the commandments only, see Jules Toner, "The Deliberation," p. 211, note 12.

[10] *DirAutog*, [22]. See the directories of Polanco, no. 82 (*DirSpEx*MHSJ, p. 312), Dávila, [112–114], (ibid., pp. 514–515); Cordeses, [115–118], (ibid., p. 553); and Official Directory of 1599, [178–186] (ibid. pp. 697–699).

paring to do so has reached the requisite openness to the Holy Spirit.[11] (3) Further, for one who intends to seek God's will and has reached openness to the Holy Spirit, the expression can mean the time when God has given the spiritual experience or experiences on the basis of which one can now discern God's will.[12] (4) Likewise, for such a person it can mean the "tranquil time" required for beginning and continuing the third mode of election, the time when the person desiring to find God's will is in an undisturbed state of mind.[13] (5) Again, "time for a sound election" can refer to the moment when evidence appears to be sufficient to justify terminating the discernment process by making a decision and choice.[14] (6) Finally, the phrase can mean a period of time during which the election process is carried on.

Among these possible meanings, the fourth and fifth are the principal ones in Ignatius' writings. Which of these two meanings (or of the others) Ignatius had in mind in any particular passage must be worked out by a careful study of the context.

A "mode of election" is a way of arriving through a process of discernment at a time for election in the sense of a time for making a decision and choice (the fifth meaning above). Whether this definition can hold for the first mode of election as well as for the other two is a question that will have to be taken up when that mode is analyzed.

It is true that in many situations sound discernment of God's will can and should be carried out quickly and without careful reflection on the method by which it is done. Nevertheless, in making a study of the three modes, it will be advantageous to have in mind a difficult and prolonged process in which each step is meticulously carried out with reflective attention in right order. Only by doing so can we be sure of seeing what is necessary or at least very helpful in any search to find God's will, whether it is carried out with

---

[11] *SpEx*, [1, 169, 179]; *DirAutog*, [17].

[12] *SpEx*, [175–176].

[13] Ibid., [177].

[14] Ibid., [175–177, 182–183, 188]. Note that only in this fifth meaning of "time for an election" can the term "election" be understocd as "choice," and that even here decision, the concluding judgment, is equally or more likely to be the meaning.

reflective attention to method or with the unreflective ease of experience and good habits when quick decisions are called for.

Chapter 8
The First Time and Mode

*T*here are three brief mentions by Ignatius of the first time for election: his statement in the *Spiritual Exercises*, [175]; the description of a first-time election (without naming it as such) in his own life, which he gives in his autobiography;[1] his passing comment in his autograph directory about three modes of election,[2] along with the direction that, if God does not move the person in the first time, he or she should go on to the second.[3] The first of these texts enables us to see certain essential factors in a first-time experience, but leaves us with many questions about that experience, especially with the question whether it, along with choice, constitutes the first-time

---

[1] *Autobiog*, [27].
[2] *DirAutog*, [17].
[3] Ibid., [18].

107

election, without any added factor.[4] Putting aside for now the question about first-time election, let us try to understand the experience which Ignatius describes, the factors in it, and their relationship. Only after doing so can we decide whether or not these factors alone, along with choice, constitute a first-time election.

The First-Time Experience: Its Essential Factors

The first time for a sound election, says Ignatius, is "a time when God our Lord so moves and draws the will that, without doubting or the power of doubting, the faithful person follows what is shown, as St. Paul and St. Matthew did in following Christ our Lord."[5] Taken out of context, the Spanish text[6] could be translated in another way: "a time when God our Lord so moves and draws the will that, without hesitating or the power of hesitating,[7] the faithful person carries out what is shown, as St. Paul and St. Matthew did in following Christ our Lord." Such a translation would, however, eliminate not only all active discernment but even the exercise of free choice. The first time would be no election or any part of an election by the human person. It is true that in the first time the person experiences being chosen by God rather than choosing; but chosen by God's non-necessitating will, which calls him or her to respond by free choice.[8]

In the first-time experience, then, there are three essential factors. For the moment, I am not concerned with the relationship of these factors to one another, their order of dependence. I am only

---

[4] In trying to answer these questions, not much help can be found either in the early directories or in later scholarship. The directories, which are very enlightening on questions about the second and third modes of discernment, are almost entirely silent about the first. Polanco says it is to be mentioned by the director "in passing" (*obiter*); that is all (no. 80, in *DirExSp*MHSJ, p. 311). Miró, except for referring to the three times, says nothing (nos. 84–85, ibid., p. 400). Dávila says only that it is extraordinary and not to be prayed for, and not to be much talked about by the director ([119], ibid., p. 516). Cordeses, like Polanco, merely tells the director to mention it in passing ([129], ibid., p. 555). The Official Directory repeats Dávila's comment a bit more expansively ([187], ibid., p. 701). Later scholarship offers interesting and stimulating speculations, but I have come across little by way of careful exegesis of the few lines which Ignatius wrote on the first time.

[5] *SpEx*, [175].

[6] *El primer tiempo es, cuando Dios nuestro Señor así mueve y attrahe la voluntad, que, sin dubitar ny poder dubitar, la tal anima devota sigue a lo que es mostrado; así como San Pablo y San Matheo lo hizieron en seguir a Xpo nuestro Señor* (*SpEx*MHSJ*Te*, p. 268).

[7] Thus L. Puhl.

[8] See above, pp. 28, 31.

concerned to note each factor so that it can be clear what acts of intellect and will are in the experience and what are not. After that is clear, the analysis can be carried further in an effort to show the interrelationship of the three essential factors, so that the essential structure of the experience may appear.

Something is said to be shown to the person. In context, there can be no doubt that "what is shown" is some act which God wills for the person to choose to intend.[9] Second, the will of the person is "moved and drawn" to this act precisely as to what God wills for him or her to choose freely (in other respects the person could be repelled by the act). Third, the person so moved is "without the power of doubting." Without the power of doubting what? In context, two things: that the volitional movement is from God and that what is shown is truly God's will. That is to say, the person has an absolutely certain judgment of what God wills for him or her to choose in this situation for choice.

If, however, Ignatius' too-brief description of the first time should leave any uncertainty about the above three essential factors, then the account which he gives of a first-time experience in his own life should remove all question. He does not name it as a first-time experience, but it is obviously such—and the only one of which we can be sure.[10] Here is how he relates it.

> He was persevering in abstinence from eating meat and was so firm in it that he in no way thought of changing. One day when he was getting up in the morning, some meat prepared for eating appeared before him as though he saw it with his bodily eyes, without his having any preceding desire for it. Moreover, along with [the vision] came, at that time and from then on, a complete

---

[9] It is necessary to keep reminding ourselves that discernment is limited to the choice of efficaciously intending. See above, pp. 66, 68.

[10] Some assert that Ignatius' visions at the Cardoner River and at La Storta (*Autobiog*, [30] and [96]) were first–time experiences. (For some references to this opinion, see Harvey Egan, *Mystical Horizon*, p. 135.) But the first of these experiences was a mystical enlightenment about God and the Christian mysteries with no indication in Ignatius' account that it had anything to do with making an election. Something can be said for the second as involving an election, but nothing which is finally convincing that there was an election or that, if there was, it was a first–time election and not a second–time election by consolation without preceding cause. See Harvey Egan's comments on its resemblance to but difference from a first–time experience (ibid., p. 139).

consent of the will to eating it. Although he recalled his earlier intention, he was unable to doubt about the matter, but decided that he ought to eat meat. Afterwards, when giving an account to his confessor, the confessor said he should seriously consider whether by chance that experience was a temptation; but he, examining it thoroughly, could never call it into doubt.[11]

In this account the three essential factors found in the *Spiritual Exercises*, [175] appear clearly, and an ambiguity about how to translate that sentence is removed. For Ignatius does hesitate to choose and to act until after conferring with his confessor and after examining the experience for some time, as his confessor advised, in order to see whether he was being deceived. What he could not do, even when making this examination, was to doubt that the experience was from God and revealed God's will to him.

Besides the three factors found in the *Spiritual Exercises*, [175], there is here an additional factor, the imaginative vision. There is, however, no good reason for thinking that this factor is an essential one; its absence would take nothing away from what is shown to be God's will or from the certainty that it is. The vision is a mere symbolic accompaniment in Ignatius' imagination.[12]

Are there any other essential factors of a first-time experience besides the three already discovered? As we shall see, many authors think that the first time always includes spiritual consolation, even spiritual consolation without previous cause. At present, it is enough to say that Ignatius' general description of the experience in the *Spiritual Exercises* contains nothing about spiritual consolation; nei-

---

[11] *Autobiog*, [27].

[12] In discussing Ignatius' first time for an election, Thomas Green in *Weeds Among the Wheat* speaks of "miraculous visions and voices" and says that, if these are genuine, no doubt about God's will is possible (p. 87). Some clarification seems needed. First, Ignatius' description of the first time (*SpEx*, [175]) does not include these sensational events. When they do accompany a first–time experience, they are merely incidental, not the source of the first–time experience of certainty. (See above, pp. 107–113.) Further, one may have such "miraculous signs" as Green mentions and not have a first–time experience; for one may not be given clarity about their meaning or, most importantly, unshakeable certainty about the origin of the signs or about what is indicated by them as God's will. To establish critically that the "visions and voices" are genuinely divine in origin and so argue to a conclusion that what is indicated by them as God's will is to be accepted as such with assurance is not at all the same as the first–time experience Ignatius describes.

ther does his concrete description of his own experience as related in his autobiography. The question whether we should, nevertheless, include it as an essential factor will be taken up a little later.

The Relationship of the Essential Factors in a First-Time Experience

It remains to ask how these three factors in the first time are related to each other. The question can be put another way. The main factor in the experience as a time for election is, of course, the indubitable judgment that "what is shown" as God's will really is his will. But how is some particular act shown to be what God wills the person to choose? And how is the person to whom it is shown certain that it is God's will? Is there an unmediated divine revelation to the person's intellect by which a particular act is shown to be God's will and, because it is known as God's will, moves the person who loves God toward choosing to do it? Just the reverse seems to be the case. For Ignatius says that God so moves and draws the will that the person cannot doubt that what is shown is his will. What is shown as God's will appears in the experience precisely as the object of the volitional drawing and not otherwise; and the certain judgment that this object really is what God wills is consequent on the drawing experienced in the will, presumably in some way dependent on it. This dependence of the judgment on the volitional response is even clearer in the vulgate version:

> The first time will be when the divine power so impels the will that all doubt by which the person might less readily follow the impulse, even the ability to doubt, is taken away.[13]

It is, in this statement, by God's impelling the will that doubt and the ability to doubt are removed, which is to say that certitude is given to the assent of judgment.

An Illustration

The foregoing descriptive analysis will perhaps be more in-

---

[13] *Tempus primum erit, quando voluntatem divina virtus sic impellit, ut omnis dubitatio, immo etiam dubitandi facultas, animae sublata sit, quominus sequatur impulsionem talem* . . . (*SpEx*MHSJ*Te*, p. 268).

telligible to the reader (and be supported) by the clear and detailed narration of one person's experience and of the life-long consequences of it.[14]

A religious experience occurred in November of Malia's senior year of high school. Religious life as a life style had never been a consideration for her. She remembers asking out of curiosity what kind of a girl could become a nun. After naming some qualifications, sister turned to Malia and said, "someone like you. You could become a sister." Malia's response was a definite and silent, "no way!" Malia also recalls praying intensely to God and expressing her desire to do whatever he wanted her to do EXCEPT become a nun. These were the only times the subject ever came up and they were soon forgotten.

It happened on a Sunday morning, the last day of a weekend retreat made by the seniors. Malia had stopped to make a visit in the chapel. As she began to kneel down she experienced a powerful shock—like a lightning bolt that went straight through her from head to feet. She felt her whole being lifted up in a surging "yes!" She had no control over it. It was much like riding the crest of a wave—one must go with it. There were no images, no words, no arguments, no doubts, no reasoning process to make. It was decided—period! She knelt there a few seconds absorbing the impact. There was a sense of great peace and joy and direction. In fact, it was the only time she had ever experienced such certitude.

Along with the call to religious life was also the name of the religious community. All that was needed was for Malia to follow through on the decision.

The decision was tested many times. In the course of the year the certitude never changed, neither did the

---

[14] The account given here is just as it was written by the person who had the experience. "Malia" is a pseudonym. I am especially grateful to the one who gave me this account because it is so difficult to find satisfactory accounts of such experiences. Those which can be found in the literature and proposed as first–time experiences are almost always lacking enough descriptive detail to enable one to be sure of their genuinity, or are clearly not genuine.

deep inner peace and joy. Malia's parents reacted with disapproval and anger at her decision. Her encounters with her mother were painful. Her father refused to speak to her during the year and announced that he would not give her financial support.

All her life Malia had been brought up to please her parents. As the oldest child she held a special place in the family and was extremely sensitive to the financial struggles and dreams of her parents. This was the first time she had ever dared to go contrary to their wishes. As painful as it was she could not shake off the certitude and peacefulness.

It was this certitude and deep peace that carried her through the year, enabled her to leave home, and helped her weather the homesickness and discouragement in the novitiate. For years after, Malia would feel the powerful impact of the experience whenever she recalled it. It was a gift, and she confesses that she would never have made it [through those years] without it. It gave her a basic joyous outlook and confidence in life and the secure sense of being loved by God—a love that she could feel in a tangible way. In her late thirties, Malia went through a period of spiritual desolation. Part of the desolation, the most painful part, was the loss of that sense of God's loving presence. And yet, in the midst of her confusion, guilt, and emptiness, the certitude of her vocation was left unshaken. It could not be doubted—when she had to believe that God was there, she knew he had chosen her to be his as a religious.

As she reflects on this, she believes that certitude comes from the fact that essentially the decision was God's; she only freely consented to accept it, to ride along on the crest of it.

Some Further Questions regarding the First Time

The foregoing description gives us all that Ignatius told us about the essential factors in the first-time experience and their relationship. One might take off from what Ignatius has said and engage in interesting speculations. (Some do so without always making clear where Ignatius' teaching stops and their own speculation begins.) My concern is only to understand what Ignatius himself said that will help us recognize the first-time experience and know how to respond to it.

However, several questions come to mind about matters which Ignatius did not explicitly touch on, questions which need to be addressed because the answers are needed for recognizing the first-time experience and for understanding what to do when it is recognized. If some or all of these questions cannot be answered with assurance, it may nevertheless be practically helpful to present possible and reasonable answers for the reader to consider. With this understanding of what we are about and why, the following questions will be addressed: (1) Is consolation (with or without previous cause) an essential factor in the first-time experience? (2) Is the first-time experience always apparent to reflective attention? (3) Does the first-time mode of election include a critical reflection on the first-time experience? (4) Are the first-time experience and mode of election rare?

1. Is Consolation an Essential Factor of the First-Time Experience?

There is an imposing array of authors who see high and intense consolation, usually consolation without previous cause, as belonging in one way or another to the first time. Thus, it is said that the first time "is beyond doubt a high form of consolation"[15] or that it "corresponds to a time of intense consolation, is a rare moment of high consolation or felt union."[16] Others specify the consolation as without previous cause, but differ about its relationship with the first time. Some seem simply to identify the two.[17] Others keep the two distinct. One merely says, without explanation, that the first time

---

[15] Brian O'Leary, "The Discernment of Spirits in the *Memoriale* of Blessed Peter Favre," *The Way*, Supplement 35 (Spring, 1979), p. 82.

[16] James Walsh, S.J., "Discernment of Spirits," *The Way*, Supplement 16 (Summer, 1972), p. 64.

[17] Hervé Coathalem, S.J., *Ignatian Insights*, trans. Charles McCarthy, S.J., 2nd ed. (Taichung, Taiwan: Kuanchi Press, 1979), pp. 187–188.

must be seen in relationship with consolation without previous cause, that the latter must be taken into account in order to understand the former.[18] Another asserts that consolation without previous cause "belongs to" the first time. By that phrase he means that, although consolation without previous cause and the first time for election have much in common, are even in some respects identical, they also differ; nevertheless, the first time "always" includes consolation without previous cause, but not vice versa."[19]

If we look at Ignatius' statement of what he means by the first time,[20] we find there no mention at all of consolation, with or without previous cause.[21] This is in sharp contrast to his statement of what he means by the second time.[22] Here consolation and desolation are said to be distinctive factors, presumably distinguishing this time from the first as well as from the third. If Ignatius thought consolation was also a factor essential to the first time, we would expect him to mention it or at least clearly imply it. If he meant to distinguish the first time from the second by types of consolation—the former being without previous cause and the latter with previous cause—not to say so anywhere would be grossly negligent. It is also significant that, in the *Spiritual Exercises*, [336], where Ignatius speaks of how to evaluate impulses which come during or immediately after consolation without previous cause, the impulse seems to be quite different from that in the first time, depending as it does on the consolation for certifying it as from God—clearly the second-time experience.

Nothing that has just been said implies that a consolation with-

---

[18] J. Clémence, "Le discernement des esprits dans les Exercices spirituels de saint Ignace de Loyola," RAM vol. 27 (1951), p. 355, note 34; vol. 28 (1952), p. 67, note 99. See also Bertrand de Margerie, S.J., *Theological Retreat*, trans. A. Owens, S.J. (Chicago: Franciscan Herald Press, 1976), pp. 155–156.

[19] Harvey Egan, *Mystical Horizon, pp. 140–141, 153.* Anyone who holds, as Egan does, that consolation without preceding cause is the first principle of *all* Ignatian discernment must somehow join this consolation with the first–time election if the latter is to have any validity.

[20] *SpEx*, [175]. See above, pp. 107–108.

[21] It is for this reason that Thomas Green, consistently with his restricted usage of the term "discernment" (see below, Appendix B, pp. 324–325), declares that Ignatius' first–time election is not a discernment. There is, Green rightly says, no consolation or desolation to discern about (*Weeds*, pp. 83–84). But what about the movement of the will which Ignatius stresses as essential to the first–time experience? Do we not have to discern whether it is a genuine first–time experience? (See below, pp. 121–127.)

[22] *SpEx*, [176]. See below, pp. 130–131.

out previous cause may not be given concurrently with the first-time experience. That is altogether possible. But the question at issue is whether consolation without previous cause is a *necessary* factor in the first time. Even if we should make the supposition that, in his mystical experiences at Cardoner and at La Storta, Ignatius had first-time experiences[23] and during them experienced consolation without previous cause, this supposition would in no way logically entail the conclusion that such consolation is always in fact included, much less that it is an essential factor, in the first time. It would only justify concluding that the two graces can be and sometimes are given together. We would still have to ask for evidence that Ignatius thought that the first time must or at least always does include such consolation.

It is altogether likely that the certitude of what God wills, which is given in a first-time experience, and the realization of God's love shown in giving such certainty of his will would issue in spiritual consolation. But such consolation would be with previous cause, a consequence of the first-time experience, not a factor in it; it would not be a help to find God's will but an experience of peace and joy as a result of having found it. This appears to be the case in the illustration of Malia's first-time experience narrated above.[24]

What appears from the *Spiritual Exercises*, [175-176] and [336] is confirmed by an examination of the account Ignatius gives of his own first-time experience in his autobiography,[25] the only clear account we have of any such experience in the life of Ignatius.[26] In it there is not the least hint of a consolation. All Ignatius mentions in his account is a vision of the meat, complete consent of will to eating it, inability to doubt that he should eat it, and, consequently, a decision to eat it.

The least that can be said is that in none of the texts which expressly touch on the first time is there any positive ground for including consolation in the *essential* structure of the first time. Given that we are talking about essentials, Ignatius' silence in all these key texts seems to say much more than that. It seems to give

---

[23] See above, note 10 of this chapter.
[24] See above, pp. 111–113.
[25] See above, pp. 109–110.
[26] See above, note 10 of this chapter.

solid reason for saying that consolation is not an essential factor in the first-time experience.

Further, if, despite its glaring absence from what Ignatius says about the first time, we should make the hypothesis of a consolation with or without previous cause as an essential part of that experience, what function could it have in reaching a certain judgment? As we have already seen, the volitional movement toward the act to be chosen as God's will precedes and grounds the judgment of what God's will is and itself seems to be self-authenticating. Further, if the person's belief that the volitional drawing experienced in the first time is from God were to depend on having consolation, the first mode of election would be indistinguishable from the second; what is more, it could not have the indubitable certainty Ignatius attributes to it. For, while Ignatius does say that a genuine consolation without previous cause is in fact certainly from God, he does not say that it is known with indubitable certitude by the one who receives it to be a genuine consolation without previous cause. There are manifold reasons for thinking it could not be so known.[27]

One way, it is true, of interpreting consolation and desolation in Ignatius' writing can escape these difficulties and escape all the arguments I have based on the *Spiritual Exercises* and the *Autobiography*. It is the way of interpreting Ignatius to mean that consolation or desolation is constituted by any affective tendency toward or away from God, without regard for what consolation and desolation mean in ordinary language; without regard for feelings of peace, joy, delight, sweetness, and so on, or the contrary. Anyone who so interprets Ignatius could logically assert that the volitional drawing in the first time not merely comes with consolation without previous cause but *is* such a consolation, even though there are no euphoric feelings whatsoever. Since this volitional drawing is without previous cause, it could be called a consolation without previous cause. However, I have already explained more fully the interpretation of Ignatian consolation which excludes as essential to it feelings of peace, joy, and delight, and presented what seem to be insuperable objections to that interpretation.[28] On that basis, I have

---

[27] See below, pp. 278–280.
[28] See Jules Toner, *A Commentary*, pp. 283–290.

to say that, while the volitional movement in the first time is without previous cause, it is not a consolation and does not necessarily involve a consolation with or without previous cause.

The contrasting real experiences of two persons, both spiritually mature and well balanced, may serve to clarify (not to establish) what I see as Ignatius' thought on the distinction between, and independence from each other of, the first time and consolation without previous cause. One of them had a very serious decision to make, a decision that could change her whole life. During the long time, at least a year, of seeking God's will for this decision, the person from time to time experienced intense, overwhelming spiritual consolations. To my judgment, they were genuine mystical experiences of a high order, coming after years of prayer of quiet and of extremely painful purifications—certainly what all commentators on Ignatius would, I think, accept as consolations without previous cause. But none of these consolations ever seemed to bring the slightest light on the question of discernment; they happened with no relationship to any decision making. The other person had similar experiences in prayer over a period of years and then one day had an experience which fits Ignatius' description of the first time (although he had no knowledge of the three Ignatian times for election and could not name the experience as first-time). The certitude about God's will was such as to make doubt impossible; it was a greater certitude than any he had ever had before (in the practical order). He, of his own accord, made clear to me that the experience was without any notable sweetness or joy; it was characterized merely by quiet and clarity. He even contrasted it with the great consolations he had experienced previously. Here, then, we see, on the one hand, a series of what seemed to be consolations without previous cause which bring no light to the ongoing search for God's will and, on the other hand, a first-time election which is devoid of consolation without previous cause and, perhaps, of any consolation whatever—unless that which follows on finding God's will.

2. Is the First-Time Experience Always Apparent to Reflective Attention?

To ask whether the first-time experience is always apparent to reflective attention is not at all the same as to ask whether it is always a conscious experience. The first time, as Ignatius describes it, is unquestionably a conscious experience. But most of what is in our consciousness at any time is not in our reflective attention.[29] Some elements of conscious experience may remain so hidden in the flowing complex mass of consciousness as not to come into reflective attention at all. Even when an element of conscious experience is in reflective attention, it may remain on the fringe of attention and hardly be noticed. Very little of our conscious experience comes into the focus of attention.[30] The question being raised now about the first time is whether this experience always comes into the focus of attention.

Most of us get the impression in reading about the first time that it comes suddenly and dramatically, forcing itself into the center of attention, as in Ignatius' experience and the experience of Malia related above. Perhaps, however, there are other experiences which fit the description of the first time in *Spiritual Exercises*, [175], but they are led up to so gradually and finally happen so quietly and hiddenly at such a deep level of consciousness as to escape any clear thematic attention. Perhaps, beneath some surface swirls and backwashes, a quiet but powerful volitional undercurrent tends in one direction, bringing a conviction that it is the way God is calling. Perhaps the conscious conviction hidden from reflective, thematic attention shows itself in the forefront of consciousness, not so much by a positive tendency to and conviction about any specific object as God's will, as by its negative power in situations where even attractive alternatives are rejected without adequate reason or any second-time experiences, but with inescapable certainty that these alternatives are not the way to go. Later, the positive choice to which God calls may gradually come to be more manifest and manifestly indubitable. Even some first-time experiences which are clear and dramatic may be only the sudden bursting into the center of reflective attention of a drawing and certainty which were already present in

---

[29] All conscious acts, of course, involve reflection in order to be conscious; but sometimes, by a further conscious act of reflection, we can attend to prior conscious acts. The question I am asking concerns this further conscious act of reflection on the preceding acts of will and intellect which constitute the first–time experience.

[30] For a fuller discussion of this point, see Jules Toner, *The Experience of Love*, pp. 61–65 and *A Commentary*, pp. 41–42.

the hidden way described above. When the latter event takes place, one who is not sensitively in touch with inner experience may not notice that the sudden experience is only a new reflective grasp of what has been going on for some time, which explains so much of his or her past ways of acting.

What I have been suggesting is very different from an opinion which I have seen expressed—namely, that any enduring inclination which gradually becomes accepted with great assurance is a first-time election. Such a way of thinking fails to take account of several possibilities. Even when it seems that no reasoning led to the assured judgment because no formal process has been undertaken, there could have been prolonged informal reasoning going on in which time after time a person, so readily and so quickly as to seem to escape reasoning, sees how everything about his or her personality, inclinations, spiritual experience, and vision of life points toward a way of life, a certain kind of work within that way of life, and so on, as more for God's service and glory. Or again, the certitude may come from many delicate experiences of spiritual consolation with drawing of the will which, without any formal discernment of spirits, gradually generate a firm sense of rightness in following the repeated drawing. What, therefore, appears to superficial reflection as a first-time experience may well be the result of a second-time or a third-time process or both together. There is only one case in which an enduring inclination, when finally accepted with certainty, can be a first-time experience. That is the case in which the certainty comes without dependence on spiritual consolations and desolations and without dependence on reasons, which characterize the third mode of election.

All I have been proposing about a hidden first-time experience is speculation without support from what Ignatius himself said. Still, I think there is nothing in it that cannot fit with what Ignatius said, and much that does seem to fit with the experiences of good and intelligent persons who are seeking God's will in their lives. I am, then, suggesting that we should consider whether there are not two ways of the first time. In fact, I would go further and express a suspicion (it is no more than that), for whatever it is worth, that, while the first-time experience in the dramatic form is relatively rare[31], many more decisions regarding God's will are of this other sort. If so, this could explain why some choose to begin and to persevere in difficult enterprises (especially undertaking a vocation in life) for God without being able to formulate any communicable evidence other than simply, "I am certain this is God's will for me."

3. Does the First-Time Election Include or Exclude a Critical Reflection on the First-Time Experience?

To this point, analysis has been restricted to the first-time experience, without explicit attention to the first mode of election. Now it is time to ask some questions about the latter. Does the first-time election include or exclude anything beyond the first-time experience described above and the act of free choice, to which all else in any election of any mode is ordered? In other words, is the first-time mode of election constituted solely by the passively received volitional movement and illumination with certainty regarding God's will, or is some active seeking, some discernment, required—or, for that matter, is such discernment really possible? The answer to this question has crucial significance for practice and for much of what is said later in this study. Let us see the implications of an affirmative or a negative answer: what would be required if anything beyond the first-time experience is required, and what evidence can be found for either answer in the writings of Ignatius.

Assume that the first-time experience and choice constitute the first-time election. In this understanding of such an election, if the one who seemed to have a first-time experience can, in reflection on it, actually doubt or even admit a real possibility of doubting and, consequently, can and should raise real questions (not merely go through the motions) about its origin or about what is shown in it and seek to answer these questions, the experience is, by that very fact, shown to be only speciously first-time.

If this first interpretation is the right one, then the first-time election is an election inasmuch as it includes a free choice, but is not an election if that is taken to involve some deliberative activity of reason, some active discernment process, in reaching a judgment.

---

[31] See below, pp. 127–129.

It is a way of knowing God's will, but not a way of seeking and finding it. It has no more need or possibility of active discernment than perceiving that a lightning bolt has struck beside you. It is, therefore, outside all rules and method and is of no further concern in this study—except for the question about the rarity or frequency of such an election.

The action judged to be God's will may be deferred, as Ignatius deferred it when so advised by his confessor,[32] while going through the motions of critical evaluation; but no real doubt and no real question can be actually entertained or even seen as possible by the subject of the first-time experience. The confessor or spiritual director of the person who has had what appears to be a first-time experience may really question the experience and try critically to evaluate it by appropriate norms, but that is another matter altogether.

The second interpretation sees a moment of critical reflection on the first-time experience as essential for a first-time election. It does not on that account require actual doubt about what has been shown as God's will. It even allows that God's will may still *seem* to the discerner to be indubitable. But it does require that the discerner recognize that what may *seem* to be so may, on reflection, turn out not to be so and that, therefore, doing one's best to find God's will requires critical reflection on the first-time experience. Here are some of the questions to be included in such a reflection:

1. Am I unable to doubt, even if I really wanted to, that what is shown me is truly God's will?

2. Do I recall with certainty and with complete accuracy what was shown, neither adding to nor subtracting from it, not altering it in any way whatever? Is what I accurately recall fully clear to me? If either of these questions must be answered negatively, then I must wait and pray for more light.

3. If I can answer these two questions affirmatively, does what is clearly and accurately recalled as God's will fully accord with the Gospel, with the Church's teaching, and with sound, faith-en-

---

[32] *Autobiog*, [27].

122

lightened reasons?[33] If not, it cannot be from God, and the first-time experience was specious. This test will have been carried out beforehand if the first-time experience comes as a response to a question about definite alternatives with which one is faced. But if, as in the experience of Ignatius[34] and that of Malia,[35] the first-time experience came without any previous thought of a choice to be made, then this test will have to be made afterwards.

4. What about the volitional movement? Was it, in the experience, a movement to what was shown as God's will purely and solely because it was God's will? Was it an expression of pure charity? No selfish motivation can be "from above," nor be part of a genuine first-time experience.

5. Does a second and/or third mode of election clearly and strongly conflict with the first-time judgment? As we have seen, doing one's best in seeking God's will is one of the two essential conditions for sound discernment;[36] and, as we shall see, this condition calls for using all modes of discernment which are possible and reasonable to use in the situation.[37] Therefore, in weighty decisions, when one has the time and energy, the first-time experience should be tested by going through a second-time election, if God makes it possible, and also a third-time one.[38] If strong second-time and third-time evidence should conflict with the first-time experience, the genuinity of the latter is at least suspect. In putting the first-time experience to this test, the discerner is not seeking to ground the certitude given in that experience on second-time or third-time evidence; for it is hardly to be thought that the judgment reached by these latter forms of discernment could serve in a positive way to strengthen the unreflected certain assent given in a genuine first-

---

[33] For helpful criteria, see the pages on St. Paul's criteria for discernment of spirits by Jacques Guillet, S.J., in *Discernment of Spirits* (Collegeville, Minn: The Liturgical Press, 1970), translation by Sr. Innocentia Richards of "Discernment des esprits," *Dictionnaire de Spiritualité Ascetique et Mystique*, vol. 3, (Paris, 1957), pp. 44–53.

[34] See above pp. 109–110.

[35] See above pp. 112–113.

[36] See above pp. 70–71; 99–100.

[37] See above pp. 251–253.

[38] To say this may at first appear to conflict with the implication of what Ignatius says in *DirAutog*, [18]. But see below, pp. 251–253. The same principle which calls for combining the second and the third modes seems also to justify testing the first mode by one or both of the other two.

time experience itself. The aim is, rather, to reach a reflective critical judgment regarding the direct assent, which in the first-time experience appears as certain and self-authenticating, and in this way to guard against mistaking a specious experience for a genuine one.

To guard against making such a mistake is, in fact, the purpose of all the suggested tests just mentioned. If anyone should deny (as I am sure some will) that the fifth test is in accord with Ignatius' instructions, the point need not be argued here. For my present aim is only to explain how the first mode of election can be understood to include some sort of critical reflection on the first-time experience as an essential element of that mode. In this way of understanding the first mode, it is an active discernment of God's will, not a purely passive illumination.

To see this second interpretation as putting human reason above divine inspiration, as some do, is to assume what is still in question. The question that needs answering is whether the experience under reflection is in fact a divine inspiration. To put reason above a divine inspiration, once the latter is known to be such, would, of course, be foolish; but to try to make sure that one is truly receiving a divine inspiration and not some dangerous substitute is certainly wise.

If the first-time experience survives all the checking and testing of critical reflection, can one now draw a reflective judgment which is just as certain as the unreflective judgment in the first-time experience? It might at first seem so, but not when we consider how fallible is all the reflection that has been carried out. Our memory may play tricks on us, and our judgments when applying norms may be erroneous. What kind of *reflective* assent can be given then— only a highly probable one? Or is there some way of justifying a firmer assent? This question can be answered only after other factors in Ignatius' teaching are taken up.[39] In any case, however, when the unreflective certitude of what God wills endures unchanged by the testing, the person seems fully justified in choosing according to that certitude—in fact can hardly do otherwise in all sincerity.

Which, then, of the two interpretations explained above is the right one? I think we have to say the answer is uncertain. Ignatius' autobiographical account of his experience suggests that the first

---

[39] See below, chapters 15–16.

interpretation is correct, that critical reflection on a first-time experience is actually impossible. Try as he might, Ignatius says, he could not really have any doubt (and, therefore, could not do any real questioning) about what was shown to him as God's will. It could be argued, however, that his inability to doubt might be peculiar to this experience and give no grounds for generalizing about all first-time elections. A hint that we can generalize may, perhaps, be looked for in the Constitutions where Ignatius is presenting a method for electing a general of the Society of Jesus. He allows for the possibility of an election by "common inspiration."

> If all by a common inspiration should choose some one without waiting for the methodical voting, let that one be the superior general. For the Holy Spirit, who has moved them to such an election, supplies for all methods and arrangements.[40]

When Ignatius says that the Holy Spirit, who has moved the group to such an election, supplies for all methods, is he not indicating that this is a group first-time election and that such an election needs no method and no discernment process? At first reading, this seems to be the case, and some authors refer to it as such. Against such an understanding of the text, it might be said that, even if we assumed there is a group first-time experience, Ignatius took for granted that a critical reflection on the experience would take place.

However that may be, the assumption that in this text Ignatius is thinking of a group first-time experience, it could plausibly be argued, is mistaken—or at least without support. For there is not the slightest evidence that the members of the congregation would, on the basis of that general inspiration, be entirely free of all doubt; much less is there any evidence that they would be unable to doubt that God willed for general superior the man they were electing. Further, it should be noted that the members of the congregation have already gone through a third-time discernment process of gathering and interpreting information on the candidates so as to reach a judgment about which candidate is more for God's service and

---

[40] *ConsSJComm*, p. 301, [700].

125

glory.[41] The Spirit may be moving them all to a common, simultaneous third-time election. For, when Ignatius says that the Holy Spirit "supples for all methods and arrangements," he must be understood in the light of his preceding sentence, which makes it clear that the Spirit's influence does away only with any need for "methodical voting." It is only the voting process that is bypassed by the inspiration, not the third-time process leading up to the voting and determining the common judgment.

In the light of what has been said, there does not seem to be any solid evidence for denying that Ignatius thought the first-time election needs critical reflection. Is there any solid evidence for affirming that he did see such reflection as a necessary part of the first-time election? Or is the question unanswerable?

In general, it can be said that reflecting on and testing any spiritual experience, especially one that points to choice and action, seems to be in accord with Ignatius' own practice[42] and his instruction to others. In important matters, he could, on occasion, even be overly cautious in this matter.[43]

Some take the well-known passage in Ignatius' letter to Teresa Rejadell of June 18, 1536,[44] as describing the first-time experience, especially those who see consolation without previous cause as an essential factor in that experience. If they are right, then Ignatius is clearly calling for a critical reflection on any such experience before decision and choice. But the passage, it seems to me, is concerned rather with a counsel given on the occasion of consolation without previous cause in a second-time election.

Ultimately, what must be said about the first time parallels what must be said about consolation without previous cause:[45] Ignatius does not describe it adequately and what he says is not very clear. Also, in parallel with what I have said elsewhere about such

---

[41] Cons, [694, 698, 699].

[42] It also seems more in accord with the teaching of the other great spiritual directors. The opinion presented here regarding a reflective moment in a first–time election can draw strength, I think, from a parallel with chapters 21 and 22, on how to evaluate private revelations, in A. Poulain, S.J., The Graces of Interior Prayer (Westminster, Vermont: Celtic Cross Books, 1978).

[43] See the entry in Ignatius' diary for March 12, and see below, pp. 199–200.

[44] LettersIgn, p. 22.

[45] See Jules Toner, A Commentary, pp. 216–217.

consolation,[46] given our uncertainty about Ignatius' teaching on this matter and given that one cannot lose by trying to carry out such a reflection as was outlined above, prudence and the desire to do our very best to find God's will strongly urge doing so whenever one reasonably can. In fact, not to do so would seem to be rash.

4. How Frequent Is First-Time Election?

The question of the frequency of the first-time election, inevitably comes to mind and has a practical bearing insofar as the answer to it can create right or wrong expectations. What Ignatius himself thought cannot be established. He says nothing which would indicate that he thought it was usual or unusual for good Christians in general. Some point out that, according to Ribadeneira, Ignatius himself frequently experienced it.[47] But even if that should be so, this fact would tell us nothing of what Ignatius thought about its frequency for other people—no more than his mystical prayer life would tell us anything about what he thought was the ordinary prayer of others. The letter to Teresa Rejadell referred to above is cited by some as evidence that, at least up to 1539, he thought first-time elections were frequent. However, it is not at all clear that Ignatius was describing a first-time election in this letter; it seems, rather, as noted above, that he was describing a second-time election in which the consolation is without previous cause. It would be altogether unsound scholarship to base any answer to the question at issue on this letter as a principal piece of evidence.

This much is altogether clear: The tradition most immediate to Ignatius points to the rarity of the first time and to its relative unimportance within the whole teaching of Ignatius on seeking God's will. In his directory, González Dávila says that the first time is "extraordinary" and is not to be asked of God. The Official Directory of 1599 repeats Dávila's opinion. Polanco and Cordeses in their directories merely say that the first time should be mentioned in passing (*obiter*) by the director of the Exercises; after that comment they say no more. Miró, after noting that there are three times for election, goes immediately to the second without commenting

---

[46] Ibid., pp. 253–256.
[47] See Harvey Egan, *Mystical Horizon*, p. 134. The passage he refers to in *FN* 2:415, n. 8, seems to me to be highly questionable as evidence for this opinion.

on the first.[48] Achille Gagliardi (1537-1607), one of the most eminent of the early Jesuit directors of and commentators on the Spiritual Exercises, expresses the same opinion as Dávila.[49]

The general opinion at present seems to agree with the earliest tradition in seeing the first time as "a rare moment."[50] One opinion goes to an extreme beyond the general view, asserting not only that it is a "direct and actual revelation in the strict theological sense,"[51] but also that Ignatius mentioned it "more out of a certain liking for system than for its practical importance."[52] On the other hand, some not only disagree with this extreme view but think that even the common opinion is too restricted. According to these authors, it has been too much taken for granted that the first time involves an extraordinary grace such as that given in mystical vocations; it is, they say, exceptional but not so rare as it is commonly made out to be.[53] According to this view, "many more people than we imagine have such self-authenticating experiences."[54] Another opinion goes even further and claims that Ignatius thought the first-time election is of frequent occurrence.[55]

The speculation made above on allowing for first-time experiences which do not get into the center of ordinary reflective attention[56] would probably allow for a notable increase in the number

---

[48] See above, note 4 of this chapter.

[49] Achille Gagliardi, S.J., *Commentarii seu Explanationes in Exercitia Spiritualia Sancti Patris Ignatii de Loyola* (Bruges: Desclee, De Brouwer et Soc., 1882), p. 93.

[50] For example, James Walsh, "Discernment of Spirits," *The Way*, Supplement 16, p. 64; Hervé Coathalem, *Ignatian Insights*, pp. 187–188, where he gives references to a number of Spanish authors; but Harvey Egan, *Mystical Horizons*, pp. 134–138, gives references to authors who support a contrary opinion.

[51] Karl Rahner, *Dynamic Element*, p. 160.

[52] Ibid., p. 128.

[53] Hugo Rahner, *Ignatius the Theologian*, p. 145.

[54] John English, S.J., *Spiritual Freedom* (Guelph, Ontario: Loyola House, 1973), p. 212.

[55] Bertrand de Margerie holds that the first time for election is "not abnormal" in the second week of the Spiritual Exercises or in the unitive way. His whole manner of speaking suggests that "not abnormal" means normal in the sense of usual (though he thinks that the person may have difficulty distinguishing the first-time experience from other concomitants and in recognizing that the first-time has been given). His claim rests on the assumed fact that the first time "corresponds with" consolation without previous cause (*Theological Retreat*, p. 155). For the textual ground that Ignatius thought the first time to be frequent, de Margerie appeals to Ignatius' letter to Teresa Rejadell (ibid., p. 169, note 26). I have already shown why I think both the fact which de Margerie assumes here and his interpretation of Ignatius' letter to Teresa Rejadell are at least highly questionable.

[56] See above pp. 118–121.

of these experiences. Whether even with this increase they would still be rare is a question that cannot be answered without much more evidence. Certainly, Ignatius himself said nothing to enlighten us on the matter.

Chapter 9
The Second Time and Mode

*A*mong the three modes for making an election, Ignatius says that, if God does not move one in the first mode, the discerner should go to the second.[1] In the second-time experience, on which the second mode of election is founded and with which it begins, there is no volitional movement given of such a kind as to generate certainty that God is moving the person and showing his will. That is peculiar to the first-time experience. What, then, does take place in the experience which founds and initiates the second mode? How does this experience lead to a judgment regarding God's will?

To answer the latter question will require a study of how that experience is critically evaluated, how it is interpreted as evidence regarding God's will, how the evidence is to be weighed comparatively and/or absolutely, and when the discerner should conclude. Before taking up these questions, we must first have an accurate description of the experience on which these questions are a reflection.

Elements in the Second-Time Experience

Ignatius' statement in the *Spiritual Exercises* describing the second time for seeking God's will is even more compressed and cryptic than his description of the first time. It reads:

---
[1] *DirAutog*, [18].

The second is a time when sufficient[2] light and understanding are gathered, through experiences of consolations and desolations and through experience of discerning diverse spirits.[3]

This statement does no more than assert that consolation and desolation and discernment of spirits play some role in the second mode of election without saying what that role is. From this statement alone, a reader can derive little understanding of what the second time for election is or of how to carry out an election in the second mode.

Fortunately, there are elsewhere in Ignatius' writing two other remarks equally compressed but full of light on the second mode of seeking God's will. One is found in his autograph directory and the other in Rule I, 5 of his rules for discernment of spirits. When these two passages are carefully analyzed and joined with some other rules for discernment of spirits, they enable us to see what the second-time experience is, and they give us the basic idea of how to do second-time discernment. They lead us to see other elements besides consolation and desolation and discernment of spirits which are involved in the second way of seeking God's will, and they enable us to see how all these factors function together in the search.

Consider first what Ignatius says in the autograph directory for the Spiritual Exercises.

If, among the three modes of making an election, God does not move one in the first mode, let him seek persistently to find his vocation[4] through consolations and desolations in the second mode of election. Here is the way to do this. Let him continue with his meditations on

---

[2] The Spanish word *asaz* (*hasaz*) can mean either "sufficiently," "enough," or "plentifully," "abundantly." Some English translations of the *Spiritual Exercises* use it in the first meaning and some in the second. The vulgate Latin translation favors the first (*satis*). The *Prima Versio* favors the second (*multum*). The authority of the vulgate (see below, note 9) and my understanding of Ignatius' teaching on the second essential condition for sound discernment (see above pp. 99–108) lead me to the translation I have given. There are times when an election has to be made without abundant evidence, but in the circumstances, what is had is sufficient. At other times only an abundant accumulation of evidence is sufficient.

[3] *SpEx*, [176].

[4] The election of the *Spiritual Exercises* is primarily intended by Ignatius for deciding on one's state of life, but not exclusively. See [169, 171, 173, 178, 181, 189] and above, pp. 30–32.

Christ our Lord and, while doing so, observe to which of the alternatives God moves him when he finds himself in consolation, and likewise in desolation.[5]

There are three main directives given in this passage: (1) meditate on Christ our Lord; (2) when in consolation, observe to what God moves one; (3) do likewise in desolation.

The directives are for a person engaged in the second week of the Spiritual Exercises, during which the mysteries of Christ's hidden and public life are to be contemplated. Ignatius is telling the person to continue with these meditations; for it is during these meditations that signs of God's will are mainly but not exclusively hoped for; signs from God may be expected also at other times.[6] Another reason for insisting on continuing to contemplate Christ is that such contemplation intensifies our faith, hope, and love, by which we are opened to the Holy Spirit and enabled to take on the mind and heart of Christ.

It is the second directive which is mostly to our present purpose. For in this directive Ignatius both adds to the description of the second-time experience a factor which is not mentioned in the *Spiritual Exercises*, [176] and also points to the relationship between this new factor and consolation. That factor is the experience of being moved toward one of the alternatives for choice. What we have already seen in the first mode of election would make us ready to think that this movement is a volitional impulse and is the central factor in the second-time experience.

The third directive is, as will appear, of minor importance compared to the second. Enough for now to note that one not familiar with Ignatius' teaching on discernment of spirits could readily be misled by this too-brief phrase, "likewise in desolation." For, as it stands, the phrase would imply that desolation, as well as consolation, is a time for God to move the person toward one of the alternatives for choice. As we shall see immediately, such an implication would conflict with Ignatius' teaching. The passage should

---

⁵ *DirAutog*, [18].

⁶ See the directories of Polanco, no. 82 (*DirSpExMHSJ*, p. 312); Miró, no. 86 (ibid., p. 401); Cordeses, [131] (ibid., p. 556); Official Directory, [221] (ibid., p. 719).

read: Likewise, when in desolation, observe to what the evil spirit moves him.[7]

The second and third directives leave us with a critically important question: How does the person know the movement toward one alternative is from God or from the evil spirit or from some other source? The answer is implied in this passage and receives clear and explicit expression in Rule I, 5 of the rules for discernment of spirits. That rule, surprisingly, is the only place in the whole of the *Spiritual Exercises* where Ignatius throws any light on how consolation and desolation can help us in seeking God's will; and, even there, the main point is not to enlighten us on how to do this. The main point of the rule is to warn against changing during the time of desolation any previously well-made choice. In the reason given for the warning, Ignatius brings up (as something taken for granted) what seems to be still another factor in the second-time experience which initiates second-time election, namely, a counsel from the good or evil spirit; and he makes clear its relationship to consolation or desolation as a sign of its source.

> The time of [spiritual] desolation is no time at all to change purposes and decisions with which one was content the day before such desolation, or the decision with which one was content in the previous consolation. It is, rather, a time to remain firm and constant in these. For just as in [spiritual] consolation the good spirit generally leads and counsels us, so in [spiritual] desolation does the evil spirit. By the latter's counsels we cannot find a way to a right decision.[8]

To say that the good or evil spirits lead and *counsel* in consolation or desolation seems, at least at first glance, to mean the experience on which second-time discernment reflects includes some influence, divine or demonic, not only on the will but also on practical judgment.

What might cause us to take a long second look before accepting such an interpretation is the text of the vulgate version of

---

[7] *SpEx*, [314, 317, 318].

[8] Ibid., [318].

133

the *Spiritual Exercises*. There, the reason for not changing decisions during desolation is put in this way:

> For just as one is ruled not by his own impulse [*instinctu*] while enjoying the [spiritual] consolation we mentioned but by that of the good spirit, so also when finding oneself in [spiritual] desolation, he is led by the evil spirit, by whose instigation [*instigatione*] nothing is ever rightly done.[9]

Instead of "counsel" (*aconseja*), the vulgate text has "impulse" (*instinctus*) and "instigation" (*instigatione*). These words could readily be taken to mean the volitional impulse which has already been noted. Are the counsel and the movement of the will the same thing under different aspects or are they distinct elements in the second-time experience?

This question is one among many which need to be answered regarding the experience in which the second-time election originates. To answer these questions, we need a descriptive analysis of each element in the experience and of their interrelationships.

The Volitional Impulse

A movement of the will appears as the core of the whole second-time experience. For the counsel, as we shall see, seems to depend on and flow from it; and the spiritual consolation or desolation is significant only as an indicator of the source of the volitional impulse (and, therefore, of the counsel also). For, unlike the volitional impulse in the first-time experience, the impulse in the second-time experience does not itself bring certainty of its source.

Although this movement is, on the side of the recipient, a

---

[9] *SpEx*MHSJ*Te*, p. 378. An editorial note in this volume (p. 378) criticizes this translation in the Latin vulgate version of the original Spanish in the autograph text and offers a more accurate translation. However, the Latin vulgate text is always worthy of serious attention as a possible source of light on the autograph text, even possibly of correction. For it was examined and approved by Ignatius, was presented by him for papal approval, was the first published text, and was used by Ignatius and his companions when directing the Spiritual Exercises. For such reasons Lewis Delmage, S.J., goes so far as to make a case for it as the most authentic expression of Ignatius' thought. See his *Spiritual Exercises of St. Ignatius Loyola* (New York, 1968), pp. iii–iv. The generally accepted view is that the autograph text is the more authentic. See the editorial discussion in *SpEx*MHSJ*Te*, pp. 117–139, especially 137–139.

movement of his own will, it must be distinguished from any impulse in him which Ignatius calls "his own." By the latter Ignatius means an impulse which originates only from the discerner's own natural or acquired affective disposition or as a consequence of his deliberation based on information about the objective situation, together with his own ways of perceiving and thinking.[10] In the second-time experience, as Ignatius describes it, God does not merely bring it about through his overruling providence that my own impulse happens simultaneously with consolation and conforms with what he prefers and would directly move me to if he were so to move me. Rather, God is said to move me directly toward a free choice of a way of acting.

Recall the passage from the autograph directory quoted above. There, the initiative is said to be all on God's side; the human person only observes what God does in him. God does not, as some commentators say he does, give consolation and leave it up to the subject of consolation to bring his own proposals to the consolation and see whether they harmonize.[11] God is not, in this passage, said merely to give the consolation as a sign of approving the person's own thoughts and inclinations offered to him. Rather, Ignatius is saying that God himself gives the consolation and God himself also gives an impulse toward choice of one alternative in preference to others. All the person is told to do is to observe to which of the alternatives God moves him when he finds himself in consolation.

This volitional impulse is distinct not only from the subject's "own" impulses but also from the consolation in which it comes. Such an impulse is itself neither a consolation nor a desolation any more than a consolation or a desolation is an impulse to choose one alternative rather than another. Each of these elements can be without the other.[12] The same impulse to choose could come in consolation or in desolation (or for that matter, in a state of calm); and its significance for finding God's will would be interpreted differently in each case.

If we look more closely now at the impulse itself which Ignatius

---

[10] *SpEx*, [336] and in vulgate text [318].

[11] See Appendix A, pp. 319–320.

[12] For a presentation and criticism of an opposing interpretation, see Jules Toner, *A Commentary*, pp. 284–290.

says is from God, we shall see of what sort it is and is not. The impulse is not a blind inclination to act in a way that bypasses free choice; the Holy Spirit draws us toward one alternative in an object of free choice. He gives a sign of his preference and makes an appeal to our feedom. The impulse, then, is a conscious movement of the will as intellectual conation and, as such, is consciously motivated by love, the root of all volitional desires and aversions.[13]

The Counsel Given in the Second Time

What does Ignatius mean by the counsel of the good or evil spirit given in consolation or desolation? Let us first note and put aside one possible meaning as beyond or only on the extreme fringe of what Ignatius might mean. To some readers his words might suggest an extraordinary experience which mystical theologians call a "locution," which may be from God or from an evil spirit or from the person's own hyperactive imagination. It is the auditory parallel of what are commonly called "visions." This experience of a lo-cution can take the form of words heard by the ear or heard in imagination or can be a purely intellectual communication without any actual or imaginative sound of words.[14] While not excluding such an experience, Ignatius certainly does not have in mind such ways of divine or demonic counseling. There is not the slightest suggestion of any such extraordinary phenomenon in anything he says about discerning spirits or discerning God's will through con-solation or desolation.[15]

The best way to begin looking for Ignatius' meaning of "lead and counsel" in Rule I, 5 is by seeing it in continuity with Rule I, 4. The latter rule ends with a generalization about the contrary con-

---

[13] Jules Toner, *The Experience of Love*, chapters 4 and 8.

[14] For a description of locutions, a discussion of their relatively slight value in most instances, and the criteria for judging their origin, see A. Poulain, *The Graces of Interior Prayer*, chapters 20 and 22. See also St. John of the Cross, *The Ascent of Mt. Carmel*, bk. 2, chapters 19–21, 28–31.

[15] At first glance, the Official Directory of 1599 might appear to present locutions as an essential element in the second–time experience when it says that one should proceed not by any rational discourse "but only by hearing God's voice and by disposing oneself as much as possible for hearing it and for accepting that movement" ([221]). The final phrase, how-ever, makes clear that hearing God's voice is merely a metaphor for accepting a movement, a volitional impulse, such as Ignatius speaks of in his *Autograph Directory* ([18]).

sequences in our ways of thought flowing from spiritual consolation and spiritual desolation.

> For just as [spiritual] consolation is contrary to [spiritual] desolation, in the same way thoughts which spring from [spiritual] consolation are contrary to thoughts which spring from [spiritual] desolation.[16]

In context, the statement is concerned with how consolation and desolation dispose a person to think of God and self, God's attitude toward him and his relationship with God, his union with God or separation from him, his grounds for hope or despair, and so on.[17] In the following rule (I, 5) Ignatius considers another sort of "thought" which comes in consolation or desolation, namely, "counsels."[18] Further, regarding the source of thoughts, what Ignatius says in Rule 5 makes explicit and unequivocal what is only implicit in his statement at the end of Rule 4. In the latter he speaks of thoughts coming from consolation or desolation; in Rule 5 he says expressly that the counsel comes in some way from the good or evil spirit who incites consolation or desolation.

Since the second mode of election is "without reasons,"[19] the counsel in the second-time experience is not a judgment based on the signs of the times or on projected advantages or disadvantages for God's service (as it is in the third time). It is a judgment which is based on the volitional movement provided by God or by the evil spirit in consolation or in desolation. In other words, the counsel is a *sentiment*, a judgment by affective connaturality, that the object of the volitional impulse is what is to be chosen. It must be kept in mind that this sentiment is not a decision and is not necessarily even evidence for a decision about what God wills. Only when it has been critically evaluated and interpreted[20] can it become evidence

---

[16] *SpEx*, [317].

[17] Jules Toner, *A Commentary*, pp. 141–143.

[18] The first part of the rule confirms what we would ordinarily take the word "counsel" to mean, a practical judgment bearing on a decision for choice and action; for Ignatius is saying that in desolation we should not change our earlier "purposes and decisions" made in consolation.

[19] See below, p. 141.

[20] See below, pp. 142–156.

for one side to be weighed against evidence for the other side so as to arrive at a decision about what God wills.

Consolation and Desolation in the Second-Time Experience

The volitional movement and the counsel in the second-time experience come in consolation or in desolation, and their prompting source is indicated by the consolation or desolation. Therefore, after telling us to observe to what God moves us during the consolation, Ignatius says:

> What kind of experience consolation is should be made clear by examples: spiritual delight, love, hope for heavenly things, tears, and every interior movement which leaves the person consoled in the Lord. The contrary of this is desolation, sadness, distrust, lack of love, aridity, and so on.[21]

A fuller and, when studied out, much more enlightening statement can be found in Rules I, 3 and 4 of the rules for discernment of spirits.

> Rule 3. Concerning spiritual consolation. I name it [spiritual] consolation when some inner motion is prompted in the person, of such a kind that the person begins to be aflame with love of his Creator and Lord and, consequently, when he cannot love any created thing on the face of the earth in itself but only in the Creator of them all. Likewise [I call it consolation] when a person pours out tears moving to love of his Lord, whether it be for sorrow over his sins, or over the passion of Christ our Lord, or over other things directly ordered to his service and praise. Finally , I call [spiritual] consolation every increase of hope, faith, and charity, and every inward gladness which calls and attracts to heavenly things and to one's personal salvation, bringing repose and peace in his Creator and Lord.
>
> Rule 4. Concerning spiritual desolation. I call [spir-

---

[21] *DirAutog*, [18]. See also [11–12], where he gives a somewhat different set of examples of consolation and a contrasting set of examples of desolation.

itual] desolation everything the contrary of [what is described in] the third rule, for example: gloominess of soul, confusion, a movement to contemptible and earthly things, disquiet from various commotions and temptations, [all this] tending toward distrust, without hope, without love; finding oneself thoroughly indolent, tepid, sad, and as if separated from one's Creator and Lord. For just as [spiritual] consolation is contrary to [spiritual] desolation, in the same way the thoughts which spring from [spiritual] consolation are contrary to the thoughts which spring from [spiritual] desolation.[22]

These descriptions of consolation and desolation still leave very much that needs to be explained if one is to have anything approaching an accurate and sufficiently thorough understanding of their meaning in the writings of Ignatius.[23] I have tried to give some help toward such an understanding in my study on his rules for discernment of spirits.[24] To repeat here the textual and the descriptive analysis of experience given in that work is out of the question. All I can do is refer the reader to that earlier work and call attention to what seem to me the more important concepts and distinctions that are needed if we are wisely to employ consolation and desolation for discernment of spirits in the second mode of seeking God's will, and if we are to develop a sound theology of Ignatian discernment of God's will. In fact, these concepts and distinctions seem to be essential for the latter purpose. Without them, many theoretical problems must be left unresolved, and many confusions, inconsistencies, and bad practical conclusions can follow.

---

[22] *SpEx*, [316–317].

[23] In her study of literature on discernment in books and periodicals published in North America and in the English periodical *The Way* since Vatican II, Susan Rakoczy states that this literature, when dealing with the criteria for discernment, "does not exhibit a high degree of conscious theological reflection on their meaning and function." There is, she says, a "lack of analysis of the emotional states described as the 'fruits of the Spirit,' e.g., joy, peace, patience, etc. This is especially apparent in the treatment of the experience of 'peace' which is emphasized as the primary criterion for discernment. . . . there is little phenomenological analysis of how 'true' and 'false' peace can be distinguished" ("The Structures of Discernment Processes and the Meaning of Discernment Language in Published U.S. Catholic Literature, 1965–1978: An Analysis," unpublished dissertation, School of Religious Studies of the Catholic University of America, Washington, D.C., 1980, pp. 182–183). Hereafter referred to as *The Structure of Discernment Processes*.

[24] Jules Toner, *A Commentary*.

The following concepts and distinctions are of fundamental importance: (1) the proper and the broad or loose meanings of consolation and desolation in the most general sense (without any specification as spiritual or non-spiritual);[25] (2) spiritual consolation or desolation as distinct from non-spiritual;[26] (3) essential Christian spiritual consolation (which cannot be absent in a Christian believer's consciousness) and contingent spiritual consolation (that which comes and goes; it is only the latter kind of consolation that Ignatius is talking about in the experience which initiates the second mode of discerning God's will);[27] (4) the ordinary sources of spiritual consolation or spiritual desolation;[28] (5) the demonic deceptions beginning from spiritual consolation;[29] (6) the complex and confusing mingling of spiritual and non-spiritual consolation and desolation in a concrete experience;[30] (7) the difference between Ignatian spiritual desolation and the passive dark night described by John of the Cross.[31]

Readers who are familiar with Ignatius' rules for discernment of spirits may expect some treatment of a distinction between consolation with and without previous cause—the more so since it is the opinion of some recent authors that Ignatius thought consolation without previous cause to be the first principle of all discernment and, therefore, necessary for any second-time discernment of God's will.[32] In the earlier work referred to above, I have already developed my reasons for thinking that consolation without previous cause is not the first principle of all Ignatian discernment and, in fact, that the distinction between consolation with and without previous cause

---

[25] Ibid., pp. 82–90.

[26] Ibid., chapters 5–6. See the excellent observations by John English in *Spiritual Freedom*, pp. 223–224, where he gives an illustration and shows how to uncover the spiritual or non–spiritual character of a consolation. See also Brian O'Leary, ''Discernment of Spirits in the *Memorial* of Blessed Peter Favre,'' *The Way*, Supplement 35, p. 84, for an example by Peter Favre in his own life.

[27] Jules Toner, *A Commentary*, pp. 90–93.

[28] Ibid., pp. 109–112, 138–141.

[29] Ibid., chapters 10–11.

[30] Ibid., pp. 70–78 and chapters 10–11.

[31] Ibid., appendix 2. Failure to note the difference could cause grave harm and great pain to persons who are going through the passive dark night or, on the other hand, lead one who needs repentance or more effort or simply patience to think he or she is becoming a mystic.

[32] See below, Appendix A. See also Jules Toner, *A Commentary*, appendix 4.

has no *fundamental* importance for Ignatian teaching on discernment of spirits or discernment of God's will.[33]

Putting together the several essential factors of the second-time experience in their relationship with one another, we get the following summary description. There is an experience of *spiritual consolation* or *desolation*. During that consolation or desolation, there is a *volitional drawing* toward choice of one alternative. (How the affective feeling of consolation or desolation and this volitional impulse are related in the second-time experience will be taken up below.) Arising from this volitional attraction is a *sentiment*, a judgment by affective connaturality, which, inasmuch as it is thought to be from the Holy Spirit, who prompts the volitional movement, and is directed toward a choice among alternatives, is called a *counsel*.

A Negative Element in the Second-Time Experience

The early directories stress over and over a negative characteristic of the second mode of election. Its significance cannot be fully shown until we examine the relationship of the three modes of election.[34] Presently we are only trying to get clear what does and does not go on in the second time. This negative element is capsulized by the directories in such phrases as *sin razones* or *sine ratiociniis*, *non vacans discursibus propriis*, *sine ullo discursu*, and so on.[35] What all these phrases indicate, even stress, is that the second-time election excludes any evidence of the kind which, as we shall see, is sought in the third-time—principally, projected advantages or disadvantages of each alternative for the service and glory of God. For that is what the authors of the directories and Ignatius without doubt meant by *razones* ("reasons"). We could call spiritual consolation and desolation with volitional impulses reasons for drawing a conclusion regarding God's will, but to do so would not be Ignatian terminology.

---

[33] *A Commentary*, chapter 10 and appendix 4.

[34] See below, chapter 13.

[35] See, for example; Polanco, no. 82 (*DirSpExMHSJ*, p. 312); Miró no. 86 (ibid., p. 401); Cordeses, [130] (ibid., p. 556); Official Directory, [190, 220, 221] (ibid., pp. 701, 717, 719). See also Hugo Rahner, *Ignatius the Theologian*, p. 146.

Reflection on the Second-Time Experience

Active second-time experience begins with the time after reception of the second-time experience, when that experience is reflected on. The time during which the experience is given is not a time to reflect on it (unless something appears which is clearly from an evil force).[36] To begin reflecting on the experience while it is happening will only hinder it and possibly end it altogether. When the experience has ceased, then is the time or occasion critically to examine[37] and evaluate it and, if genuine, to interpret it as evidence pro or con about an alternative for choice.

This time for reflection must be a tranquil time.[38] Some speak as if a tranquil time for rational reflection were peculiar to the third mode of Ignatian discernment. That this is not so can best be shown after seeing what is involved in the second mode besides the second-time experience and after studying what Ignatius means by saying that the third time is a "tranquil time."[39] It is enough for now to observe that critical evaluation and interpretation of the second-time experience (as of any other experience) cannot ordinarily be done well except with a tranquil mind and heart.

Critical Examination and Evaluation

The purpose of a critical examination and evaluation of the second-time experience is to make sure that it is accurately remembered and that the components in the experience are truly such as to be data for the second mode of discerning God's will. For this purpose, some questions need to be answered; some of these questions overlap, but all need explicit attention.

1. Is the consolation or desolation during which the person experiences the impulse and counsel a spiritual one? A truly spiritual consolation is of the kind indicated by Ignatius in the examples he gives in the quotations presented above.[40] A study of these leads to

---

[36] *SpEx*, [333–334].

[37] On the necessity for careful examination of second–time experiences, see Dávila, [134–139] in *DirSpEx*MHSJ, pp. 519–521.

[38] G. Bottereau, S.J., "La Confirmation divine d'apres le Journal Spirituel de Saint Ignace de Loyola," RAM (1967), pp. 43–44. Bottereau sees this point indicated in *SpEx*, [14, 318, 336].

[39] *SpEx*, [177]; and see below, pp. 163–167.

[40] See above, pp. 138–139; see also *DirAutog*, [11, 12, 18].

some generalizations. Briefly put, the consolation is spiritual if it is rooted in living faith and of itself tends towards an increase of living faith and of facility in the expression of living faith in deeds and endurance.[41] Living faith is "faith working through love."[42] A desolation is spiritual when it is truly the contrary of spiritual consolation; when it is God-centered, but centered on God who is felt to be absent and not loving toward the desolate person; when it is a faith experience, but an experience of living faith felt as endangered or even actually diminishing and, therefore, bringing on gloom, confusion, anxiety, and, above all, discouragement about loving and serving God, making it difficult or at least painful to do the deeds which express living faith and to endure in God's service.[43] Only a spiritual consolation or desolation can be an essential factor in the second-time experience.[44]

2. If the consolation is spiritual, there is a further question: Is the spiritual consolation prompted or occasioned by an evil spirit? Is all that flows from it characterized by continuity, "the beginning, middle, and end"[45] in accord with the Holy Spirit? Or, in the process of thoughts and affections flowing from the spiritual consolation, is there anything evil, anything distracting from good, or a tendency toward what is less good than what the discerner had been doing or intended to do? Does the process lead to any weakening of faith life or any disquieting affections, disruptive of the peace which comes from living faith? If so, then the original spiritual consolation can be thought to have arisen under the prompting of the evil spirit; consequently, the impulse that comes during the consolation is to be distrusted.[46]

---

[41] Jules Toner, *A Commentary*, pp. 109–113.

[42] *Gal.*, 5:6.

[43] Jules Toner, *A Commentary*, pp. 143–144.

[44] This is not to say that a natural consolation or desolation never has value for discerning God's will. It can be important data in the third mode of seeking God's will. It can be objective data about the person's temperament or character, data which may be a significant indication of God's will for this individual when put into the whole context of reasons for and against some course of action. But it does not mark any volitional impulse as a divine movement in the way a spiritual consolation can.

[45] *SpEx*, [333].

[46] Ibid., [333–335]. For a discussion of how and why an evil spirit might prompt true spiritual consolation and of what it means to say that the signs of an evil spirit are in continuity with a true spiritual consolation, see Jules Toner, *A Commentary*, pp. 222–235.

3. Is the alternative to which the impulse in consolation is directed good of itself and a real option for this agent in the concrete? What this question means has been explained above where God's will as an object of discernment is discussed.[47]

4. Is the person moved to the alternative solely or at least primarily inasmuch as it seems to be or could be God's will? It is true that the object of the impulse from the Holy Spirit may, in fact, coincide with the object of my own natural impulse motivated by self-love; but the two motivations differ, and a selfish motivation calls into question the origination of the impulse from the Holy Spirit. If the impulse experienced in what seems to be spiritual consolation is toward choice of what I like solely or predominantly because I like it, or away from choice of what I dislike solely or predominantly because I dislike it, either the consolation itself is not genuinely spiritual or the requisite conditions for spiritual discernment are not pure or firm enough to prevent egoism from asserting itself even during a genuinely spiritual consolation. In other words, discerning the source of an impulse by appeal to the consolation in which it is experienced is appropriate only when the impulse toward a choice is, of itself, toward what God wills, solely or predominantly because he wills it.

5. Even when the impulse is rightly motivated and the consolation is truly spiritual and not prompted by the evil spirit, we still cannot think the consolation validates the impulse as coming from God unless another question is answered affirmatively. Did the volitional impulse and counsel come *during* the actual spiritual consolation, not only immediately before or only immediately after (during the afterglow)? Only the impulse and counsel which come *during* the actual consolation can reasonably be thought to come from the Holy Spirit.[48]

6. Further, even if the impulse with counsel came during the consolation or desolation, did it flow from the consolation or desolation as from a matrix? (This relationship between impulse with counsel and consolation or desolation can be discussed better in our

---

[47] See above, p. 28.
[48] For why this is so, see below, pp. 148–149.

144

next step, where we consider how to interpret the second-time experience in order to find evidence regarding God's will).[49]

7. Finally, are the object of volitional impulse and the consequent sentiment or counsel accurately grasped, without addition or subtraction?[50] Perhaps I have joined to it something which, in my ordinary way of thinking is closely associated with, even inseparable from, that to which I was moved. For example, I am moved to live a life in which I am always aware of God; immediately, I think that God is calling me to a life of less-active service, perhaps even to a cloistered life. But the inspiration may be rather to a life of contemplation in action. Perhaps what I am moved to suggests something else that I desire very much, and I immediately joined the latter to the former. For example, suppose I am discerning whether God wills for me to stay in hospital administration or to volunteer for teaching in a mission school in Africa. I have plentiful second-time experiences in which I am drawn toward the former, but I understand the drawing to be toward administration at the hospital where I am presently working and where I would very much like to remain. I immediately conclude that God wills for me to stay here where I have been working—something for which I really have no evidence at all. I may, as a consequence, dismiss out of hand any considerations which indicate that I could give a more-needed service as administrator elsewhere and God might be calling me there. On the other hand, God may be moving me to something I fear so much that I block it out and delete it from my memory of the second-time experience, though not so completely that I cannot recover it by careful recall.

Again, the root of my misunderstanding the second-time movement and counsel may lie in a failure to understand or at least to attend to the concrete situation in which the need for discernment and choice arises. Since the evidence for decision in the second mode of discernment is not (as it is in the third) reasons based on the objective situation for choice, it might seem that there is no need in the second mode for a careful understanding of that situation. But the truth is that the understanding of the real concrete situation

---

[49] See below, pp. 146–152.
[50] SpEx, [336]; Jules Toner, *A Communtary*, pp. 249–253.

145

is an important safeguard against a misinterpretation of divine counsels.[51] Failure to understand one's own limitations and gifts, the needs of the world and the Church, the signs of the times, and so on may lead to misunderstanding the divine counsel or to mistaking a counsel from the evil one for a counsel from the Holy Spirit. I may, for instance, experience in consolation a drawing toward a course of action which, when considered either in isolation from any real situation or in relation with a falsely understood concrete situation, appears as very good. In the real concrete situation, however, the action may be certainly rash or unjust or involve a withdrawal from another course of action of greater value for God's service. A clear grasp of the real situation would enable me to see that this second-time experience is not from the Holy Spirit. (The necessity of understanding the situation is seen also in Question 3, above.)

If the answer to any one of the foregoing questions is negative, there is no use in going further. The experience is not a genuine second-time experience, and it can provide no evidence by this way of discernment for what God wills. If all the questions are answered affirmatively, then the second-time experience certainly provides data to be interpreted as evidence of what God wills.

Interpretation of Second-Time Experience as Evidence of God's Will.

We have found the essential elements in the experience which is the starting point for the process of seeking God's will in the second mode, described each of these elements in some detail, and seen how the elements are to be critically examined. If the critical examination shows that the experience really was a second-time experience, the question remains: how does this experience provide evidence of what is God's will? In trying to understand how to interpret second-time experience, attention will, to begin with, be limited to the impulse and counsel which come in spiritual consolation, giving our best efforts to this. Afterwards, more briefly, the impulse and counsel which comes in spiritual desolation can be

---

[51] Movements of spirits, says Dávila ([138], *DirSpEx*MHSJ, p. 521), are to be tested by a threefold light: the word of God, the Church and its public magisterium, *and human reason*. See also *LettersIgn*, p. 197.

attended to. Just as Ignatius explains desolation by contrast with consolation,[52] so also he sees counsel from the evil spirit as intelligible by parallel and contrast with counsel from the good spirit.[53]

Interpretation of Second-Time Experience with Consolation

In the Ignatian texts already noted, we find the basic principle for interpreting second-time experience as evidence regarding God's will. In the *Autograph Directory* Ignatius tells the discerner that he should "observe, when he finds himself in consolation, to which alternative God moves him."[54] In the *Spiritual Exercises* he says, "Just as in [spiritual] consolation the good spirit more leads and counsels us, so in [spiritual] desolation the evil spirit [more leads and counsels us]."[55]

The word "more" (*más*) in this passage holds implications of great significance. It is repeated in the *Autograph Directory*, when Ignatius tells the discerner to observe to what alternative for choice God gives him the "greater sign" (*más señal*) of his will.[56] The implication in both texts is that consolation gives no absolute assurance that the Holy Spirit is the prompting source of the counsel. Until shown otherwise, the consolation favors that interpretation but does not exclude our being lead by "our own" thoughts and desires or even by the evil spirit. That is why no single second-time experience can ordinarily, if ever, yield adequate evidence regarding God's will and why Ignatius looks for plentiful light and understanding[57] from many such experiences. Whether even this plentiful light can justify a conviction about what God wills is a question to be taken up later.[58]

The second thing of importance in the text being studied is the phrase "in consolation." The minimal meaning is "during consolation," while the actual consolation is being experienced. If the impulse and counsel come before or after, even immediately after,

---

[52] *SpEx*, [317].

[53] Ibid., [318].

[54] *DirAutog*, [18].

[55] *SpEx*, [318]. The vulgate text omits the qualifying adverb *"more" (más)*, but it is in the *prima versio* as well as in the autograph text.

[56] *DirAutog*, [212].

[57] *SpEx*, [176], and see above, note 2 of this chapter.

[58] See below, chapters 15–16.

but not during the actual consolation, then the consolation cannot serve to interpret the counsel as one given by the Holy Spirit. Ignatius points out a way in which we are easily deceived in our interpretation, namely, by confusing the afterglow of spiritual consolation with the actual spiritual consolation itself. For a spiritual consolation to indicate that the Holy Spirit is here and now influencing a person, the consolation must here and now be actual; but it frequently happens that when the experience of actual spiritual consolation has ended, the affective feelings continue to reverberate. Such feelings are not spiritual consolation in the proper sense of the term. If one wishes to call them such because they have some relationship to a spiritual consolation which is now ended, it makes no difference for the point now at issue. The point is that they do not attest to any *present* influence of the Holy Spirit. Therefore, they offer no ground for thinking that an impulse and counsel which come during them is from the Holy Spirit until shown otherwise.[59]

If we ask why the impulse and counsel in actual spiritual consolation is more probably from God, about all Ignatius says expressly is that spiritual consolation is a sign of the person's being under the influence of the Holy Spirit.[60] He never develops what he says, but he seems to be trusting Christian tradition rooted in Holy Scripture and Christian experience over the centuries or, more exactly, his own experience as understood in light of Scripture and tradition.

Basing ourselves on what he wrote, we can work out a fuller answer than he was concerned to give to the question of why the impulse and sentiment are very likely from God if they are experienced in spiritual consolation. Briefly, it comes to this. Spiritual consolation is rooted in living faith; it grows out of it and expresses it. Since living faith comes only from the action of the Holy Spirit, so does the spiritual consolation which is rooted in it.[61]

It would be a misunderstanding of Ignatius to think that for him the only sign or even the principal sign of the Holy Spirit acting

---

[59] SpEx, [336]. See Jules Toner, A Commentary, pp. 245–253.

[60] SpEx, [315, 316, 318, 329–331, 335].

[61] Jules Toner, A Commentary, pp. 109–115. This is so even when the spiritual consolation is prompted by an evil spirit. See SpEx, [332–333] and A Commentary, pp. 227–229.

on us is spiritual consolation.[62] There are ways in which both good and evil spirits influence a person without penetrating the affective sensibility in any way notable enough to be called consolation or desolation in the ordinary meaning. While a person is in spiritual calm or even feeling spiritually desolate, the Holy Spirit can be acting powerfully in the intellect and will, affecting faith, hope, charity, courage and active energy, and so on.[63]While a person is in spiritual calm or even feeling genuine spiritual consolation, anti-spiritual thoughts and inclinations can arise from his own egoism,[64] and the evil spirit can still be active in his deceptions.[65]

Given that spiritual consolation can be one sign, a very useful one, that an attraction during it is from the Holy Spirit, is it enough that the drawing and counsel take place during it? After all, during spiritual consolations I may experience, and sometimes do experience, conflicting volitional impulses; one of these may be from the Holy Spirit, while another, as just observed, from my own egoism, which can still influence my impulses during such consolation.[66] If mere temporal simultaneity with spiritual consolation is not enough to indicate that the impulse and counsel are from the Holy Spirit, what more is required? It is necessary that the impulse and counsel form an integral experience with the consolation. This does not mean that they are elements of the consolation in the proper sense of the term—although the total integral experience may be called conso-lation in the broad or loose sense of the word.[67] What it means is that, while each element of the total experience remains fully dis-tinct, all of them are so closely integrated as to form a whole in which the feelings influence the thought and impulses. This seems to be what Ignatius has in mind when he speaks of a drawing "in" consolation or desolation, and even more clearly when he speaks of contrary thoughts which spring from (*que salen de*), flow, or grow

---

[62] Unless one conceives of any and every movement of the mind and heart toward God as spiritual consolation, an interpretation which I find to be in conflict with the text of Ignatius. See *A Commentary*, pp. 284–290.

[63] Ibid., pp. 63–76.

[64] Except when the consolation is the kind in Ignatius' first description in *SpEx*, [315]. See *A Commentary*, pp. 96–97.

[65] *SpEx*, [332–333].

[66] See above, note 64.

[67] Jules Toner, *A Commentary*, pp. 86–87.

from consolation and desolation.[68] As we have already shown, these thoughts can include plans and counsels.

The relationship of these elements can be understood more fully by recalling what I have spoken of elsewhere as the essential structure of the total complex experience of consolation.[69] In this structure are affective feelings of peace, delight, warmth, sweetness, and so on; their subjective grounds; their subjective consequences. The feelings constitute the consolation in its strict or proper sense. They are grounded in prior acts of intellect, imagination, and will. In spiritual consolation they are ultimately grounded in living faith, the principal work of the Holy Spirit in us. These feelings, in turn, dispose the subject for consequent ways of perceiving, reasoning, loving, desiring, and so on. They sensitize him to the impulse and counsel of the Holy Spirit and make it seem easy and joyful to do God's will even at great cost. So it is that the time of spiritual consolation is a time at which the Holy Spirit is likely to give an impulse and counsel. What it means, then, for the impulse and counsel to be integral with the spiritual consolation may be expressed by saying that the feelings of consolation with their grounds in living faith form a matrix, or conscious surrounding, within which the impulse and counsel originate.

The point of all this analysis is that when, and only when, the volitional attraction and the counsel are integral with spiritual consolation, the whole experience can rightly be interpreted as from the Holy Spirit and, therefore, as some evidence for what God wills.

This understanding of Ignatius' teaching is confirmed by a passage in one of his letters which has become a classic for those interested in his teaching on discernment of spirits and of God's will.

This passage, it is true, seems to be describing an unusual experience, what Ignatius calls consolation without previous cause; but, *mutatis mutandis*, it can be generalized to cast light on impulse with counsel given in any consolation which is spiritual.

It remains for me to speak of how we ought to understand what we think is from our Lord and, under-

---

[68] *SpEx*, [317].
[69] Jules Toner, *A Commentary*, pp. 109–113.

150

standing it, how we ought to use it for our advantage. For it frequently happens that our Lord moves and urges the soul to this or that activity. He begins by enlightening the soul; that is to say, by speaking interiorly to it without the din of words, lifting it up wholly to this divine love and ourselves to his meaning without any possibility of resistance on our part, even should we wish to resist. This thought of his which we take is of necessity in conformity with the commandments, the precepts of the Church, and obedience to our superiors. It will be full of humility because the same divine Spirit is present in all. But we can frequently be deceived, however, because after such consolation or inspiration, when the soul is still abiding in its joy, the enemy tries under the impetus of this joy to make us innocently add to what we have received from God our Lord. His only purpose is to disturb and confuse us in everything.

At other times he makes us lessen the importance of the message we have received and confronts us with obstacles and difficulties, so as to prevent us from carrying out completely what has been made known to us.[70]

As in Rule I, 3 for discernment of spirits, Ignatius in this letter first describes consolation in terms of its grounds, God speaking interiorly without words and lifting the person wholly to his love; but he then refers to the experience of consolation properly speaking when he speaks of the soul still "abiding in its joy." Besides the thought ("enlightening") which grounds feelings of consolation ("joy"), another thought (*sentido*) is given. That the latter thought is a counsel for action is clear on several counts. First, Ignatius begins by saying that this consolation which he is describing happens when God intends to move the person to one action or another. Further, the thought has to be in conformity with the commandments, with the precepts of the Church, and with obedience to su-

---

[70] *LettersIgn*, pp. 22–23.

periors,[71] all of which have to do with actions to be done or left undone. Again, at the end of the passage, he speaks of Satan, "the enemy," trying "to prevent us from *carrying out* completely what has been made known to us" (emphasis mine) by taking something away from God's message or by turning us back from execution by putting obstacles in the way.

How are the consolation and the counsel related? Both come from God, who not only consoles but also "moves and urges" to some act. He gives a thought about doing something. The thought about what to do is *his* thought (*su sentido*) communicated to the human person, *not* the person's own thought brought to the consolation as a touchstone for testing. Satan attempts to make us add to what God himself has communicated or take away from it so as to prevent us from doing what has been shown to us *by God*, what we have "perceived from God, our Lord." It is during consolation that the thought, the counsel, is given; it would not seem to be stretching the text to suggest that the consolation appears as the matrix from within which the divine counsel arises. It is when he wants to move and urge to some action or another, Ignatius says, that God gives the consolation. The consolation is not peace and joy over the thought of doing this or that action; it is joy simply because one is lifted wholly to God's love. Within that experience of joy, an impulse and counsel are given by God.

Are There Two Ways of the Second-Time Election?

There is a passage in Ignatius' autograph directory which, in some of the directories written by the early Jesuits, is taken to indicate a second way of going about a second-time election[72] that is somewhat different from the way I have just described. The latter

---

[71] Ignatius is writing to one who has a vow of religious obedience and assumes, of course, that the superior's authority is exercised justly, within the scope of authority granted by the Church through the constitutions of the religious community.

[72] The directories of Polanco, Dávila, Cordeses, and the Official Directory of 1599 all seem to assume that this passage, *DirAutog*, [21], refers only to the second–time election. The context, however, favors seeing it as referring also to the third–time election; for it appears not immediately after the paragraph on how to do the second–time election, [18], but, rather, immediately after the following two paragraphs, [19–20], which treat of the two ways of third–time election; and it says nothing that would restrict its reference to the second–time election.

way is based on paragraph [18] in Ignatius' directory; the other way is based on paragraph [21]. In paragraph [21] Ignatius says:

A way of going about the election is to offer one alternative to God one day and the other on another day. Thus, on the one day it will be [life according to] the [evangelical] counsels and on another day [life according to] the commandments [only], observing to which offering God our Lord gives a greater sign of his holy will. This method may be compared to offering various foods to a prince and observing which of them pleases him.

According to González Dávila, Ignatius in the earlier paragraph [18] is saying that, when the discerner is in consolation, he should propose both alternatives together with indifference and observe to what he is more moved.[73] In the latter paragraph [21], Dávila understands Ignatius to be saying that the discerner offers *one* alternative at one time *as if already determined to it*, and the other alternative in the same way at another time, hoping to see which offering will receive a greater sign of God's acceptance.[74] The Official Directory of 1599 makes pretty much the same distinction.[75] The Latin text of the autograph directory appears to support this interpretation. For in it paragraph [21] begins, "This way can *also* be used"[76] (emphasis mine), implying a way of going about a second-time election that is different from the way given in paragraph [18].

There are difficulties to be raised regarding Dávila's statement

[73] Dávila, [122–126] (*DirSpEx*MHSJ, pp. 517, 518).
[74] Ibid., [124–126].
[75] Official Directory of 1599, [194–195, 220] (*DirSpEx*MHSJ, pp. 703, 705, 717).
[76] *Potest etiam uti hoc modo* (*DirSpEx*MHSJ, p. 77).

which are peripheral to the question now under discussion.[77] For our present purpose, the main thing to note is that, even if we are to understand that Ignatius proposes two modes of second-time election, they are distinct merely by reason of different mechanics, as it were, not at all different by reason of different kinds of second-time experiences and evidence. There is no reason for thinking that the "sign" (*señal*) sought in paragraph [21] is different from that sought in paragraph [18], namely, the volitional movement or impulse from God that results in a counsel and is shown to be from God by the spiritual consolation in which it comes.

Interpreting Second-Time Experiences of Counsel with Desolation

To complete our analysis we must now ask what role Ignatius assigns to spiritual desolation in the second mode of making a sound election. How can desolation provide any evidence for what God wills? Ignatius does not say much that serves to answer this question beyond pointing to a parallel (left undeveloped) between discerning by consolation and by desolation.[78] That parallel will suffice as a basis for an answer.

Since the spiritual desolation is from the evil spirit and/or one's own sinfulness as its prompting source, it is a sign that the impulse

---

[77] Although peripheral to the present question, these difficulties are, nonetheless, important for an accurate understanding of how to do an Ignatian election. First, Dávila thinks that Ignatius is saying we should make the offering of alternatives during spiritual consolation and see to what God moves or inclines us. However, in paragraph [18], where Ignatius tells the discerner to observe to what he is moved during consolation, he says nothing about making an offering; whereas, in paragraph [21], where he suggests the offering, he says nothing about doing so during consolation. He simply suggests that "on one day" the discerner offer one of the alternatives and "on another day" he offer the other alternative and see for which of them he receives a greater sign of God's will. In context, then, paragraph [21] seems to mean that the offering is to be made without regard for the discerner's affective state with a hope that, as the day of prayer goes on, consolations with impulse toward the offered alternative will be given by God if the offered alternative is what he wills. In fact, the context does not indicate that the greater sign is limited to greater second–time experiences of consolation and impulse—and this is the second difficulty about Dávila's statement. For Ignatius does not speak immediately after paragraph [18] about making the offerings. Rather, in paragraphs [19] and [20], he speaks about moving on to the third–time election and, immediately after that, suggests the offerings, without any indication that they are peculiar to the second–time election. The most reasonable interpretation, therefore, is that the greater sign of God's will can be either greater second–time experiences or stronger third–time reasons—or both, when the two modes are combined (see below, pp. 251–254.).
[78] *SpEx*, [318] and *DirAutog*, [18] (*DirSpEx*MHSJ, p. 77).

and the counsel are more probably from that same source.[79] This holds, however, only if the desolation is truly a spiritual one[80] and if the impulse or counsel comes during it and is integral with it, that is, from it as a matrix.[81] Given that these conditions are fulfilled, the experience can be interpreted as some probable evidence against thinking that the action to which the person is moved is God's will. It can, consequently, by contraindicative, also be some evidence in favor of the opposing alternative for choice as being God's will.

For a number of reasons, the positive and even the negative evidence regarding God's will based on a counsel in spiritual desolation is, however, very untrustworthy.[82] This is especially so if we take seriously, as Ignatius did, the reality of personal evil spirits, who take advantage of our weakness and sinful tendencies to prompt spiritual desolation and temptation, and to deceive us. Elsewhere I have given my opinion that it is still possible for one who does not believe in such spirits profitably to use the Ignatian rules for discernment of spirits; but I also said that the use would not be the same in all cases.[83] Here is a case in point.

For, if we are up against a personal and clever antagonist when we try to interpret the significance of our inner motions during desolation as evidence regarding God's will, it becomes necessary to take into account possible errors by the evil spirit, as well as his strategies, his shifting positions, and mingling of truth with falsehood in order to confuse us. Then the whole matter of interpreting the impulse and counsel in desolation becomes much more complex and uncertain than it would be if we were interpreting inner motions taking place only according to some stable laws of human psychology and spiritual life.

First of all, even if we should think counsel in desolation to be as valid for indicating Satan's intention as counsel in consolation

---

[79] *SpEx*, [315, 317, 318, 333].

[80] See above, pp. 139–141.

[81] See above, pp. 148–152.

[82] What has been said so far about how to interpret a second–time experience with spiritual desolation as evidence of God's will is, I think, well founded on what Ignatius says. What I shall now add regarding the great uncertainty of such evidence and the consequent dangers to be taken account of when using it is my own opinion—developed in accord with Ignatius' principles but not found expressly in his writing.

[83] Jules Toner, *A Commentary*, pp. 34–36. See also pp. 56–59, 141–142.

is for indicating God's intention, Satan himself can be mistaken about what God wills, about what would turn out to be more for the glory of God. So, he can mistakenly move us toward what is in fact God's will or away from what is in fact not God's will. Further, even assuming Satan is not mistaken, all we have is some indication that this alternative is not what God wills. Therefore, unless there is only one other real alternative open to us, we are not sure which of the other proposed alternatives we have evidence for is God's will.

Even if there is only one other real alternative for choice and even if we assume that the evil spirit is not mistaken about what is God's will, even then could we have any solidly probable grounds for thinking that what he counsels in desolation is opposed to God's will? Could he not, with devious purpose, prompt in desolation a counsel which he thinks is God's will, the same counsel already received in spiritual consolation? For, if he is dealing with one who understands and follows the fundamental principles of Ignatius, could he not by such counsel hope to confuse his victim, make him doubt the counsel received in consolation, call into question what actually was genuinely spiritual consolation, and become discouraged about discernment altogether? Could he not, for the same purpose, at one time himself prompt spiritual consolation with a counsel and at another time prompt desolation with the same counsel, leaving anyone but the most adept at discerning spirits in a confusing and discouraging tangle? Perhaps even the adept discerner may find it next to impossible to be sure whether Satan is showing his true intent in the counsel given.

All in all, therefore, the seeming evidence for God's will by contraindication in desolation is ordinarily not easily to be trusted except when it supports solid evidence from spiritual consolation. Then it may help somewhat toward the abundant light and evidence Ignatius sees as necessary for a conclusion about God's will. For the rest, we will do much better simply to fight against spiritual desolation and to base our second-time decisions on counsels received in spiritual consolation.

Weighing Evidence and Concluding

Rarely, if ever, will a particular second-time experience provide more than some bit of probable evidence, which is by itself inconclusive. That is to say, it is insufficient for even a sound probable conclusion. In any second-time discernment that is of great consequence and does not have to be made quickly,[84] only a notable accumulation of evidence through manifold experiences can justify a conclusion. The second time for a sound and trustworthy election, Ignatius says, is a "time when light and understanding are gathered sufficiently [plentifully] through experiences of consolations and desolations."[85]

If no second-time experience can ordinarily provide more than a bit of probable evidence, may we expect to find conflicting second-time evidence? That Ignatius allows for this to be so is assumed in his autograph directory.[86] There, as we have seen, he advises one seeking God's will to offer the alternatives, one at one time, the other at another time, and observe to which offering God gives the "greater sign" of his will. If we are to observe on which side God gives a *greater* sign, the implication is that we may get a lesser sign on the other side. But does God then give a person conflicting signs? Should we take Ignatius' words at face value or should we see here one of those almost inevitable inaccuracies of expression consequent on his exaggeratedly compressed style? What he says here could be a parallel of the inaccuracy noted above where he says that, when one is in consolation, he should observe "to what alternative God moves him, and likewise in desolation," as if desolation were also a sign of God moving him—a clear contradiction of his teaching elsewhere.[87] On the other hand, there could be some parallel with what he says about God's moving different persons in conflicting directions (for his own good reasons).[88] There is strong extrinsic evidence for the latter interpretation: all the important early directories assume that the discerner may have second-time evidence for each of the opposing alternatives.[89]

To reach a sound conclusion, the accumulated evidence will,

---

[84] See below, pp. 307–308.

[85] See above, note 2 of this chapter

[86] *DirAutog*, [21].

[87] See above, pp. 132–133, and see *SpEx*, [318, 329, 333, 336].

[88] See above, pp. 47–53.

[89] See below, note 91 of this chapter.

of course, have to be weighed: if there is conflicting evidence, in order to see which side is weightier; and, in every case, in order to see whether the evidence is enough to justify a conclusion.

Weighing evidence will have to take into account not only the frequency of second-time experiences and their duration but also certain characteristics of each of the several distinct factors in such experiences. Thus, the depth, fullness, and intensity of the spiritual consolation[90] must be attended to, as also the power of the volitional impulses, the clarity and firmness of the counsel.

Weighing evidence has to be done in a variety of situations. When there is evidence on both sides, the evidence for each side may sometimes be so nearly equal to the other that no decision can yet be made.[91] The discerner has to decide whether to continue in the second mode of discerning or to move on to the third. When the balance of evidence clearly favors one alternative, two questions can still arise. Is the weight of evidence on that side sufficiently greater? Or, if the evidence on one side is much weightier than on the other, is it solid enough to rest an important decision on it?

Consequently, the discerner will sometimes find it hard to decide whether he should make a decision or continue waiting for more and stronger second-time evidence or go on to the third mode of discernment. To answer this question depends very much on the importance of the issue and on how much time and energy the discerner has.[92] To recognize when one is delaying too long in the quest of too much evidence and when one is impatiently jumping to a precipitous conclusion calls for sensitivity to the actual situation and a power of sound judgment; no set of rules can substitute for these qualities.

However, in Ignatius' own discernment, one thing appears to be the "clincher" for him in deciding whether or not to bring his discerning to a decision. It is a state of mind which he mentions under a number of aspects: a sense of security in having made a

---

[90] See above, pp. 103–107 and below, pp. 176–178.

[91] Polanco, no. 82 (*DirSpEx*MHSJ, pp. 311–312); Miró, no. 87 (ibid., pp. 401–402); Dávila [122, 126] (ibid., pp. 517–518); Official Directory of 1599, [222] (ibid., p. 718). In fact, Polanco, no. 83 (ibid., p. 313) and the Official Directory of 1599 [223] (ibid., p. 718), allow for occasions when the signs for each alternative are so nearly equal as to make a decision impossible in the second time.

[92] See below, pp. 307–308.

good discernment and found God's will; freedom from anxiety about opposing God's will; a sense of finality, of completeness, of being relieved from any need to seek further evidence. In short, it is an untroubled assurance that he has done all he ought to do and has successfully finished the task of seeking and weighing evidence.

Thus, in his account of his discernment about whether to oppose the project of making Francis Borgia a cardinal, Ignatius tells how he wavered back and forth for some days before coming to a decision, now wanting to oppose the project and now fearing that by doing so he might oppose God's will. On the third day, he says, he found himself with a judgment so "conclusive" and with a will "so tranquil" that he was sure he should conclude his discernment and act on it.[93] In the discernment about poverty recounted in his spiritual diary, when coming to a decision prior to seeking confirmation, Ignatius uses such expressions as these: "freed from the desire of going any further with the election";[94] "all desire [of continuing the election] left me, the matter seemed to be clear"; "a matter not worth further examination. I considered it completed . . . with great tranquility of mind."[95]

Two comments on this sense of assurance are needed. The first is that the assurance of having done all that is called for in seeking God's will must be distinguished from the assurance of having found God's will in the judgment reached. Both are involved in the experience just described; but for the present I want to stress only the former, which can be understood in the light of the second condition for sound discernment as already explained.[96] Ignatius' thought on assurance of having found God's will is to be taken up later in Chapters 15 and 16.

This much, however, can be said now: The decision reached at this point of the second-time discernment process is a tentative decision, waiting on confirmation before becoming finalized for choice, always with the possibility of disconfirmation. It is true that a notable group of writers thinks that Ignatius saw no need for confirming the conclusion of a second-time discernment; only a

---

[93] See above, p. 49.
[94] Entry for Feb. 8.
[95] Entry for Feb. 9; and see below, pp. 212–214.
[96] See above, pp. 99–100.

third-time discernment, they think, needs confirmation—by consolations and desolations, as in the second mode. If they are right, then the decision reached at this point is a final decision in a second-time election; but, when confirmation is discussed, I will show why I think their opinion is a mistaken one.[97]

Before taking up any questions about confirmation of a decision, however, it will be better to study Ignatius' teaching on the third-time mode of election. There are several good reasons for this. First, as will be shown, since Ignatius does in fact seek confirmation for decisions in the second as well as the third modes in the same way, it will be more economical to study confirmation in relation to both modes at once. Second, as will also be shown, since Ignatius seeks confirmation by the kind of evidence found in the third mode as well as in the second, it is better to wait until that kind of evidence has been analyzed before taking up the subject of confirmation. Third, as will be shown, while Ignatius sees the second and third modes of election as fully distinct, nevertheless, in practice, he combines them in the discernment process which leads to the tentative decision for which confirmation is to be sought; the confirmation is, then, of the conclusion of this combined process. Consequently, we will now attend to the third mode of election and take up confirmation afterwards.

---

[97] Entry for Feb. 9. Fuller and more frequent descriptions of the same kind are to be found in later entries where Ignatius is deciding on when to terminate the process of seeking confirmation for his decision and to finalize it. These will be presented in chapter 11, especially on pp. 212–214, and will throw much light back on the present discussion.

Chapter 10
The Third Time and Mode

*P*aralleling his brief statement in the *Spiritual Exercises*[1] on when it is the first and when the second time for making a sound election, Ignatius makes a brief statement on when it is the third time.[2] What he does not do for the first or second time, he does for the third: he follows that statement with many paragraphs of detailed instructions on how to carry out the third-time election process.[3] These paragraphs are intended to throw light on the preceding statement about the third time. Now, however, the focus of our attention is only on that opening statement itself. It reads:

> The third is a tranquil time when one considers first
> for what a person is born, that is, to praise God, our Lord

---

[1] *SpEx*, [175–176].

[2] Ibid., [177].

[3] Ibid., [178–188].

and to save his soul; and, when desiring to do this, the person elects as a means to help serve God and save his soul a way of life or state in life[4] within the boundaries of the Church. I said a tranquil time, a time when a person is not stirred up by diverse spirits and has free and tranquil use of his natural powers.[5]

In other words, the third mode of seeking God's will is through comparative evaluation of alternative ways or states of life or other alternatives for choice, precisely inasmuch as they are means to praise and serve God and to reach salvation. These alternative means are, of course, all real options for the discerner. The elective evaluation of these alternative means, Ignatius says, presupposes a consideration of the ultimate end of life, a desire for that end, and a tranquil state of mind. When these three factors are present, it is a time for a sound election in the third mode.

Consideration of What a Person Is Made For

The "tranquil time" is mentioned first in Ignatius' statement, but its importance can be understood only in relation to the other elements; therefore, it will be discussed after these. Within the tranquil time, the discerner is to consider what a person is born for, the ultimate end of human life. That is, as Ignatius says here, to praise God our Lord and save our souls—or, as we saw earlier, the greater glory of God in us.[6] Such consideration is the first step in all deliberation about means, and the third mode of discerning God's will is a deliberation about means to be chosen.

It is true that in the first two modes of discernment Ignatius presupposes that one understands what he is born for; after all, it is stated in the first sentence of the "principle and foundation" of the *Spiritual Exercises*,[7] and it is stressed over and over in the exercises leading up to the election.[8] But consideration of it is not an essential constitutive element of the first-time or the second-time experience

---

[4] See note 4 of chapter 9.
[5] *SpEx*, [177].
[6] Ibid., [23, 179, 180, 183, 185]; and see chapter 2.
[7] Ibid., [23].
[8] Ibid., [155, 157, 166, 169].

or essential to the discernment process of reflection on these experiences. It may come into play, but it need not; it may remain a tacit presupposition. Not so in the third mode.

Volitional Impulse in the Third Time

Volitional impulse or desire, however, is in one way or another both a necessary presupposition of discernment in every mode and an element in each time for discernment.

It is, we have seen, central to Ignatius' understanding of the primary condition for seeking God's will, no matter what mode of seeking. For that condition is openness to the Holy Spirit; and such openness, on its positive side, is constituted by and proportionate to the desire to know and do God's will. This desire, in turn, springs from and is proportionate to one's love for God in Jesus Christ. When the love and its consequent desire to do God's will are deep and intense enough to overrule all other desires, they render the discerner indifferent to any alternative to choice until it is judged to be what God wills.[9] Since the desire for or impulse toward whatever is God's will is rooted in a love which, in turn, is rooted in faith, it is, like the faith and the love, a divine grace, an impulse from the Holy Spirit.

In continuity with his emphasis on this *general* impulse from the Holy Spirit to whatever may be God's will, Ignatius makes this impulse, as *specified* to a particular concrete alternative for choice, the center of attention in his descriptions of the first-time and second-time experiences. In both of these some spiritual experiences are given which can be signs that a specified impulse is from God. In the third time, there is the general impulse from living faith to do God's will, whatever it may be, and a particular impulse, therefore, toward each alternative inasmuch as it is possibly what God wills; but, in contrast with the first-time and second-time experiences, there is no indeliberate impulse to any alternative as that which God does will.

"A Tranquil Time": What It Is and Why

Along with a consideration of the end and a desire for that end

---

[9] See above, pp. 74–77.

and for whatever more conduces to it, there is a third element which appears as essential in Ignatius' description of the third time for a sound election. It is the one he mentions first, "a tranquil time."

> I said a tranquil time, a time when the person is not
> stirred up by diverse spirits and has free and tranquil use
> of his natural powers.[10]

In this explanatory statement, there are two constitutive elements or factors: first, the discerner is not stirred up by diverse spirits; second, the discerner has free and tranquil use of his natural powers. Let us consider each of these factors in turn.

Just as the words "peace" or "peaceful" are commonly used in different meanings, so also are "tranquil" or "tranquility." All these words can refer to euphoric affective feelings, a consolation, or merely to the absence of affective excitement, or even to a motionless condition in beings without consciousness.[11] It would not be surprising to find different meanings in Ignatius' use of the words. Which one applies here?

Some interpret the tranquility of the third time as spiritual consolation. Karl Rahner is ambiguous on this point. He first says that "the experience of not receiving consolation is itself a factor in the Election made according to the third mode"; and, therefore, he thinks of the discerner in that mode as having to "fend for himself" without divine aid.[12] He then, however, immediately suggests a different interpretation openly in contradiction to the one just given. In this second interpretation, the tranquility of the third time may "be regarded as a sign of motion by the good spirit,"[13] a motion so delicate that the discerner "does not notice it at all and so he thinks that he has found the right solution by pondering and calculating acutely and lucidly, pencil in hand, without being moved by any spirit at all."[14]

---

[10] *SpEx*, [177].
[11] Jules Toner, *A Commentary*, pp. 87–89.
[12] Karl Rahner, *Dynamic Element*, p. 168.
[13] Ibid.
[14] Ibid., pp. 168–169.

164

Is the Third Mode of Election Really a Hidden Second Mode?

Harvey Egan is altogether clear in what he says on this point. For him, the time of tranquility in the third mode is a time of being moved by diverse spirits to consolation without high crests or to desolation without deep troughs.[15] He even goes so far as to say that the third time is a deficient mode, not only of the second time but of the first time too and, therefore, includes consolation without previous cause,[16] which, in his view, belongs to the first time.[17]

Piet Penning de Vries also asserts that tranquility in the third mode is consolation, but a consolation that is really a moment of desolation!

> Sometimes God comes to us through consolation. Sometimes the soul is not moved by diverse spirits, but makes use of its natural powers, freely and calmly. Consolation also accomplishes a task during these periods. Properly speaking this is a vaguer form of the time of election. Here peace is a moment of consolation, but the consolation is not sufficient and so this really means a moment of desolation.[18]

This is quite confusing. Perhaps he means that in the third mode there is a consolation which does not come from any movement of good or evil spirits. But, then, how can he assert that the peace of the tranquil time in *Spiritual Exercises*, [177] cannot be very different from the tranquility and quiet of consolation described in [333]?[19] Further, why is it called a desolation simply because the consolation is "not sufficient"?

Perhaps he has been influenced by Gagliardi, who conceived of tranquility in the third time as a desolation, but different from the desolation described in *Spiritual Exercises,* [317]. For the latter, he says, is prompted by the evil spirit and of itself tends to evil, whereas the former is from God and is the state of soul that results

---

[15] Harvey Egan, *Mystical Horizon*, p. 147.

[16] Ibid., pp. 152–153.

[17] See above, pp. 114–115.

[18] Piet Penning de Vries, S.J., *Discernment of Spirits*, trans. W. Dudok Van Heel (New York: Exposition Press, 1973), p. 62.

[19] Ibid., p. 68, note 2.

165

when God withdraws consolation, and it does not of itself tend to evil.[20]

The foregoing ways of understanding the tranquility of the third mode are contrary to the common understanding, and the immediate context of the *Spiritual Exercises*, [177] makes them entirely unacceptable.[21] In that context, Ignatius is distinguishing the third time from the second as he has just distinguished the second time from the first. When he says that by a tranquil time he means a time when the person is not stirred by diverse spirits, the obvious reference is to the consolations and desolations from good or evil spirits by which in the previous paragraph he characterized the second time for election.[22]

Ignatius has two reasons for excluding consolation and desolation from the third time. One reason, as the first factor in his explanation of a "tranquil time" indicates, is that, in this mode of election, a different kind of evidence from that in the second mode is sought. The evidence in the third mode of election is precisely the evidence which is excluded from the second mode of election; namely, reasons (*razones*) in the sense of projected consequences of alternative actions inasmuch as these are judged to be more or less conducive to God's service and glory.[23] Consequently, the data of consolation and desolation with impulse, which are in the second-time experience and are interpreted as evidence of God's will by discernment of spirits, are excluded—at least as a source of evidence;

---

[20] Achille Gagliardi, *Commentarii seu Explanationes in Exercitia spiritualia Sancti Patris Ignatii de Loyola*, pp. 146–147, 153.

[21] Gagliardi, however, seems to have only a different terminology—one, it must be noted, which fits with such passages as *SpEx*, [322], where it reads as if loss of consolation were equivalent to falling into desolation.

[22] Those who interpret "tranquil time" in reference to the third time of making an election as meaning a time of consolation appeal to certain phrases in *SpEx*, [180–184]. Their interpretation of these phrases seems so clearly in conflict with the whole context that one wonders if it would ever occur to anyone except a very logical person who saw himself forced to it by the need for logical consistency with other elements in his interpretation of Ignatius' thought. In opposition to this interpretation, Polanco (no. 89, *DirSpEx* p. 316), tells the director of the Spiritual Exercises not to allow the exercitant to enter on the third–time election while still having spiritual movements of consolation or desolation. Miró (no. 90 in *DirSpEx*MHSJ, p. 403) warns against allowing the exercitant to move into the third week of the Exercises while still engaged in the third mode of election: his reason is that the exercises of that week usually bring sorrow and sadness over the sufferings of Christ—a form of spiritual consolation, as Ignatius says in *SpEx*, [315].

[23] *SpEx*, [180–182]; and see above, on the second time being without reasons, pp. 141–142.

otherwise the election would still be the second time instead of the third. Spiritual consolation and desolation may serve for confirmation or disconfirmation of a decision already reached by third-time evidence[24] but are not necessary even for that.[25]

The other reason for excluding consolation and desolation from the third mode of election is linked with the reason for the second factor in Ignatius' explanation of a tranquil time. The free and tranquil use of one's natural powers for rational investigation and reflective evaluation needs a quiet state of mind, not agitated by consolation or desolation or by any other kind of emotional excitement.

Second Factor in a Tranquil Time

By "natural powers" in this context, Ignatius surely means those powers used in the third mode of discerning God's will: insight, reason, imagination, memory, and will (firmly set on the greater glory and on finding the significant facts and reasoning correctly). By "free and tranquil use" of these powers, he means their unimpeded and undisturbed functioning in searching out and arguing the advantages and disadvantages of alternatives for God's service.[26]

This meaning of the phrase goes beyond the exclusion of second-time spiritual movements as evidence in the third mode of discernment. It also excludes these diverse movements of spirits as impediments to the free and tranquil rational process of seeking information, interpreting it as reasons pro and con, comparatively weighing these reasons, and concluding. That is why Polanco and Miró in their directories are insistent that in the Spiritual Exercises the exercitant should not begin the third-time election while the various movements of the second time continue.[27]

Further, and for the same reason, it is not only the spiritual motions characteristic of the second time which are excluded from the third time. Also excluded are any other spiritual or non-spiritual

---

[24] See below, pp. 207–209.

[25] See below, pp. 204–205.

[26] SpEx, [180–181]. The word "tranquil" applied to the use of the natural powers in third–time discernment confirms the foregoing interpretation of "tranquil time"; for to speak of a "consoling" use of these powers would, in this context, make no sense whatsoever.

[27] See above, note 22.

167

disturbance; for example, worry, preoccupying concerns, fatigue, distracting surroundings, anguish, anger, or any highly exciting emotions of delight, joy, and so on.

Two Questions for Clarification

Two further clarifications are needed. The first concerns the exclusion of consolation or desolation, spiritual or non-spiritual, from the third time for election. Is this exclusion to be understood as absolute, as total, or only as relative to the purpose for which Ignatius requires tranquility? In other words, could the discerner be in the Ignatian third time while experiencing a consolation or desolation which is not a second-time experience and does not interfere with the unimpeded and untroubled use of the natural powers? What I have said above could easily mislead the reader to think that I am asserting an absolute exclusion. Others do seem to say so. As one commentator puts it, "This third time is one of peace and calm. The person is in a flat calm: no storms, nor even any breezes, disturb his tranquility."[28] While basically agreeing with this statement, I think it goes too far. Could we not allow for some slight breezes of consolation or desolation or some other slight emotional excitement?

There is sound reason to think so. Surely, at least "essential consolation"[29] from living faith will continue during the third time; for the whole process is founded on and enlightened by faith, from which flows essential consolation. What about "contingent consolation"? Even this, in light of the reasons for excluding spiritual movements, may have a place in third-time discernment. A gentle, quiet, low-key consolation or a very slight desolation might not significantly hinder one's search for information and for reasoning on it. Should we not in fact ordinarily experience at least some mild spiritual joy and peace when searching for God's will in the third mode with faith in him to lead and guide us? This spiritual joy and peace is neither constitutive of the "tranquil time" for an election in the third mode nor evidence for either alternative; it is only an accompaniment, desirable but not necessary. When given, it can be

---

[28] John J. English, *Spiritual Freedom*, p. 212. See also Hervé Coathalem, *Ignatian Insights*, p. 48. Coathalem says that the person "experiences a 'dead calm' or 'time of tranquility,' with no wind favorable or contrary making itself felt."

[29] Jules Toner, *A Commentary*, pp. 90–93.

168

very supportive for carrying on the hard work sometimes required in this mode of discernment. It can also serve as a sign of what spirit is influencing one's reasoning, along with other more certain signs such as charity and humility.

The second question for clarification regards the implication of the phrase "use of his natural powers." Does this phrase imply that Ignatius thought discernment had to be carried out "on our own,"[30] without divine help? Given the relationship which Ignatius sees between the person and God in discernment, such a conclusion could make sense only on the supposition that what he calls the third mode of election is not really a mode of election at all but only a device to prepare for and lead to the second mode. This supposition has been widely held of late by eminent interpreters, but the evidence against it is massive. Since almost all of this evidence is presented and discussed in detail in other contexts, there is no need to repeat here all that has been or will be said at length elsewhere. For now it will be enough to state what has been or will be established and give references to where this has been or will be done.

In his preliminary remarks concerning the whole of the Spiritual Exercises, Ignatius urges that the exercitant remain as much as may be in solitude. He gives several reasons for this.

> The second [reason] is that being withdrawn in this way [from distracting concerns], the mind free from and undivided by [attention to] many matters, concentrating on one thing only, that is to say, on serving his creator and benefiting his own soul, *he uses his natural powers more freely in seeking diligently that which he so greatly desires.*[31]

What the exercitant so greatly desires and seeks is, at each stage of the Exercises, the special grace appropriate to that stage.[32]

---

[30] Karl Rahner thinks so. See *Dynamic Element*, pp. 97, 168. William Peters's interpretation agrees with Rahner's. He thinks the discerner in the third–time election is "relying on his own natural powers" and, therefore, can have no justifiable confidence in a decision reached in that way. This mode of discernment, says William Peters, in contrast with all the early directories and the main Ignatian tradition, lies outside the "long retreat," that is, the full Spiritual Exercises. See *The Spiritual Exercises of St. Ignatius: Exposition and Interpretation* (Jersey City, N.J.: Program to Adapt the Spiritual Exercises, 1967), pp. 126–127.

[31] *SpEx*, [20], emphasis mine.

[32] Ibid., [45, 48, 51, 55, 91, 104, 139, 152, 180, 193, 221, 233].

To think that Ignatius means for the exercitant to seek these graces by use of his mere natural powers unaided by the Holy Spirit would be obviously unacceptable. There is no good reason to be found in Ignatius' writing for thinking that such an interpretation of the phrase "free and tranquil use of his natural powers" when describing the third time for election is any more acceptable.

All trustworthy discernment must be under the guidance of the Holy Spirit.[33] That is why openness to the Holy Spirit is one of the essential conditions for sound Ignatian discernment.[34] But Ignatius presents the third mode as a distinct and autonomous mode of seeking and finding God's will,[35] one that he trusted for himself and for others.[36] The *ultimate* ground for this trust in a decision reached by discernment is not the evidence, whether second-time or third-time, but God's benevolence, his fundamental will for us to find and choose what is for his greater glory in us.[37] Once we understand that, it is not difficult to understand how any reasonable way of seeking evidence which we pursue to the limit of our ability can be used by the Holy Spirit to lead us to a true conclusion. There is no good reason within the framework of Ignatius' thought to assume that the Holy Spirit influences our will (volitional impulse) and affective sensibility (spiritual consolation) but not our memory, reason, and judgment or that in using these we are left on our own. Rather, Ignatius believes that whenever we open ourselves to the Holy Spirit, in spiritual consolation or desolation or in calm, he is present to help us find the Father's will.

In ultimate analysis, God guides our natural powers in both modes of discernment or in neither. For in both modes our natural powers have an essential role; and there is the very same ground for believing in divine guidance of them in the third as in the second mode. As we have seen,[38] the second-time experiences, from which the second mode of discernment begins, provide data which must be remembered, critically evaluated, interpreted, and weighed. Does

---

[33] See above, pp. 36–44.
[34] See above, chapter 6.
[35] See below, pp. 246–250.
[36] See below, pp. 257–269.
[37] See below, pp. 281–282 and chapter 16, especially pp. 289–296.
[38] See above, chapter 9.

170

the Holy Spirit leave us on our own when using our natural powers in these ways? If so, why should we think the conclusion of a second-time discernment is of more value than the conclusion of a third-time discernment? If, on the other hand, in the second mode our natural powers are guided by the Holy Spirit, then why not in the third mode? That Ignatius did think the reasoning in the third mode is under the guidance of the Holy Spirit is shown, as we shall see, by his confidence in the conclusion of such a discernment[39] when the conditions for it are fulfilled.[40]

To sum up, the third mode of discernment involves such natural human powers as attention, memory, foresight, circumspection, understanding, and illation. In this mode of discernment, they function integrally with Christian faith, love, and hope. A discerner begins from a faith vision to search for God's will and continues to do so within a faith perspective. The discerner is motivated by charity to seek for God's will and carries out the search with loving openness to the Holy Spirit and with hope, founded on Christian faith, that the Holy Spirit will surely guide the search.[41] Consequently, Ignatius believes that, although it is the natural powers which are operating (and need good natural conditions for operating), they operate under direct or indirect divine influence.[42]

In What Sense a Tranquil Time Is and Is Not Distinctive of the Third Mode of Election

The understanding of what Ignatius means by calling the third time for election a tranquil time and why he sees tranquility as essential for it will now enable us to see in what way this tranquility is distinctive of the third time and in what sense it is not. A tranquil time is necessary for carrying out the process by which the discerner

---

[39] See below, pp. 257–265.

[40] See chapter 6.

[41] What Robert Ochs, S.J., says about the deistic strain in most of us, though not focused on discernment of God's will, has relevance to it. See his booklet *God Is More Present Than You Think* (New York: Paulist Press, 1970), pp. 30–40. See also pp. 13–29, where he talks about God's will.

[42] See above, chapter 4. I do not mean to imply that the Holy Spirit always preserves even those most open to him from getting false data or from reasoning erroneously. (See below, pp. 290–293.) I do mean that, within the limits of discernment (see above, chapter 5), through the working of our natural powers such as they are, the Holy Spirit guides those who are open to him to true conclusions. (See below, chapters 15–16.)

reaches a conclusion in the second mode of election, and even in the first if it really involves an active discernment of God's will.[43] Whenever there is a rational reflection, a time of tranquility is needed to do it well, a time free of stirrings by good or evil spirits and a time when the natural powers are able to function freely. Why, then, does Ignatius speak of the third time as a time of tranquility, as though tranquility were peculiar to this time for election? He does so because the first two modes begin with the experience of affective feelings and/or affective acts, and cannot begin without them; while the third mode cannot begin until a time when these spiritual stirrings and all non-spiritual disturbances have quieted down, leaving the person in a tranquil state.

The Third-Time Process: A First Way

After stating what he means by a third time for a sound and trustworthy election, Ignatius also gives relatively detailed instructions on how to carry out the third-time process of election. In fact, he gives instructions on what he calls two ways or forms of doing it.[44]

In the first and basic way, the discerner is to recall what the real options are in the situation for choice,[45] open himself to the Holy Spirit,[46] and pray to God to move his will toward and show him what is for the greater glory.[47] After these preparatory steps, he is to reason on the matter for the election "well and faithfully,"[48] looking over every aspect of the situation and drawing out evidence.[49] Evidence in the third mode is principally the greater advantages or disadvantages, for the glory of God which are foreseen as likely or certain consequences of each alternative.[50] These are to

---

[43] See above, pp. 121–127.

[44] *SpEx*, [178–188].

[45] Ibid., [178].

[46] Ibid., [179].

[47] Ibid., [180].

[48] Ibid.

[49] Ibid., [182].

[50] Ibid., [181]. For illustration, see Ignatius' third–time election on poverty in *Cons*MHSJ, I, pp. 78–81.

be weighed and a decision made in favor of the alternative to which *reason* is more strongly moved by this evidence.[51]

Relevant Data

In order to make sound projections regarding future consequences, one has to be well informed about the relevant past and present. About the present situation which calls for a choice, the discerner must take into account its concrete circumstances of time and place and of persons, their strengths, weaknesses, needs, resources, and responsibilities.[52] He must also note the possible and reasonable alternatives which this situation opens up. Further, the discerner must be informed about the past insofar as it helps to understand the present situation for choice and to project the future (for example, events leading to the present situation, experiences of past situations of a like nature, results of experiments made,[53] and so on). Sometimes the information is evidently valid; sometimes careful critical evaluation by appropriate principles and methods is called for.

In every instance the disposition of openness to the Holy Spirit is requisite; without it we risk missing or screening out real alternatives or significant information about the alternatives to which the Spirit might lead us. The light of the Holy Spirit is needed through all this early part of the third-time process, not merely later on at the time of interpreting the information and finding reasons. It is by his leading and guiding light that we find and understand and give significance to the manifold bits of information that will ultimately lead us to see reasons one way or the other.

The Main Norm: The Greater Glory

The main norm or principle which covers the selection of information and the interpretation of it as evidence regarding God's will is the greater service and glory of God—the *magis* principle, as it is called, the greater-glory principle.[54] Every real alternative for choice in a third-time discernment must be conducive to the

---

[51] *SpEx*, [182].
[52] See above, p. 27.
[53] See, for example, Ignatius' instruction on doing penance, *SpEx*, [89].
[54] The classical statement is in *SpEx*, [23]. See also [152, 155, 179, 182, 183, 185].

glory of God in human persons. When under some aspect a particular alternative is *more* conducive to that glory than other alternatives, we have a reason in support of thinking it is God's will. For, as we saw earlier, God always wills for us to choose what is for his greater glory in us, our greater glory. Therefore, to be relevant to the search for God's will, information about our alternatives for choice must illuminate an alternative not only as a means to God's glory but also as certainly, or likely in some respect, more for that glory than any other real alternative in this concrete situation. Attending to all the ways in which a proposed course of action would promote or not hinder the glory will merely clutter up the deliberation with useless information and may lead to spurious reasons.[55]

At first hearing, the greater-glory principle may sound rigid and frightening. It is absolute, and Ignatius is unyielding in applying it, but not rigid. On the one hand he sees it as the expression of divine love, which inexorably seeks to fill all of us to the full with God's life and joy and will not be content with what is less good for us.[56] On the other hand, he sees that divine love accepts us as we are, with our peculiar gifts and limitations and different stages of growth. If making a choice which, in the abstract, would be more for the glory would in the concrete go beyond my present psychological and spiritual strength and be spiritually harmful for me, that choice is not for the greater glory and is not God's will for me. Neither does the greater-glory principle always require choosing hard things. Sometimes it does require very hard choices, at other times thoroughly delightful and easy ones, far more delightful than the alternatives rejected. What counts is not whether the alternative for choice is pleasant or unpleasant, but whether it is more conducive to the glory. For instance, the fact that I like or enjoy doing a certain work is *of itself* not significant for discerning God's will about what work I should undertake. But the added consideration that I will be more effective in God's service when doing a work that I like to do is significant. Other factors in the situation being equal, it may be of decisive significance. At another time the principle may demand

---

[55] Some do find it helpful to begin by brainstorming, putting down whatever comes to mind as reasons and then carefully sifting out for consideration those which fit with the greater-glory principle.

[56] See above, pp. 21–24.

that I choose to do an unpleasant work because it is more needed for God's service and I am capable of doing it without effects on myself contrary to God's glory in me.

In every case, accepting and living by the greater-glory principle is from our side the expression of our love for God and for all persons. So, whatever the object for choice, the measure of our love for God and neighbor will measure the fundamental satisfaction we will find in choosing and acting by the greater-glory principle. Whatever I choose by that principle, no matter how undesirable in some other respect, will always be what I most want insofar as I am a true disciple of Christ.

Supplemental Principles or Norms

While the greater-glory principle is the primary and only absolute principle Ignatius gives for third-time discernment of God's will, he also sees other principles which are supplemental to it.

Some supplemental norms or principles are obviously dependent on the greater-glory norm and have no force apart from it. They are merely specifications of it, specific ways in which one alternative can be more conducive to the greater glory than the others, helps for applying a more general norm to concrete cases. They cannot function in discerning God's will unless the discerner sees how, in any particular concrete case, meeting this supplemental norm is more for the glory. Clear illustrations of such norms can be found in the Constitutions of the Society of Jesus where Ignatius is instructing Jesuit superiors how to make decisions about the distribution of manpower. There he gives a series of norms which he clearly relates to the greater-glory principle as their source of significance. Workers, he says, should be sent where there is greater need for them, where there is a greater opportunity for fruitful work, where there is a greater debt of gratitude owed to the people, where more universal good can be achieved, where the enemy of Christ seems to be more powerful, where works of more lasting value can be undertaken, and so on.[57]

The "signs of the times," or what God is doing in the Church and the world, when used as norms for discernment and choice, are

---

[57] *Cons*, [622–624].

sometimes obvious specifications of the greater-glory norms; for example, the movement of the Holy Spirit toward promotion of justice in all aspects of human life as a necessary expression of Christian faith.[58]

Other supplemental norms are, in ultimate analysis, reducible to the greater-glory norm, but the discerner does not have to see as yet *how* in the concrete case meeting this norm will actually be more for God's glory. What God's providence has already done in our past can sometimes serve in this way. An illustration can be found in *The Deliberation of the First Fathers*. When the pope was beginning to send the first companions of Ignatius to all parts of the world, they all gathered together to discern whether God willed for them to hold together in a body with a special concern for one another, letting neither distance nor anything else separate them.[59] The ultimate and absolutely important question was whether it would be for God's greater glory that they should try to maintain their relationship. But, when giving their reasons for an affirmative response, they did not begin by answering that question. It was what God had done in bringing such an unlikely group together that first suggested to them that it was his will for them to remain together. Their second (and, no doubt, more important) reason was that holding together would make them more effective in God's service.

> In the end we established the affirmative side of the
> question, that is, that inasmuch as our most kind and
> affectionate Lord had deigned to gather us together and
> unite us, men so spiritually weak and from such diverse
> geographical and cultural backgrounds, we ought not split
> apart what God had gathered and united; on the contrary

---

[58] " . . . discernment takes place in society, by persons formed by the culture and values of their community. . . . [One] dimension of attentiveness to social reality is the ability to 'read the signs of the times.'. . . Examples of positive signs include movements for the dignity and liberty of persons, promotion of the rights of women, breakdown of class and race differences, the call to human solidarity, movements to eradicate hunger and to work for world peace. . . . Some signs are clearly negative. . . . Others are ambiguous. . . . In order to utilize the 'signs of the times' as part of a discernment process some principles of interpretation are necessary. . . . The interpreter must guard against any simplistic judgment about what they signify" (Susan F. Rakoczy, *The Structures of Discernment Processes*, pp. 48–51).

[59] *Deliberatio Primorum Patrum*, [3], in *Cons*MHSJ, I, p. 3; Jules Toner, "The Deliberation," p. 190.

we ought day by day to strengthen and stabilize our union, rendering ourselves one body with special concern for each other, in order to effect the greater spiritual good of our fellow men. For united spiritual strength is more robust and braver in any arduous enterprise than it would be if segmented.[60]

A Special Magis Principle: The Greater-Union or Greater-Likeness Principle

There is another principle or norm proposed by Ignatius which is of major importance in his thought on discernment of God's will. When explaining openness to the Holy Spirit as the primary condition for sound discernment, we came upon Ignatius' ideal disposition for discernment and choice, what he calls the "third mode of humility." Included in that elective disposition is a norm. It can be called a special *magis* norm, the greater-likeness or greater-union norm; for it presents greater likeness to Christ in his poverty and humiliation as a norm for deciding and choosing, not in every situation for choice, but in one special kind of situation.

That special situation has two essential characteristics: first, the alternatives in some way involve riches as opposed to actual poverty, or honors as opposed to humiliation or opprobrium; and, second, the greater-glory norm cannot be applied. Conceivably, there are two cases in which the greater-glory norm could not be applied: first, when, despite one's best efforts, the evidence that one alternative is more conducive to the glory of God cannot be discovered or, second, when there is no such evidence to be found because the alternatives are objectively equal for the service and glory of God. Reasons were given when discussing the third mode of humility for thinking that the latter case is purely hypothetical, never to be found in actuality, and proposed by Ignatius only in order to present a really possible mode of love.[61] The first case, however, is a real possibility. When the discerner cannot find evidence to show that one alternative is more conducive to God's glory, the greater-likeness norm calls for a judgment in favor of what more

---

[60] Jules Toner, "*The Deliberation,*" p. 192.

[61] See above, pp. 92–93.

177

assimilates the discerner's life to the life of poverty and humiliation which Christ chose as his way of bringing God's truth and life to the world and which he called blessed.

Even in some cases where the greater-glory norm does apply, the greater-likeness norm can still serve to confirm a decision according to that former norm. A clear illustration of this use is to be found in Ignatius' *Spiritual Diary*, when he was discerning about what kind of poverty to propose for the Society of Jesus.

> . . . the thought of Jesus occurring to me, I felt a movement to follow him, it seemed to me interiorly, since he was the head of the Society, a greater argument to proceed in complete poverty than all the other human reasons, although I thought all the reasons for the past elections tended toward the same decision.[62]

Taking account of what has just been said and of what was said earlier about the third mode of humility as a disposition for seeking God's will, the relationship of the greater-likeness norm to the greater-glory norm can be clarified. The latter is absolute, overriding, always primary. The greater-likeness norm is secondary; it can never, in any choice, have equal weight with the first *magis* principle; it can never justify a choice of actual poverty and humiliation over riches and honors if the latter are seen to be more for the service of God in a particular situation for choice, with all its concrete circumstances, including the agent's responsibilities to others[63] and his or her own stage of psychological and spiritual development. It is not needed when the choice of poverty and humiliation is seen to be for the greater glory.

Not only is the greater-likeness secondary to the greater-glory norm; it also seems reducible to the latter as a special case of it, although Ignatius never said so. For, although neither alternative appears more for God's glory than the other, nevertheless, as seen earlier, the act of choosing humiliation and poverty with Jesus rather than riches and honors involves the actuation of a more intense love

---

[62] Entry for Feb. 23.

[63] *SpEx*, [168], *Cons*, [101]. Note Ignatius' practice of defending his own companions' reputation for good morals and sound doctrine when that was for the greater service of God (for example, see *Autobiog.*, [86] and [98]).

for him than would the opposite choice.[64] But this more intense love is more for the glory of God.

An Illustration of the Several Norms Used in One Discernment by Ignatius

There is a document in which we can see how Ignatius used the several kinds of third-time norms.[65] It is not included in Ignatius' *Spiritual Diary* but does seem to be the "elections" to which he refers time after time while making the discernment which he recounts in the diary.[66]

The question for that discernment was, in Ignatius' own words, "whether the churches [of the Company of Jesus] should have any income and whether the Company [of Jesus] could receive help from it."[67] In the document to which he refers again and again as "the elections," he sets down the pros and cons for having or not having income. Most of the reasons are based clearly and directly on the greater-glory norm (with its dependent, more specific forms). Some, however, are based on the norm of what God has already led to as his will. Thus, in his list of "advantages and reasons for not having any revenue," we find the following:

> 13. All ten of us [Ignatius and his first companions], without exception, choosing this kind of poverty [without any income] took as our head the same Jesus, our Creator and Lord, with the intention of going out under his banner to preach and exhort in accord with our calling.

> 14. We ourselves requesting poverty of this kind, the bull was granted to us, and after waiting a year for it to be expedited, persevering the while in unchanging assent, we received confirmation from His Holiness.

> 15. It is connatural to God our Lord to be constant, and to the enemy [Satan] to be inconstant and fickle.

---

[64] See above, pp. 90–92.

[65] "Deliberacion sobre la Pobreza," *Obras Completas*, pp. 297–299.

[66] For example, see the entries for Feb. 8–11 and 16. See ConsMHSJ, I, pp. xciii–xciv; here the editor identifies the *Deliberatio S.P.N. Ignatii de Paupertate* (ibid., pp. 78–81) as the documents referred to by "elections" in these passages.

[67] *Autobiog*, [100].

Other reasons on this list are based on the special norm of greater likeness to Christ poor and humiliated. Thus,

> 11. Poverty with no income is more perfect than poverty with partial or full income.
> 12. Taking for himself this kind of poverty, our universal Lord set the same before his apostles and beloved disciples, when sending them to preach.

Sometimes reasons based on the greater-likeness norm are fused with reasons based on the greater-glory norm.

> 1. The Company [of Jesus] will attain greater spiritual energy and greater devotion by resembling and coming close to the Son of the virgin, our Creator and Lord, so very poor and in such great afflictions.[68]
> 4. It will help to humble us more and unite us more with him who humbled himself above all others.

We also find the norm of greater likeness used with the norm of what God has been doing, as is clear in Reason 13 given above to illustrate the latter norm.

Weighing Evidence and Coming to a Conclusion

After telling us what kind of evidence according to what norm to look for in the third mode of discernment,[69] Ignatius points out the next step to be taken.

> Fifth [point]. After going back and forth [over the advantages and disadvantages] in this way and having reasoned on the matter proposed [for election] from all sides, to observe toward which alternative reason leans. Thus, in accord with the prevailing movement of reason, and not in accord with any sensual movement, a decision on the matter proposed ought to be made.[70]

---

[68] Compare with the entry in Ignatius' diary for Feb. 23. (See above, p. 178.) In the reason given there, he does not mention any spiritual advantages, and the reason seems to draw its peculiar strength from seeing Jesus as head of the Society of Jesus. (See below, pp. 208–209)

[69] SpEx, [180–181].

[70] Ibid., [182].

Here again Ignatius stresses what he urged just before this passage, namely, reasoning over the matter "well and faithfully."[71] He is not satisfied that the discerner put down a set of well-pondered reasons carefully based on the relevant norms. He wants him to go back and forth over those reasons, looking at them from all sides (as he himself did time and again for long periods, with much prayer, in the discernment recounted in his diary).[72] The discerner should also make sure that it is the stronger reasons and not any selfish or sentimental inclination which lead him to a decision.

The problems in judging which reasons are stronger and whether strong enough to justify a decision are parallel with those in the second-time election. What was said there about weighing second-time evidence and coming to a conclusion (tentatively, before seeking confirmation)[73] holds here *mutatis mutandis* for third-time evidence. Thus, there will be evidence for each alternative; under some aspect each will appear to be more for God's glory than the others. Judgments have to be made about the comparative weight of the opposing sets of reasons; about the weightier set, whether it is sufficiently weighty to justify a decision; finally, about the time to end deliberation and actually make a decision to be offered to God for confirmation. There is no need to repeat what has already been said about these steps in the exposition of discernment in the second mode.

Only the last step of seeking confirmation from God has yet to be studied. Before turning to that, it will be better to take up the second way of the third-time discernment. For, as we shall see, at the conclusion of the instructions on the latter way, Ignatius refers the discerner back to the sixth and final step of the first way, that of seeking divine confirmation, telling him to act as directed there. If we defer the study of this final step in seeking God's will, we can deal with it in relation to both ways of the third-time election, as well as to the second time of discovering God's will.

---

[71] Ibid., [180].

[72] See also Ignatius' remarks on his election which led to offering his resignation from the office of general of the Society of Jesus. There he speaks of deliberating "on various occasions over months and years," "at many different times." (See below, pp. 263–264)

[73] See above, pp. 156–159.

The Second Way of Third-Time Election: Conflicting Interpretations and Basic Questions

The function of what Ignatius calls the second way of third-time election and its relationship with the first way are understood diversely by writers on Ignatian discernment. By seeing the contrast between these conflicting interpretations, we will see what basic questions need to be answered when we examine the four ''rules'' and the ''note'' which constitute Ignatius' directions for this second way.[74]

According to one interpretation, the second way of the third mode is not independent of the first. It presupposes the first way and is a continuation *and necessary completion* of it. This interpretation attributes to the reasoning and decision of the first way some positive value for finding God's will, but it sees these as incomplete until the discerner's motives are tested by the second way. On the basis of *Spiritual Exercises*, [184], it is said that the second way of the third mode of election does not begin from indifference but from felt preference for one of the alternatives, whether this preference results from the first way or from some other source. The second way is thought to be a way of finding whether this preference is from God or from disordered affectivity.[75]

According to another interpretation, the whole third-time method (both first and second ways of the third-time election) of seeking God's will by the use of any kind of evidence proper to it is of no positive value for finding God's will, apart from its relationship to the second-time election. The first way of the third-time election, therefore, is not an incomplete election which can be completed by the second way; the whole so-called third-time election is merely a preparation for, or a device leading to, a second-time election by spiritual consolation. In this view, to think of the second way of the third-time election as completing an election already well started in the first way would be giving the third-time election a value it does not have.[76]

---

[74] *SpEx*, [184–188].

[75] Edouard Pousset, *Life in Faith and Freedom*, pp. 125–128. Thomas Green leaves me unsure on this point but gives the impression that he sees the second way of third–time election as independent of the first way. (See *Weeds Among the Wheat*, p. 86.)

[76] See below, pp. 236–241.

In contrast with the two preceding interpretations, another one sees the whole third-time election (first and second ways) as fully distinct from and independent of the second-time election and, further, sees the two ways of the third-time election as distinct from and independent of each other. In other words, each can be a fully autonomous mode of election. The second way is not thought of as concerned with testing the motives of the preceding first way or of merely leading to a second-time election by consolation. Rather, this interpretation understands Ignatius to be presenting some exercises which, by themselves, can enable one to find God's will by "spontaneous reactions and intuitions of Christian good sense."[77]

In partial agreement with some elements in each of the three preceding interpretations but also in sharp contrast with other elements, I would like to present another interpretation of the second way of third-time election which, I think, results from more careful analysis of Ignatius' words in *Spiritual Exercises*, [184-188] and attention to a fuller context in the *Spiritual Exercises* and other Ignatian documents. In contrast to the first two interpretations presented above, I hope to show that this second way has no necessary relationship to the second-time mode of election. (As we shall see, it can even be totally independent of any second-time kind of evidence as confirmation.[78]) In contrast with the third interpretation presented above, I hope to show that this second way is entirely dependent on the first way of the third-time election but not necessary to the latter. That is to say, the first way can be complete without the second but not the other way around. The first way is essential to the third mode of election; the second way presupposes the first and is merely an aid when the latter is not succeeding, or it can be used to make the conclusion of the first way even more sure.

The disagreements among the foregoing interpretations point up several fundamental questions that need to be answered regarding the second way of the third-time election. When, under what circumstances, is the second way of third-time election to be undertaken? When it is undertaken, what is its function in the search for finding God's will? Is it or is it not an autonomous mode of election?

---

[77] Hervé Coathalem, *Ignatian Insights*, pp. 190–191.
[78] See below, pp. 205–210.

When to Undertake the Second Way of Third-Time Election?

There is a clear indication in the Ignatian text of the order in which each way or mode of election is to be taken up, and this order indicates under what circumstances the second way of the third-time is to be undertaken. If, Ignatius writes, the person is not moved by God in the first time for election, he should go to the second.[79] If he does not succeed in the first or the second mode of making an election, there are two ways available in the third.[80] The first of these is the way of "intellectual discourse through the six points" which are given;[81] ultimately, the last way which one can use is that of the four points,[82] that is, the second way of third-time election.

If the second way of third-time election were an essential part of the first, there would be no point in calling it the last way available for seeking God's will. Such a way of speaking implies that the preceding first way of the third-time election is sufficient by itself but not always so. When it is not sufficient, the second way is the last help Ignatius has to offer. Some early directories support this interpretation, but add that, even when the first way of the third-time election is sufficient, one may use the second in order to make doubly sure of the decision reached[83]—even ought to use it, in some cases, in order to be doing the very best one reasonably can.[84]

The Function of the Second Way of Third-Time Election

The second and central basic question asked above concerns the function of this second way of third-time election. Is this final way of seeking God's will designed to help us find evidence for what God wills by interpreting spiritual movements of the affectivity or by reasoning about advantages and disadvantages for God's ser-

---

[79] *DirAutog*, [18].

[80] Ibid., [19] and *SpEx*, [178].

[81] The "six points" are in *SpEx*, [178].

[82] Ibid., [20].

[83] According to Polanco (no. 90, *DirSpEx*MHSJ, p. 317), if the conclusion of the second way of the third–time election agrees with the conclusion of the first way, it makes the latter *more* certain—a clear indication that it may well be used even after a successful first way. According to the 1599 directory, [199] in *DirSpEx*MHSJ, p. 707, when no decision is reached by the first way of the third time, the second way is to be used, but also even if a decision is reached by the first way [223] (ibid., p. 719); for, if the two ways concur, the directory says, that is a good sign.

[84] See below, pp. 251–253; 303–308.

vice or by some other way, for example, that of Christian intuition? Each of these possible functions has some backing among commentators. The only way to answer the question at issue is to make a careful analysis of the "four rules and a note," which contain Ignatius' instructions for this second way.

The first rule[85] is that the motive for choosing should "come from above, from the love of God." By this, Ignatius means that the one making an election should "first" (*primero*), that is, before coming to any decision or choice, have an inner perception that the love he has, greater or less, for any alternative in the election "is solely on account of his Creator and Lord." That is, he must be sure it is only his love for God and the desire for God's glory consequent on that love which roots his affection toward any alternative. The first rule is, then, plainly yet another insistence on purity of heart and indifference to all motives apart from love for God. As we have seen, Ignatius urges over and over again the necessity of these dispositions for beginning and continuing and concluding any election by any mode.[86]

Analysis of the next three rules uncovers no reasonable ground for understanding them as anything more than three exercises calculated to help the discerner attain and maintain the purity of heart called for in the first rule.

Thus, in the second rule, Ignatius proposes that I (the discerner) consider some person, real or imaginary, whom I have never seen or known but for whom I desire the perfection of Christian life— one, no doubt, in the very situation for choice which I now face. All things considered, whatever I would counsel that person to choose for the greater glory of God is what I should choose.[87] What this rule gives us is not a way of securing any different data or evidence than that obtained in the first way of the third-time discernment. It is simply a device for gaining objectivity and honesty with oneself so as to see the data and their meaning, unobscured by rationalization springing from my desires and fears. It is the device

---

[85] *SpEx*, [184].

[86] To interpret this rule as if the affection Ignatius is speaking of were some second–time evidence for judging that one alternative for choice is God's will, as some do (for example, Karl Rahner and Edouard Pousset), seems to be ignoring the immediate context and also what Ignatius says elsewhere. See below, pp. 188–189.

[87] *SpEx*, [185].

used by Nathan to make David look honestly at the heinousness of his sins against Uriah[88] and used by Christ to show Simon the Pharisee how his assumptions blinded him.[89]

Much light on this second rule is found in the *Deliberation of the First Fathers*. There we are told how Ignatius and his companions had for several days tried to discern whether God willed for them to take a vow of obedience to one of their group. Failing to reach a conclusion, they recessed the discernment to reflect on their method of seeking God's will.[90] After much discussion they settled on some additions to it. One of these was a set of three preparations.[91] The first preparation was a way of overcoming an obstacle to indifference regarding the vow of obedience by use of the "counterattack principle."[92] The second was a way of making sure that the advantages or disadvantages anyone proposed for or against the vow of obedience would be his own, coming from his prayer and reflection rather than from hearing what others thought. The third was the very exercise we are considering: "Each one would think of himself as a stranger to our group who would have no expectation of joining it."

Given what precedes in the context of this deliberation and especially what follows, there can be no doubt that this third preparation was intended neither for receiving the counsel of the Holy Spirit through spiritual consolations (as in second-time election) nor for arriving at an intuition without reasoning. All that Ignatius and his companions planned to do from here on (and all they actually did) was to go on finding and weighing advantages and disadvantages for the service and glory of God.[93] On the basis of these they

---

[88] II *Sam.* 12:1–4.

[89] *Lk.* 7:36–47.

[90] *Deliberatio Primorum Patrum*, [4–5] in *Cons*MHSJ, I, p. 4.

[91] Ibid., [6], pp. 4–5.

[92] On the principle, see Jules Toner, *A Commentary*, pp. 160–162. On its application in the deliberation by Ignatius and his companions, see Jules Toner, "The Deliberation," pp. 198–200; 211, note 12.

[93] *Deliberatio Primorum Patrum*, [6–8] in *Cons*MHSJ, I, pp. 4–7; Jules Toner, "The Deliberation," pp. 201–205.

made their decision,[94] a decision that determined the course of all their lives.

The third and fourth rules cannot be understood in context as anything other than exercises for the sake of gaining greater freedom from inordinate affections which hinder an honest, objective, clear assessment of the advantages and disadvantages for the service and glory of God, as in the first way of a third-time election.

The third rule[95] bids the person to imagine himself on his death bed and to consider what at that time he would wish to have chosen. In that imagined situation, insofar as he can make it real to himself, he will not anticipate any more temporal satisfaction or pain from either alternative. All that is finished. So he is free from selfish desire or fear in relation to either alternative. The only thing that matters is the greater glory of God and the discerner's salvation.

In the fourth rule[96] Ignatius suggests a final exercise. It is very much like the preceding one, but it focuses on the day of judgment rather than on death—and this does make a difference. Since the discernment is concerned with finding among alternatives which are for God's glory the one which is more for the glory, the judgment is not concerned with being assigned to heaven or hell. It is, rather, a matter of coming face to face with the infinitely beautiful God who has entered into friendship with me and loved me "to the end." It is a matter of imagining myself in his presence and looking back with him on how I have loved him, either with fidelity, generosity and courage or with selfish reservations and a love stunted by cowardice and pettiness. The thought of some punishment to be imposed might not shake me very much. I might be quite ready to take that as a trade-off for what I intensely want now. But when, in the imaginary experience of judgment, my infinitely lovable and loving Savior has to look at my ignoble and niggardly love, when all my brothers and sisters, who will then love me beyond measure and I them, will have to know that I backed away from choosing what would be for the greater glory of God in all of them—these experiences in an imaginative rehearsal will surely help me overcome

---

[94] *Deliberatio Primorum Patrum*, [8] in *Cons*MHSJ, I, p. 7; Jules Toner, "The Deliberation," pp. 205–206.

[95] *SpEx*, [186].

[96] Ibid., [187].

whatever present disordered desire or fear may be hindering me. With such clarity of mind, what I would then wish to have chosen I will choose now.

If the foregoing interpretation of the Ignatian second way of the third-time election should need any support, it is to be found in a later passage in the *Spiritual Exercises*, the "rules for almsgiving."[97] These are instructions on how to go about preparing oneself for discerning God's will regarding the distribution of alms. What Ignatius says here makes even clearer what he intended to achieve through the exercises presented in the four rules for the second way of third-time election. That those very same rules are being used here is expressly stated;[98] and each one of them is now restated in terms of discerning how to distribute alms. The entire purpose of the rules is clearly to help the person reach freedom from the disordered affections which blind him to what is truly for the greater service and glory of God.

Two situations are called to special attention, both of them situations in which most persons would find it very difficult to maintain indifference to all but God's greater service. In one there is question of using for one's own needs what might be used for alms to others.[99] In order to be able to discern with openness to the Spirit in this situation, Ignatius recommends an attitude of self-diminishment and an endeavor to approach the pattern of Christ's poverty.[100] The other situation occurs when, among the prospective recipients of alms, there are persons who are bound to the giver as friends or blood relatives.[101] What Ignatius says regarding the latter makes clear beyond all question what he saw as the function of the four rules, namely, to dispose the person for third-time discernment as done in the first way.

> When any person perceives that he is drawn to and
> is affectionate toward any other person to whom he wishes
> to dispense (alms), let him delay and ponder well the

---

[97] Ibid., [337–344].
[98] Ibid., [338].
[99] Ibid., [343].
[100] Ibid., [344], and see [189].
[101] Ibid., [338].

foresaid four rules, examining and testing his affections
by them. Let him give no alms until in conformity with
them he has entirely stripped off and cast away his disordered affection.[102]

There is in this passage no suggestion of anything to be
achieved by using the "four rules" (taken from the second way of
third-time election) except the freeing of oneself from disordered
affections. Achieving this, of course, also prepares one to receive
consolations and impulses from the Holy Spirit; but there is nothing
here or in the instructions for the second way of the third-time
election which indicates that as the sole or main purpose of these
four rules. In context, their purpose is to prepare one for a better
discernment by the first way of the third mode of election[103] or,
perhaps, as some think, for an intuition for what is more conducive
to God's glory.

The Question of Intuition in a Third-Time Election

Ignatius makes no explicit assertion or denial of such an intuition as the aim of the second way of the third mode of election.
The context, however, seems to argue against such an aim. For, if
it were true, there would be no apparent reason for speaking of a
second way of the third mode of election rather than a fully distinct
fourth mode. What would the so-called second way have in common
with the first way of the third mode?

However that may be, in the light of our experience, it seems
altogether unrealistic, at least in a situation that involves the least
complexity, to expect that purity of heart will, without any weighing
of reasons, enable a person to see what is for God's greater glory.
Take the case of distributing alms. Surely it would be rash to think
that one who has attained great purity of heart will, by that very
fact, see how to distribute goods for the greater service of God
without finding out the needs of various possible recipients and the
likely consequences of fulfilling these needs, or weighing these considerations in terms of the advantages for God's glory in the lives

---

[102] Ibid., [342].

[103] They can also be used as a way of testing and seeking to confirm or disconfirm a decision
reached by the first way. See above, note 83.

189

of the recipients and others. Even one main proponent of intuition by Christian common sense as the goal of this second way becomes uneasy when the decision is "rather complicated" and indicates that it is ordinarily better to combine the two ways of the third-time election and have recourse to the director of the Spiritual Exercises.[104]

There is, it should be noted, a cognitive experience which so resembles intuition as easily to be mistaken for it, and could even be called intuition in a manner of speaking. It is really only an amazingly quick and unreflective form of reasoning on objective data. The third mode of discerning God's will could be carried out in this way by a person who is gifted for such reasoning, but it could be mistaken even by himself as well as by others for an intuition.[105]

Ignatius concludes his instructions on the second way of third-time election by telling the discerner to make an election in accord with the rules given above and to offer his decision to God as in the sixth point of the third way, begging God to accept it and confirm it.[106] What constitutes this confirmation and how important it is for Ignatian discernment will be considered in the following chapter.

---

[104] Hervé Coathalem, *Ignatian Insights*, p. 191.

[105] What I am referring to is like or includes what John Henry Newman calls "natural inference." See his *Grammar of Assent* (Garden City, N.Y.: Image Books, 1955) pp. 260–269.

[106] *SpEx*, [188].

Chapter 11
Confirmation or
Disconfirmation Prior to
Finalizing the Tentative
Decision

*W*hen I am preparing to seek God's will, Ignatius would have me offer to God all my will and liberty so that God may dispose of my person and of all I have according to his will.[1] When I am actually seeking God's will, Ignatius would have me offer the alternatives to God so that he may lead me to know which one he prefers.[2] Likewise, after I have reached a decision, Ignatius would

---

[1] *SpEx*, [5].

[2] *DirAutog*, [21].

have me offer it to God, begging him to confirm it if it is his will or disconfirm it if it is not.

> When that election or decision has been made, the person who has made it should with great diligence go to prayer before God our Lord and offer him the said election so that, if it be for his greater service and praise, he may be pleased to accept and confirm it.[3]

This brief statement occasions and leaves unanswered many serious questions which need answering and are answered in conflicting ways by Ignatian commentators. Happily, however, we do have a detailed account by Ignatius himself of his way of seeking confirmation from God for what he counted as a very important decision. Before presenting the questions which need to be addressed and trying to evaluate the diverse answers given to them, two things need to be done. First, any ambiguity about what kind of confirmation is being sought must be removed; much confusion can result from lack of precision on this point. Second, the main source of our knowledge about how Ignatius himself sought confirmation must be examined. After these preliminary steps, we can put the important questions in order and attempt to find the answers.

Confirmation of Judgment and Confirmation of Will

Confirmation of the judgment reached by discernment must be kept distinct from confirmation of the will courageously and energetically to carry out what is judged to be God's will.[4] Both of these must be kept distinct from other kinds of confirmation mentioned by Ignatius.[5] As will appear, all of these can get confused and cause misinterpretation of what Ignatius means in this final step of seeking God's will. For the moment our concern is with the distinction between confirmation of judgment and confirmation of motivation to execute it.

These two kinds of confirmation, it is true, can influence each

---

[3] *SpEx*, [183].

[4] See Ignatius' remarks to Francis Borgia on the need for volitional confirmation by consolations, *LettersIgn*, p. 181.

[5] For example, confirmation of holy desire (*Autobiog*, [5–10]); of faith (ibid., [29]); of being reconciled with God (*Diary*, March 15); of security regarding the future (ibid., Feb. 24).

other: a firmer assent to an act as God's will surely makes for a firmer will to do it in a person who loves God; and, in some cases, the experience of a firmer will to do what God wills can also be a confirmation of the assent. Take, for example, the experience of struggling toward and arriving at a tentative decision, with fear of the painful consequences attendant on carrying it out, and then experiencing the grace of God taking away all fear and making the difficulties and pain to be borne for love of God and neighbor seem easy and sweet.[6] Despite their mutual influence, however, the two kinds of confirmation are truly distinct.

In the *Spiritual Exercises* the volitional confirmation to which Ignatius mainly attends is that which is needed before reaching a judgment, in fact before even seeking to reach one. For, as already seen, before beginning the election and during it, the discerner must have already chosen in principle and have a firm will to carry out whatever the discernment process will lead him to judge is God's will.[7] All the meditations and contemplations before the election begins are for the sake of confirming the person's will in this attitude by purifying and intensifying the person's love for God in Christ; but one who has been confirmed in this way has not yet come to any judgment about what God does will in the matter for discernment. Again, volitional confirmation is needed after the finalized conclusion of the discernment. Because our will easily falls away from its resoluteness, confirmation of a volitional resolve may be needed for ensuring prompt, energetic, and persevering execution. The third and fourth weeks of the Spiritual Exercises can serve this purpose. But before seeking such volitional confirmation, one must have come to a finalized judgment on what God wills.

The conclusion for which Ignatius, in *Spiritual Exercises,* [183], recommends seeking confirmation is not finalized; it is as yet tentative. That is to say, even though the conclusion is based on sound and sufficient evidence, it does not yet actually inform choice and efficacious intention; it is held from doing so while awaiting divine confirmation, and it is still open to the possibility of disconfirmation.

---

[6] Official Directory of 1599, [196].

[7] See above, pp. 77–79.

The rest of the election process after this tentative assent is not, properly speaking, for the sake of attaining or strengthening volitional consent to do what God wills; it is entirely, or at least mainly, for the sake of strengthening the tentative intellectual assent and thus enabling the discerner to finalize the decision for choice.[8] As indicated above, confirmation of the assent may result in confirmation of the will to carry out the act assented to as God's will. Further, when confirmation of the assent is by spiritual consolation, then by its very nature it also brings confirmation of the discerner's will to carry out what God wills. But the confirmation directly and explicitly sought in the last step of the election process is confirmation of the judgment which constitutes the conclusion of that process. If *Spiritual Exercises,* [183] leaves any doubt of this, we shall see now that the account of Ignatius' own discernment in his *Spiritual Diary* does not.

Source of Evidence to Answer the Questions about Confirmation

Outside the brief directive in *Spiritual Exercises,* [183] quoted above, there is nothing else in that document which can be of much help for answering the many questions regarding confirmation which occur; and there is very little help in that directive itself. Neither is there any help to be found in the *Autograph Directory.* In fact, there is only one primary source that can be of notable help, namely, Ignatius' *Spiritual Diary.* Without that we would never be able to know from Ignatius himself how he thought on the questions before us. We do, of course, still have the early directories to help us; and on some points we will have to look for light in them. In the diary we have a detailed, step-by-step account of a discernment that lasted at least forty days. A great part of it, perhaps the greater part, after the eighth day is given over to an account of Ignatius' seeking

---

[8] "It is possible that certain minimizing interpretations of the word *confirmar,* used in no. [183] of the *Exercises,* are due to the influence of the vulgate, which translates it by the word *stabilire.* But the meaning of Ignatius seems to us to be attested by too many other uses to permit us to reduce this *confirmation* to the strengthening of the will or the facility of execution, although these last elements constitute a part of the grace asked by St. Ignatius" (Maurice Giuliani, S.J., "Movements of the Spirit," in *Finding God in All Things,* trans. William J. Young, S. J. [Chicago: Henry Regnery Company, 1958], p. 273, note 17).

confirmation for the truth of his decision reached on the eighth day.[9] This long description of his search for confirmation provides evidence for answering most of our questions.

Giving answers to the questions about confirmation with reference made to the diary could never convey Ignatius' understanding of confirmation as convincingly as going through his experience step by step. Therefore, the best way to proceed is to defer trying to answer any questions until after looking at the day-by-day account of what Ignatius wrote during his search for confirmation.

The Question for and the Phases of Ignatius' Discernment

The question about which Ignatius was seeking to find God's will concerned the practice of poverty in the Society of Jesus. It was a somewhat complex question and had a somewhat complicated history in the years during which the Society of Jesus was being established.[10] It seems better for our present purpose (which is to understand Ignatius' discernment method rather than his thought on poverty) simply to say that the question was whether poverty in the Society of Jesus should be more or less complete, more or less strict.

The account in his *Spiritual Diary* can be analyzed and divided in a number of ways. For our purpose I find four main parts or phases.[11]

The First Phase

It is in the first phase, February 2–11, that we find the clearest picture which we have anywhere of how Ignatius himself carried on an election, brought it to a decision, offered the decision to God, and received signs for God's acceptance confirming his decision.

For seven days, February 2–9, Ignatius was powerfully led by both second-time and third-time[12] discernment to the same conclusion, that "perfect poverty" (neither full nor partial income) was what God willed. On the evening of February 8, he found himself

[9] Whether the discernment begins on Feb. 2 or before, we do not know for sure; consequently, the discernment leading to the tentative decision may have taken more than eight days.

[10] See George E. Ganss, *ConsSJComm*, p. 253, note 5; I. Iparraguirre, S.J., *Obras Completas*, pp. 294–295, 309; *Cons*MHSJ, I, pp. xciii–xcv, 35–37, note 3.

[11] A different and more detailed division by I. Iparraguirre can be found in *Obras Completas*, pp. 314–315.

[12] See below, pp. 205–209.

with no thought whatever in conflict with that decision and no desire of proceeding any further with the election. On the evening of the following day, February 9, he considered that the question did not merit further thought, that the search was finished.

On February 10 he began offering his decision to God in prayer so that he might accept and confirm it. Morning and evening on that day, Ignatius went over his reasons and offered to God his decision for perfect poverty, and he received signs of divine acceptance: devotion, tears, peace, clarity of understanding regarding the decision, a sense of security of having made a good election.

On February 11, without any consideration of reasons or any offering or petition for divine acceptance, he received intense mystical consolation and with it firmness in the decision made. Later he took out his written reasons in order to go over them with prayer for power to discern well, but with an attitude of reviewing what was really already settled. He experienced devotion, certain understanding, and clarity of vision. At the very time that he lost all desire for further reasons, he received a new confirmation by reason based on the mission of the apostles. He recalled how Christ sent the apostles to preach in poverty and how they were confirmed in this by the Holy Spirit sent from the Father and the Son. Deeply moved, he again offered his decision for perfect poverty, holding it as "ratified and valid, and so on." Shortly thereafter, in the midst of profound mystical consolation, he saw the whole election as "something completed," and later experienced "great tranquility and security of soul, like an exhausted man who takes a good rest, neither seeking nor caring to seek any further, considering the matter finished except for giving thanks."

Second Phase: February 12–18

Surprisingly, however, Ignatius did not terminate the election. The disturbing events of the following day initiated a new and somewhat confused phase of his quest for confirmation.

Ignatius began the day of February 12 with fervent thanks and with consolation. But later on, he experienced a "temptation" (Ignatius' own word) to back off from the decision already reached, confirmed, and counted as finished. The temptation was to allow some mitigation of perfect poverty. This event seems to have been

196

concurrent with a racket in the house which greatly disturbed him and caused him to leave his prayer and go to stop it.[13] This act of leaving prayer he counted as a fault needing forgiveness and reparation. His notations for February 13 are entirely taken up with his fault and seeking pardon, and so on.[14]

During the next three days, February 14–16, he received great consolations with assurance of being forgiven for his fault; and on each day he declares that he had no doubt about his decision for perfect poverty. On the last of these days, February 16, he reviewed the pros and cons for an hour and during that time saw any mitigation of the strictest poverty as a snare and obstacle of "the enemy" (Satan). But later on the thought came to look over the elections for two days. At this thought, even though he wanted to repel it, he lost the intense devotion he had been experiencing and saw such a thought as a temptation. He resolved to examine the reasons no more, but to offer the decision for two more days.

On February 17, in consolation, he considered "the matter" (the election) settled. He offered the decision which he considered accepted by God, gave thanks with great consolation, and soon lost all desire even to make further offerings. He considered the matter closed, and he resolved to finish the election on the next day.

Ignatius' intention was to end the election on this day (February 18) with Mass in honor of the Holy Trinity. The day began with overflowing consolation (which he interpreted as confirmation) and thanksgiving to God. He experienced a strong impulse to beg each person of the Trinity to confirm him—but understanding at the same time that they had already done so. During the Mass which was to bring the election to an end, he experienced abundant divine con-

---

[13] See William Young, trans., *St. Ignatius Own Story*, p. 5, note 6; I. Iparraguirre, *Obras Completas*, p. 324, note 38.

[14] Ignatius' response to this fault and especially to the later one on Feb. 18 may well seem to most readers exaggerated and to imply a distorted notion of God. A careful and sympathetic consideration will, I think, change that interpretation. For one so extraordinarily gifted by God, so intimately united with him, given so many and such intense experiences of God's beauty and goodness and love and majesty, his heart so deeply in love with God, his whole consciousness so purified and sensitized to the evil of even the slightest thing not fully in accord with God—to such a one, these faults appear in a way that others less gifted can hardly understand. On the other hand, note that Ignatius does not at all see God as angry, punishing, vengeful. Throughout the time of seeking "reconciliation" after his faults, he continually experiences God as loving him tenderly and pouring out gifts of love on him without measure.

solations. However, at times the consolation faded somewhat. The lessening of consolation at times during the Mass rendered Ignatius dissatisfied with the confirmation. As a result, he felt "indignant" (*indignándome*) with the Trinity. He wanted to be done with the long and wearing discernment, but some bit of doubt remained. The experience of devotion lasted all day, but in some little ways it was attacked; and this left him in fear of erring.

These reasons and his need to feel fully reconciled once again with the persons of the Trinity after his fault in becoming impatient and angry with them—all these made Ignatius again delay finalizing his decision. So begins a third phase of the election.

Third Phase: February 19–March 11

During this period many exalted mystical consolations are given him, but there is no indication that they have any relationship either to his decision on poverty or to his reconciliation with the persons of the Holy Trinity. There are also some other experiences of the same kind which are spoken of as confirmations; but it is dubious whether most or any of these, with one important exception, refer to his election on poverty. Rather, they seem to refer to his being confirmed as fully reconciled.[15] Even though he indicates in these passages that he sees no need for further confirmation (whether of his decision or of his reconciliation), he continues to defer finalizing his decision. The election seems bracketed while the reconciliation is being completed and, after that (so the notation for March 2 could be interpreted), while he waits for a visitation from God to set the time for finishing the election.[16]

As just mentioned, there is during this period one clear experience of being confirmed in his decision for perfect poverty. On February 23, while he was preparing for Mass, the thought of following Jesus as leader of the Company of Jesus occurred to him as "a greater argument for complete poverty than all the other human reasons." This insight, he thought, would surely strengthen him against any temptation.

---

[15] See entries for Feb. 24, 25, 26, and March 5.

[16] This interpretation is strengthened by Ignatius' wavering about concluding the search for confirmation, which he recounts in the entry for March 12.

Fourth and Final Phase: March 12

Although the day of March 12 began with "great devotion," Ignatius soon and suddenly found himself in the depth of a spiritual desolation. He felt so estranged from the divine persons that, despite the daily, intense, and overpowering experiences which had been given him, it seemed he had never had any personal experience of them and never would in the future. Thoughts against Jesus arose in him. His mind was confused with ideas going in all directions about what to do to improve the situation, finding no peace any- where. With this desolation begins a fourth phase of his discernment, a very brief one (part of one day), full of confusion and struggle, at the close of which Ignatius at last overcomes all hesitation and reaches his goal.

He is caught in tension between opposing thoughts and desires. On the one hand, he thought that he was wanting too many signs of confirmation from God, that the right decision was really very clear. He had a strong desire to end the election, to be done with it. On the other hand, he was fearful that, if he ended it now in his present condition rather than at a time of consolation, he would later be dissatisfied. On the one hand, he felt that God would be more pleased if he finished without hoping or seeking for more proofs. At the same time, on the other hand, he saw in himself a hope that God would condescend to his desire to end the election at a time of great consolation.

Becoming reflectively aware of this tension within him was the turning point. He immediately chose to side with what he thought would be more pleasing to God, to end the election without seeking consolation or any further sign. Wondering whether he should wait until evening to conclude, he decided that to do so would entail looking for more confirmation when there was no need for it. At that point he considered the whole discernment to be concluded. "Finished" (*finido*), he added with finality.

Two more things, however, then happened which throw light backward on his experience. First, when he sat down to eat, the tempter tried to make him hesitate again over his decision. By this time Ignatius was so clear about what had been going on that he was able to follow his own counsel given to others.[17] Immediately and without any disturbance at all, rather with confidence of victory, he responded, "*A tu posta*" (in this context, freely but accurately translated, "To hell with you").

The second enlightening event happened fifteen minutes later, when Ignatius had further insight into his whole experience of seeking for confirmation. What he says is so significant that it is best left in his own words.

> A quarter of an hour after this, an awakening with understanding and clarity to how at the time that the tempter insinuated into me the thoughts against the divine persons and my mediators, he put or wished to put in me a doubt about the matter [the decision]. On the contrary, when I experienced the visits and visions of the divine persons and my mediators, I was entirely steady and confirmed about the matter. I understood this with spiritual delight and with great security of soul, my eyes filled with tears.[18]

The implication of this "awakening" is surprising. What we would expect Ignatius at this stage of his life to be immediately alert to whenever it happened, he was in fact not alert to during desolation or even during the great movement of consolation, but only in a period of calm when his power of critical reflection on experience could come into play.[19] What he saw in this moment of calm reflection is illustrative of his rules for discernment of spirits[20] and confirms the whole interpretation already offered of what was happening after February 11. For, even if one directly refers these words of Ignatius only to what happened earlier on this day, March 12, what happened then clearly has continuity with, is a climactic experience of, what happened on February 12 and February 16–18 and all that followed from these events. Even he, no longer in the spiritual immaturity of his early years, was deceived and misled by the evil

---

[17] *SpEx*, [325].

[18] Entry for March 12.

[19] See above, pp. 142, and below, p. 234.

[20] Especially rules I, 1–2, 5 and II, 1 (*SpEx*, [314–315, 318, 329]).

spirit until, during a time of calm reflection, he saw what had been going on.

Basic Questions about Seeking Confirmation of a Discernment

Drawing on the *Spiritual Diary* as our source of light, we can now hope to find accurate answers to some basic questions about confirmation of a discernment. Without these answers, the step of seeking confirmation cannot be well understood or well carried out. The following questions will be taken up in the order given: (1) Is seeking confirmation peculiar to the third mode of discernment? (2) Is seeking confirmation necessary? (3) Is actually receiving confirmation necessary? (4) What counts as confirmation? (5) How is confirmation to be sought? (6) When is the search for confirmation to be terminated?

Some interpreters give an affirmative answer to the first three questions. For they believe that Ignatius had slight regard for the third mode of election[21] and even considered it to be of no value except as leading back to the second,[22] and therefore that the discerner who has not been given a first-time experience will have to have evidence of the kind peculiar to the second mode, namely, spiritual consolation and desolation, in order to reach a decision which can be taken seriously. On the other hand, a decision reached by the second-time evidence has no need for more evidence of this kind as confirmation. For those who think this way, the answer to the fourth question also seems clear: confirmation is constituted only by spiritual consolation and desolation. If these answers are correct, then little needs to be said by way of answer to Question 5. Question 6 I have not found seriously treated in the writings with which I am familiar. Although the above answers to Questions 1–4 are admirably coherent, I have found much evidence which calls them into question as expressing the thought of Ignatius.[23]

---

[21] See below, pp. 255–257.

[22] See below, pp. 236–241.

[23] It is interesting to note that those who want to limit seeking confirmation to the third mode have no problem about seeing the election in Ignatius' *Diario Espiritual* as primarily a second–time election. Yet, Ignatius spent most of his time in that election seeking confirmation!

1. Is Seeking Confirmation Peculiar to the Third Mode of Discernment?

Given what Ignatius says in *Spiritual Exercises,* [183] and [188], there can be no question whether he wants the third mode of election to include an offering of the decision reached by that mode and a search for divine confirmation of it before finalizing it. The question is whether the second mode of election should also include seeking confirmation and, after that, whether such confirmation has to be given in order to have a trustworthy conclusion. Because in the *Spiritual Exercises* Ignatius speaks of confirming a decision only in his instructions for the third mode of election, a conclusion could easily be drawn that seeking confirmation is peculiar to that mode.

The *Spiritual Diary* of St. Ignatius, however, leaves little room for doubt about his thought on this point. It is true that his provisional or tentative decision reached on February 9 rested on a combination of the second and third modes of discernment. But to say that the long quest for confirmation which followed was only for the sake of confirming the results of the third mode would not make sense. Why should he seek to confirm the conclusion from the third-time evidence by more consolation when he already had abundantly sufficient second-time evidence to justify the same decision to which his third-time evidence pointed? If the decision had rested entirely, or almost entirely, on third-time evidence, then, within the way of thinking now under examination, it would make sense to seek confirmation by second-time evidence. But the entries for February 2–9 in the diary show plentiful second-time evidence for the decision prior to seeking confirmation for it. If Ignatius had thought confirmation was to be sought only for a third-time discernment, then there would have been no point in seeking confirmation as he did after February 9. The diary, therefore, clearly shows that Ignatius wanted confirmation for a conclusion reached by the second as well as by the third mode of discernment.

2. Is Seeking Confirmation Necessary?

Seeing what Ignatius requires in order to reach the decision before seeking confirmation for it, one may well wonder whether he put great importance on the confirmation. The documents leave

202

no doubt that in fact he did so. The tone of the passage in which he directs the discerner to seek confirmation is earnest and urges diligent prayer and offering. Seeking confirmation is to be no easy-going step, much less a formality. The directive after the second way of the third mode of election[24]—to go back to the last step of the first way, that is, to seeking confirmation—suggests an insistence on this step. Most of all, his attitude toward confirmation is seen in his diary, which shows that, despite the massive and one-sided evidence (both second-time and third-time) which supported the decision he had made, he considered the search for confirmation to be of capital importance. He would certainly not spend many days and so much emotional energy on something he did not consider to be requisite for a sound discernment. The intensity of his desire for confirmation appears in his prayer for it.

> Later, while preparing the altar and vesting [for Mass] I had a strong impulse to say: "Eternal Father, confirm me; Eternal Son, confirm me; Eternal Spirit, confirm me; Holy Trinity, confirm me; my only God, confirm me!" I said this with great earnestness and with much devotion and tears, very often repeated and very interiorly felt. Saying once, "Eternal Father, will you not confirm me?"[25]

But why did he put such emphasis on seeking confirmation? If after a careful and prayerful discernment process the evidence is already strong enough to justify a decision, why insist on holding that decision only tentatively while seeking confirmation by more evidence? Those who think that Ignatius had little or no trust in a third-time election for finding God's will, that only the third-time election needs confirmation, and that confirmation is constituted by second-time evidence alone—those who think this way have a logical explanation for his insistence on confirmation; namely, without confirmation by second-time evidence the decision by third-time evidence has no solid support.[26] But if, as has been and will be more

---

[24] *SpEx*, [188].

[25] Entry for Feb. 18 in William Young, trans., *The Spiritual Journal of St. Ignatius Loyola*, p. 12.

[26] See pp. 255–257.

fully argued, this whole way of thinking conflicts with what Ignatius actually wrote, then that answer to our question is of no help.[27] The only acceptable answer that comes to mind is based on a principle which is one of his essential conditions for trustworthy discernment of God's will, namely, that we must make all reasonable human effort do our very best.[28] In accord with this principle, we may well think that the discerner should always try to make assurance doubly sure by seeking confirmation.

Does this principle require us to think that, for Ignatius, seeking confirmation is a necessary step in any and every sound discernment process? Ignatius himself never explicitly says so, and the principle itself leads to a negative response. For, according to the principle, we must make our best *reasonable* effort in seeking God's will. In some cases it seems reasonable and, therefore, necessary for a sound discernment to seek confirmation, and in some cases it does not. To seek confirmation for the decision from every minor and brief discernment would be an unreasonable drain on time and energy, hindering other more important matters. But when the decision is of sufficient importance and the discerner does have the time and energy for it, given Ignatius' practice and what he says in *Spiritual Exercises,* [183] and [188], it seems that he would think that a failure to search for confirmation was a failure to do one's best.

3. Is Actually Receiving Confirmation Necessary?

When seeking confirmation of a decision is reasonable and, therefore, necessary, is actually receiving confirmation necessary for a trustworthy final decision? This also is a question that Ignatius does not bring up; but here too we can derive an answer from his fundamental principles on discerning God's will. The fundamental belief on which all Ignatian discernment depends is belief that God loves us so much that in every situation for choice he wills for us to choose what promotes the greater sharing of all in his glory.[29] Ignatian discernment also rests on the belief that only trust in the guidance of the Holy Spirit can justify us in thinking we can find

---

[27] See. pp. 257–273.
[28] See pp. 99–100.
[29] See chapter 2.

or have found God's will, but that we can be justifiably confident of the Holy Spirit leading us if we do our reasonable best.[30] It follows that if, after a decision by a well-made election, we do our reasonable best in seeking confirmation but without success, then the decision made is to be trusted and acted upon. For if the decision were not for the greater glory, we could rightly believe that the Holy Spirit would, one way or another, give some disconfirmation.[31]

Lest this view be misunderstood, it is important to be clear that doing our reasonable best may, in some cases, mean continuing for a long time in search of confirmation or deferring the search to a later date. It all depends on how important the decision is, how soon the decision has to be made, how much time and energy the person can reasonably devote to it, and so on. This way of thinking is supported by the practical directions given in Polanco's *Directory* and the Official Directory of 1599—even though they do not give the reasons I have offered or any others. Thus, when Polanco comments on *Spiritual Exercises,* [183] and indicates how to judge various experiences during the search for confirmation of a third-time election, he comes finally to what we should think if there is no confirmation or disconfirmation by any sign in affectivity or intellect. In that case, he says, "the decision must not be changed." Rather, he continues, "one must judge that God wishes for his will to be found through rational discourse" of the completed first way of the third mode; and, if the election by that way is approved of by the second way of the third mode, "so much the more certainly, it must be held that God's will has been found."[32]

4. What Counts as Confirmation?

When confirmation is to be sought, we still have to ask further questions. Is it constituted exclusively by consolations and desolations (as in second-time evidence), or does it also include reasons

---

[30] See chapter 4.

[31] This matter involves the question of what kind of assent can justifiably be given to the finalized decision of a discernment (chapters 15–16). The answer to this question presupposes what is thought about the limits of discerning God's will (chapter 5) and about confirming or disconfirming a decision already finalized for choice and even put into execution (chapter 12).

[32] Polanco's directory, no. 90; Official Directory of 1599, [232] in *DirSpEx*MHSJ, pp. 317 and 723.

(as in third-time evidence) and even such signs as can follow on choice and execution of the decision; for example, approval of authority, favorable circumstances for execution, success in reaching the goal of execution, good consequences? The question whether Ignatius counts as confirmation of a decision anything which takes place after it is finalized for choice and is put into execution will be taken up further on. For now our attention will be limited to what confirms a tentative decision before it is finalized for choice.[33]

The common opinion found in writings on Ignatian discernment of God's will is that confirmation, at least prior to choice and execution, is simply spiritual consolation. It is what we would expect those to hold who believe that Ignatius had no trust in the third mode of election and that, for him, seeking confirmation is a return to the second mode.[34] Others, however, who seem to value the third mode of election as a valid way of discernment in its own right also take for granted that confirmation means only spiritual consolation.

All that Ignatius says in the *Spiritual Exercises* is that, when a decision has been reached, the discerner ought to go to prayer and offer the decision to God, hoping the Divine Majesty will be pleased

---

[33] John Futrell speaks of "confirmation" not only after the tentative decision but also all through the process leading to that decision, while acknowledging that this is not Ignatius' way of using the term. See p. 229.

[34] Thus, Edouard Pousset, commenting on *SpEx*, [183], says that confirmation is "from some affective experience of consolation" (*Life in Faith and Freedom*, p. 213) and that "St. Ignatius here returns to the way of making a choice according to the 'second time' " (p. 125; see also p. 126). According to Piet Penning de Vries, "this confirmation is based upon consolation. And so, finally, the rational method [of third–time election] all the same escapes reasoning" (*Discernment of Spirits*, p. 65; see also following pages). According to Hervé Coathalem, confirmation before choice and execution consists in "interior dispositions of peace and joy" (*Ignatian Insights*, p. 190). Brian O'Leary declares that consolation from the good spirits "is the ultimate criterion and desirable confirmation in the decision–making situation" ("Good and Evil Spirits," *The Way*, no. 15 [1975], p. 180) and that "even when an election is made in the 'third time,' one of tranquility, it remains necessary to seek confirmation through consolation when the election is offered to God." Such confirmation, O'Leary says, "*must* be in the form of consolation" ("The Discernment of Spirits in the *Memoriale* of Blessed Peter Favre," *The Way*, Supplement 35 [Spring, 1979], p. 82). John English asserts that confirmation is "not from . . . his [the discerner's] reasoning process but from some affective experience of consolation" (*Spiritual Freedom*, p. 213). This confirmation by consolation, he adds, "takes us back to the second time" (p. 214). He even requires that the consolation be what Ignatius speaks of in the rules for discernment of spirits, II, 2 and 8, that is, consolation without preceding cause (p. 214). Nicholas King says that third–time discernment "requires confirmation in the form of heaven–sent consolation and desolation" ("Ignatius Loyola and Decision–Making," *The Way*, Supplement 24, [Spring, 1975], p. 57). Karl Rahner thinks that asking God to accept and confirm a third–time decision is a return to the second time, which means that the confirmation is constituted by consolations (*Dynamic Element*, p. 96).

to accept and confirm it, if it be for his greater service and praise.[35] There is nothing here to prove or disprove any opinion on what can constitute confirmation, and no light on the question is to be found elsewhere in the *Spiritual Exercises*. Neither do the passages on the election in Ignatius' *Autograph Directory* offer any help at all. If we had no source of light on confirmation of a decision other than Ignatius' instruction on election, we would have no explicit indication of what he had in mind as constituting it. All we could do would be to guess. The most reasonable guess might be that any of the several kinds of evidence which can lead to a decision can also confirm it. Nothing Ignatius says would ever lead us to guess that only second-time evidence could constitute a confirmation.

We might, therefore, even put together an ideal picture of being confirmed in believing a decision is true and accepted by God. It would include all the elements which we would see as contained in ideal evidence for reaching the decision before seeking confirmation. It would include impulses rooted in spiritual consolation; a clearer and firmer insight into already-acquired reasons why what I am moved to is what God wills; new confirming opinions by persons whose prayerful judgment in the matter at issue is worthy of respect; confidence whereas before one was fearful; anything else that might give grounds for thinking that the tentative decision is true and ought to be finalized.[36] Such guessing, we find, seems to be quite accurate when compared with what appears in the principal, even primary, source we have to enlighten us on the meaning of confirmation of a decision, namely, Ignatius' *Spiritual Diary*.

A very obvious form of confirmation recorded in that document is spiritual consolation. There is, as we have seen, a problem in reading the diary to distinguish which consolations confirm his decision regarding poverty, and which confirm him in his assurance of reconciliation with God after some fault which interfered with his finalizing the election. These faults seem to have no apparent relationship with confirming either his reconciliation or his decision.

---

[35] *SpEx*, [183].
[36] See Brian O'Leary, "The Discernment of Spirits in the *Memoriale* of Blessed Peter Favre," *The Way*, Supplement 35 (1979), p. 99.

There are, nevertheless, many consolations which clearly confirm his decision regarding poverty.[37]

Not as abundant as confirmations by spiritual consolations but frequent, nevertheless, are confirmations by reasons; and along with these is evidence that Ignatius desired and sought confirmation by reasons. The entries for February 6, 8, and 9 show that, in reaching the decision for which he thereafter seeks confirmation, Ignatius discerned by reason as well as by spiritual consolation, that is, by the third as well as by the second mode of election. The evidence for this is much stronger than at first appears. For on February 8 and 9, he speaks of "going over the elections" (*pasando por las elecciones*). These "elections" refer to a carefully organized list of advantages and disadvantages[38] which were drawn up before the account in the diary begins or very soon after that.[39] They unmistakably indicate a full third-time discernment which Ignatius frequently reviewed and added to during the search for confirmation. On February 10 he begins his search for confirmation by immediately turning to these reasons. On February 11 he spends three hours going over them. On February 16 he again prays over them. Taken together, these two documents, the one containing these reasons and the diary, form one complete account of his discernment regarding poverty. In the diary, the two distinct and complete modes of discerning function in combination, each strengthening the other.[40]

Besides those reasons about which we have been talking, other new ones confirm Ignatius in his decision for perfect poverty. On one occasion (February 11), when he had been going over the reasons he already had and just when he had lost all desire for reasons, other "understandings" (*intelligencias*) came to him. He understood how Christ had sent the apostles on their mission in complete poverty and how this mission in poverty was confirmed by "the Holy Spirit giving them his spirit and the gift of tongues," and also by the Father and the Son sending the Holy Spirit—so that all three persons confirmed the mission. In context, the implication is clear that, just

---

[37] See entries for Feb. 10–11, 13–18, and *Autobiog*, [100]. Desolation played some slight part in confirming Ignatius' decision: see entry in his diary for March 12.

[38] See note 65 of chapter 10.

[39] This is indicated by the entries for Feb. 8 and 11. See *Cons*MHSJ, I, p. xciii.

[40] See below, pp. 251–254.

as Jesus wished to mission the apostles in complete poverty and the Trinity confirmed the mission, so also the members of the Company of Jesus, whom Jesus now sends to preach the Gospel, should do so in evangelical poverty. In context, there is no other point to the passage. Two points are noteworthy about this passage. First, the fact that at this time Ignatius says he had lost all desire for further reasons is itself an unmistakable indication that he had been seeking reasons as confirmation and, therefore, that he did count reasons as confirmation. Second, the other "understandings" that came to him at that moment as confirmation of his decision constitute an *a pari* argument based on Holy Scripture. The confirmation is not (or at least not mainly) any consolation which accompanied the argument, but the argument itself.

On February 23, another argument (*argumento*) came to mind, one which seemed to him "to be a greater argument for living in complete poverty than all the other human reasons [*razones*]," although he thought that all his other earlier reasons favored the same conclusion. This powerful argument is simple enough and is stated by Ignatius in a syncopated form. What it comes to is this: Jesus is the leader of the Company of Jesus; Jesus during his own public life lived in total poverty; therefore, the Company of Jesus should follow Jesus in total poverty. This reasoned conclusion moved Ignatius to great firmness and left him confident that it would be enough to keep him firm through all future temptations and trials. There is more than a hint here of volitional confirmation for living out the decision, but the primary confirmation is intellectual, a confirmation of his judgment that God wills him to propose to his companions that they adopt a rule of perfect poverty in the Constitutions which he was writing subject to their approval.

The foregoing evidence in the *Spiritual Diary* leaves no doubt how greatly Ignatius valued reasons as well as consolations for confirming the tentative decision arrived at by the election process, whether a second-time or third-time process or the two combined.

It is true that, during the search for confirmation recounted in his diary, Ignatius' examination of the reasons he had already used in reaching his decision and his discovery of new reasons are sometimes followed by spiritual consolation; but to infer from that fact that the reasons were not themselves confirmations of his decisions

209

but only served as a way of leading to confirmation by consolation—such an inference would not only be arbitrary but, taken in context, would be in conflict with what Ignatius said wherever he talked about the reasons that came to him.

Besides consolation and reasons, but necessarily in conjunction with them, Ignatius mentions in passing another sign of God's will, namely, "a greater movement of the will,"[41] an intensification of the volitional impulse toward one alternative as that which God wills. Since it is this volitional movement which needs spiritual consolation or reasons "from above" to mark it as coming from God, the intensification of it could not by itself be evidence of God's will. But, if the volitional impulse forms a whole with consolation or reasons, then, even without any increase in these, an intensification of it has evidential value. I have not found Ignatius mentioning this kind of evidence in his diary after he has begun seeking confirmation; but, if it serves for drawing a tentative decision, why would it not also serve as confirmation after that decision has been made?

Finally, there is one other important factor in Ignatius' understanding of interior confirmation which appears prominently in the diary. It is the person's experience of assurance that God has accepted the decision offered, his sense of security in having found God's will. This experience, we saw, plays a decisive role in the person's knowing when it is time to bring the discernment to a tentative decision. It also plays a decisive role in knowing when it is time to cease seeking confirmation and to finalize the decision for choice of efficacious intention to act. It will be more suitably treated a little further on, when we ask about when to terminate the search for confirmation.

In sum, we have found the following possible kinds of confirmation for a decision reached by discernment but not yet finalized: spiritual consolation, new reasons, awareness of greater force in reasons already had, intensification of the movement of will (when integral with spiritual consolation or understanding of reasons), and a sense of assurance that the discerner has done all that could reasonably be done and that God's will has been found.

---

[41] Entry for Feb. 8.

5. How Is Confirmation to Be Sought?

In what way are these confirmations to be sought? Ignatius gives a general indication in the *Spiritual Exercises* and detailed indications by his own procedure shown in his diary. Further light can readily be had parallel to what we have already found about the process which leads to the tentative decision.

The person seeking confirmation should "go to prayer before God our Lord with great diligence and offer him the said decision so that his Divine Majesty may be pleased to accept and confirm it, provided it be for his greater service and praise."[42] This prayer must be made "with great diligence." Meditation and contemplation will have their place in the quest for confirmation just as they did in the election process leading to the decision. But then as now the seeker for God's will must realize what a great gift it is to find it with justifiable confidence of having done so and, consequently, must intensely desire and insistently beg God for so great a favor. The confirmation, however, is to be desired only if what is desired is truly for God's greater service and praise. Therefore, if it is not so, the discerner should desire that it be disconfirmed.

The indifference to all but God's will which is at the heart of openness to the Holy Spirit's guidance is still very necessary lest, too eager to have the seeking over with, the discerner too readily sees sufficient confirmation where there is none. In his *Spiritual Diary* we see Ignatius pleading with the Father, the Son, and the Holy Spirit as he offers his decision over and over again, always careful (perhaps too careful) not to conclude his search precipitously.

With these attitudes of offering and prayerful longing for and indifference to all but God's will, Ignatius does two things. He waits on God to give consolation and impulse (at Mass, at times during contemplation, or at other times)[43] and he actively reviews the reasons he already has while looking for new light on them, and he adds to them the new reasons that come to him. In his diary he rarely has occasion to explicitly mention making any reflective critical examination and interpretation of his second-time experiences; but we may assume he did so—though with him, so great was his

---

[42] *SpEx*, [183].

[43] See *DirAutog*, [18] and [21].

sensitivity and ability to discern spirits that these reflections could be done very swiftly and easily, with a minimum of thematic attention. (Even he, however, as we saw above, could miss a very significant aspect of his experiences and only note it later, after the discernment was over.)[44] For others less gifted than Ignatius in such discernment of spirits, it is important to call attention to the need for explicit critical reflection on the consolations received in the confirmation process, just as in the process of second-time discernment before the tentative decision. Likewise, the reasons which confirm a decision, just as the reasons which led to it, must be critically examined by the "greater-glory" and the "greater-likeness" norms[45] in order to make sure they are valid reasons; and, in weightier discernment, they must be reflected on over and over to see their comparative value.

6. When Is the Search for Confirmation to Be Terminated?

Just as in the process of coming to a tentative decision, so also in seeking confirmation for the decision, one of the most difficult steps in some cases is judging when to end the process and finalize the decision. The limited meaning of finalizing a decision in this context needs to be kept clear in order to avoid prejudging a further question, namely, whether we should look for confirmation or disconfirmation after choice and beginning execution of the chosen alternative. In the context of Ignatian discernment, to make a tentative decision prior to seeking confirmation is to hold in abeyance the actual choice and execution of what is judged to be God's will, while seeking confirmation or disconfirmation for the judgment. Finalizing the decision can have two meanings. It can mean only finalizing it for actual choice and execution while leaving it open to further confirmation or disconfirmation based on events consequent to choice of execution, leaving it in some sense still tentative. It can also mean closing off any necessity for further confirmation or any possibility of disconfirmation by consequent events. For now, I am using the term only in the first sense. The question whether the judgment so finalized needs further confirmation or is open to

---

[44] See above, pp. 200–201.
[45] See above, pp. 173–180.

disconfirmation by consequent events will be taken up in the next chapter.[46]

Ignatius' answer to the question of when to finalize the tentative decision has many parallels with his answer to the question of when to conclude the process by which the discerner arrives at the tentative decision for which confirmation is sought.[47] But, surprisingly, the documentary evidence for his answer to the latter question is much fuller than for the former and can cast much light on the former question.

How much confirmation is needed? How long should the discerner pray and wait and look for confirmation? Answers to questions such as these are influenced by several variable factors; for example, how important the issue for discernment is, how much time is available, how strong and clear the confirmations are. No formula for finding the answers is possible; ultimately it is a matter of good judgment. How difficult it can sometimes be to make a reasonable judgment comes out clearly in the *Spiritual Diary* of Ignatius. There we see him struggling painfully to do so. On the one hand, the intense and relentless character of Ignatius' quest for confirmation and his backing away time and again from ending the search show how patient a seeking is called for and how any haste to finish it off is to be avoided. On the other hand, Ignatius' critical reflection on his own search also warns us against the contrary extreme of unreasonable delay. For most of us, I think, the first lesson needs emphasis more than explanation, while the second needs explanation more than emphasis.

Unless very carefully studied and understood, Ignatius' *Spiritual Diary* could be as misleading as it is enlightening; for it could lead us to conclude that deciding when to finalize a decision is always a long and agonizing task. Several considerations warn us against such a conclusion. First of all, the decision Ignatius was making appeared to him as one of the most crucial of all the decisions he had to make in drawing up the Constitutions of the Society of Jesus. Not all decisions, even important ones, would be so demanding. Add to the picture that the decision he had reached was a change

---

[46] See chapter 12.
[47] See above, pp. 157–159.

from what he and all his companions had earlier decided on and the pope had approved.[48] Further, even regarding this crucial decision, there is reason to think that Ignatius himself believed or at least suspected that the confirmation process should have ended much sooner, even on the evening of February 11, a month before it actually did.[49] If this interpretation is correct, two days of intense seeking and of repeated strong confirmation without wavering would have sufficed even for so weighty a decision.

In any case, no matter how a reader may interpret what Ignatius says about his temptations and excessive desires for confirmation, it is interesting to note that the difficulty he experienced in deciding whether to be satisfied with the confirmation he had received or to wait and pray for more required a brief subordinate election within his main election.[50] Whether it is a question about making the first and tentative decision or the finalized decision, when it is very difficult to do so, one may need to follow Ignatius' example and make a very brief formal discernment in order to decide whether to conclude or not.

When at last Ignatius did finalize his decision, as also at those earlier moments when he thought he was ready to do so, we find him using the same ''clincher'' that he used when making the tentative decision.[51] He looks for a sense of completeness, of having done all he reasonably could or should do; a sense of ''security'' (no fear of error); a loss of all desire for more confirmation. Thus, at the times when he thought he was ready to conclude his search for confirmation, he writes of ''a certain feeling of security that it was a good election,''[52] ''great tranquility and security of soul, like an exhausted man who takes a good rest, neither seeking nor caring to seek any further, considering the matter finished except for giving thanks,''[53] ''confirmation with tears and with complete security about everything decided.''[54] Without such a sense of complete se-

---

[48] I. Iparraguirre in *Obras Completas*, pp. 294–295.
[49] Entry for March 12.
[50] Ibid.
[51] See above, pp. 157–158.
[52] Entry for Feb. 10.
[53] Entry for Feb. 11.
[54] Entry for March 12.

curity, Ignatius did not seem to be ready to make his finalized decision. Even after a passing experience of such assurance, if it was weakened for one reason or another,[55] if "some slight doubt remained,"[56] Ignatius did not want to end the process.

Recall his letter to Francis Borgia about his discernment when the pope was thinking of making Francis a cardinal. Ignatius describes how for several days he wavered back and forth, at one time fearing that what he had in mind to do might not be God's will and at other times being relieved of such fear. Finally, he tells us, on the third day during his usual prayer, he found his judgment was so "settled" and his will so "tranquil and free" from hesitation about doing what he had before been uneasy about that if he did not do it he would think he was failing to do God's will.[57] That was the time for him to make his finalized decision.

The Official Directory of 1599 confirms this sense of assurance as an Ignatian norm for the time to conclude a search for God's will. "If the divine will is so established that the person is thoroughly assured and secure and has no desire for more assurance, he can be at rest."[58]

This sense of assurance can be of great significance but can also easily be misused and misunderstood unless it is understood within the context of Ignatius' full teaching on how to seek God's will and is critically examined and interpreted by one (the discerner or a spiritual director) with sensitivity, balanced judgment, and ability to discern spirits. For the sense of certainty has no value as a signal for either a tentative or a finalized decision unless the discerner has been and is now truly open to the Holy Spirit,[59] has made every reasonable effort in the search for God's will,[60] has accumulated sufficient evidence, and has his sense of security rooted in living faith and in loving trust that God has led him to this decision.

---

[55] Entry for Feb. 16.
[56] Entry for Feb. 18.
[57] See above, pp. 48–49.
[58] [198] in DirSpExMHSJ, p. 705. See also Dávila's directory, [129] (ibid., p. 518).
[59] See chapters 4 and 6.
[60] See above, pp. 70–71.

Chapter 12
Confirmation after the
Finalized Decision

All the foregoing questions about confirmation have been concerned with confirmation or disconfirmation of the tentative decision before, and for the sake of finalizing, the decision for choice. Many writers on discernment of God's will and, I suspect, most practitioners of it think to find confirmation or disconfirmation after the decision has been finalized, i.e., has informed actual choice and virtually effective intention, or has been put into execution. In their view, therefore, finalizing the decision for choice does not terminate the discernment. They speak of such a decision being confirmed or disconfirmed (1) when it is approved or disapproved, permitted or forbidden, by legitimate authority; (2) when the circumstances for successfully acting on it turn out to be notably favorable or unfavorable; (3) when execution of the chosen act is eminently successful or unsuccessful in attaining the specifically intended goal of the chosen course of action; (4) when the results of executing the chosen act (whether successful or unsuccessful in attaining the specifically intended goal) seem to be greatly for the glory of God, or not so.

Asserting or denying that these events, consequent on the finalized decision, justifiably serve as signs of divine confirmation or disconfirmation of the decision has implications both for the practice and for the theology of discerning God's will. Each of them, therefore, deserves careful consideration.

The Question Clarified

Before considering them individually, several general preliminary clarifications are necessary. First of all, we are talking about decisions reached by a sound Ignatian discernment, that is, one in which the discerner observes the limits and fulfills the essential conditions for such discernment. The question here is not whether, after finalizing a decision in choice, we can come to see that the decision was defective because of a lack of openness to the Spirit, a slovenly and hasty discernment process, or any other defect. Of course we can. The question is: Can the finalized decision of a *sound* discernment be confirmed or disconfirmed in any of the four ways mentioned above?

Second, it will be necessary also to keep in mind that we are not talking about volitional confirmation or disconfirmation, the strengthening or weakening of the person's resoluteness of will to carry out what is judged to be God's will. Such confirmation is certainly needed and, without doubt, may be given in many ways after finalizing the decision; many things may tend to encourage or to weaken and discourage us from carrying out a decision. All that is clear. The question now concerns confirmation or disconfirmation of the finalized *judgment* which was arrived at through a sound discernment.

The question which we are asking, then, is this: After a person has, to the reasonable best of his or her capacity, been open to the Holy Spirit, gone through the discernment process faithfully, arrived at a tentative decision within the proper limits of discerning God's will, and finalized it for choice only after seeking confirmation according to Ignatius' instruction—after all that, is further confirmation of the judgment about what God wills necessary or even possible in any of the four ways mentioned above? Is disconfirmation in any of these ways possible?

Finally, if it should turn out that for Ignatius no such confirmation or disconfirmation need be looked for or is even possible in the ways we are asking about, that would not mean that these happenings, which some call confirmation or disconfirmation, are of no value for a discernment of God's will. They would still be of value for assuring the discerner that God wills for him or her to continue carrying out what he (God) earlier willed for the discerner to intend and to begin executing, or of value for alerting the discerner to the need of a new discernment to find God's will in new circumstances. But in neither case would they indicate anything positively or negatively either about the decision reached in the earlier discernment process or about what God willed for the discerner to choose at that time.

With these clarifications in mind, we can now evaluate each of the four proposed ways of confirming or disconfirming a finalized decision. In doing so, what has already been said in Chapter 5 on the limits of discerning God's will determines what has to be said now. The whole question of confirmation or disconfirmation after finalizing a decision for choice and intention of action is a question about the limits of discernment.

Confirmation or Disconfirmation by Authority

Is the decision finalized for choice confirmed or disconfirmed by the fact that just authority permits or forbids carrying it out? Let it be clear that the authority referred to in this question is authority by reason of office, an authority which imposes an obligation to obey when it is exercised within its proper limits, not authority which comes from learning or wisdom or experience or a divine gift of discernment and so on.[1]

In much of the literature on Ignatian discernment of God's will, it seems to be assumed as evident that a decision already

---

[1] Seeking advice before making a decision from those who have these latter kinds of authority can be an important, even a necessary, part of sound discernment; not seeking it may constitute a failure to do one's best in the search for God's will, a failure to fulfill the second essential condition for sound discernment.

finalized for choice and even already acted on can be and sometimes needs to be confirmed by authority before the discerner can be confident of having found God's will.[2] When, however, we take account of the limits of discerning God's will and examine this opinion in relation to several kinds of discernment, it is difficult to see how that opinion can stand.

Prohibition by authority or positive command to do the contrary of what has been decided and chosen by discernment may make action on the decision impossible or illegitimate. It may indicate what God wills the subject actually to do or not do now. But it can indicate nothing about what at an earlier moment, prior to the command or prohibition, God willed the discerner to choose to intend efficaciously. It could do so only if the conclusion of a discernment were predictive. Recall that Ignatius thought it altogether possible for the Holy Spirit, for his own good reasons, to move two persons to opposing intentions, at least one of which, therefore, would be frustrated.[3]

Further, we cannot leave out of account the very real possibility that the person in authority may have made a defective discernment or simply reacted to a situation impulsively or even with bad motives and, consequently, be opposing the subject's decision when God wanted him to choose, approve, and permit its execution. Or, for that matter, the superior could approve the subject's decision reached by a sound discernment and permit its execution when God really wanted him (the superior) to forbid what he (God) willed the subject to intend.

The general assertion that no exercise of authority can confirm or disconfirm a subject's decision about God's will which has been reached by sound discernment can, perhaps, be more clearly and convincingly established if it is shown that such confirmation or disconfirmation is, in the very nature of the case, excluded from each of the several kinds of discernment of God's will.

Consider, first, deliberative discernment. Suppose the decision

---

[2] John Futrell states this opinion clearly (MACL, p. 143; see also pp. 124, 149, and "Ignatian Discernment," p. 63). When I wrote "A Method for Communal Discernment of God's Will" (*Studies in the Spirituality of Jesuits*, vol. 3, no. 4 [Sept. 1971]), I followed Futrell on this point (p. 145). My effort to understand the limits of discernment have led me to change my opinion.

[3] See above, pp. 49–50, 62–66.

made is one which the discerner had no right to make, one that belongs to someone in authority to make. In that case there can be no sound discernment to be confirmed or disconfirmed.[4] On the other hand, if the authority does not rightfully extend to the matter for discernment, then that person's command or prohibition does not even indicate God's will now, much less confirm or disconfirm the subject's prior decision and choice. If the discernment is consultative, then the decision by the one who has authority to command or forbid what the consultative discernment recommends is irrelevant to the truth or falsity of the judgment arrived at through that discernment and cannot confirm or disconfirm it. For God's will, as object of consultative discernment, is limited to his will regarding what the discerner should advise; it does not extend to what the one in authority who is advised should choose to command or forbid.[5] Again, as just noted above, the person in authority may or may not make a sound discernment and may or may not find God's will for his decision to command or forbid.

If the discernment and decision is an entrusted one, then the person in authority who entrusted it has already made a decision beforehand to own as God's will whatever the discerner decides.[6] Therefore, his actual acceptance of the decision reached by the entrusted discernment is not a confirmation of that decision. It is fidelity to his decision made beforehand. On the other hand, his rejection of the decision by a sound entrusted discernment is not a disconfirmation of it. It might just as well be a sign of instability in the one who entrusted the discernment or show that he was not really entrusting the discernment but only looking for someone to tell him what he wanted to hear.

When all that has been said, it is still true that Ignatius did speak, for instance, of the pope confirming the Society of Jesus or confirming the Constitutions. By Ignatius' own principles, however, these confirmations could not be interpreted as confirmation of the discernments he and his companions made—no more than, if the pope had refused to confirm the Society of Jesus or the Constitutions,

---

[4] See above, pp. 51–53, 67–68.

[5] See above, pp. 54–55.

[6] See above, pp. 55–59.

would this have disconfirmed their discernment. Once we understand the limits of discerning God's will, the reason is clear and simple. It was beyond the limits of discernment for them to find what God willed for them to do beyond efficaciously intending to offer their plans and purposes to the pope for his acceptance or rejection of them; and it was beyond those limits for them to find what God willed for the pope to do, whether to accept or reject those proposals. Further, we cannot even leave out of account that the pope's approval or disapproval could be in discord with God's will; the pope could act out of bad motives, without trying to discern God's will, or could make a careless and hurried discernment without fulfilling the essential conditions for sound discernment.

Confirmation or Disconfirmation by Favorable or Unfavorable Circumstances for Execution

Is a decision regarding God's will which has been finalized for choice confirmed or disconfirmed by the fact that circumstances greatly facilitate carrying out the decision or notably impede doing so, even make it impossible? Some think this is so.

> God's good pleasure [regarding a decision reached
> through a discernment] may then be manifested not only
> by the interior dispositions of peace and joy that we feel,
> but also, and perhaps *more commonly*, by his providential
> arrangement of secondary causes whose activity helps us
> execute this program, or places no obstacles in its way.[7]

If this is so, then it would seem to follow as a correlative that finding serious obstacles in the way should be interpreted as a sign that God does not want the decision to be carried out. Much more so, if the obstacles altogether prevent undertaking what is decided.

Nowhere to my knowledge does Ignatius declare such a view or explicitly deny it. But the whole tenor of his thought seems to be that the more any work is Christlike and likely to be for God's greater glory, the more it will be opposed by "the enemy of the human race" and all the forces of evil. This way of thinking seems to be in accord with Christ's teaching to his followers, with Ignatius'

---

[7] Hervé Coathalem, *Ignatian Insights*, p. 190 (emphasis mine).

own experience, and with Christian experience over the centuries. If the circumstances for executing a discerned decision have any significance as confirming or disconfirming it, then it would seem much nearer the truth to think that, in general, the greater the obstacles to be faced or the more misunderstanding and pain to be borne, the more these circumstances confirm the decision as being God's will. The truth is, however, that no generalization about these circumstances as confirming or disconfirming a conclusion of a discernment seems trustworthy. Within the context of the discerner's life, the fact that circumstances facilitate or hinder acting on a soundly discerned decision may, by faith in God's loving providence, be interpreted as God's tender condescension to one's weakness or as his permitting a stern challenge in order to promote one's spiritual growth; but neither the one nor the other could serve to confirm or disconfirm a decision reached by sound discernment and finalized for choice.

Confirmation or Disconfirmation by Success or Failure in Attaining the End Intended

Perhaps, whatever the circumstances for execution, if and when the act decided on is actually executed, success or failure in attaining the end for which it is intended as a means is a true confirmation or disconfirmation. The end referred to here is not God's ultimate glory in general but the specified and more or less proximate end intended for God's glory. Did Ignatius think that the conclusion of a discernment is confirmed or disconfirmed by actual success or failure in attaining this end? I do not find him answering this question one way or the other. I do, however, find what seems to me strong reasons for denying confirmatory or disconfirmatory force to such success or failure, and I find nothing in my reasons that conflicts with Ignatius' teaching or practice. As I look back upon my actual success or failure, there is no way of reasonably judging that the success or failure says anything about what God willed for me to decide and choose efficaciously to intend. Suppose my chosen act has actually succeeded, and the end achieved is clearly for the glory of God. How do I know that the alternative course of action which I rejected would not have been, proximately or ultimately or both, more successful, more effective of the glory of God? How then,

222

can I judge that my success confirms the decision and choice I made? Suppose, on the other hand, my chosen act has actually failed to achieve my intended goal. How do I know that the alternative which I have rejected would not have failed more dismally? Perhaps also, my failure is accounted for by the bad will of other free agents, whom God permitted to have their way for now. Or perhaps God himself intended for me to choose and execute a course of action which would fail of the goal I intended but, in the long run and in ways beyond my foreseeing, perhaps even by reason of the initial failure, would be for his greater glory in me and all others. Do not the lives of prophets and saints exemplify this—and, above all, Christ's life and death? How then could failure disconfirm the finalized decision of discernment?

Further, Ignatius' belief that the Holy Spirit might move different persons in ways that bring them into opposition comes into play here. For when this is the case, neither person has any reason through his discernment to think that God wills his action to prevail over the other person's. All he knows, as Ignatius says, is what God wants him to intend and, if possible, carry out. One or the other person is bound to be frustrated of his goal. God may see both the success of one and the failure of the other as ways to greater glory for all of us; or he may intend to bring the opposing persons together finally in seeking a common goal of which neither thought prior to their opposition. Given all these possibilities, how could success or failure in attaining the intended end confirm or disconfirm either of the decisions?

Confirmation or Disconfirmation by Unintended Results of Acting on the Decision

Whether the intended end of the action decided on is successfully achieved or not, results other than the intended end may be observable in the lives of the discerner and others. These may be good or bad, direct or indirect, immediate or long deferred. Some see these results as divine confirmation or disconfirmation of the decision. May they reasonably be so understood? If so, are they necessary in order to evaluate the conclusion of the preceding discernment of God's will?

In answering these questions, several things must be clear.

223

First, the only aspect under which such results could even possibly count as confirmation or disconfirmation of the discernment is that of being for the greater or lesser glory of God. Under any other aspect, desirable or undesirable, splendid or revolting, results are irrelevant to Ignatian discernment of God's will.[8]

Another needed clarification is that we are not concerned with results from a planned experiment. A discerner may be unable as yet to make a trustworthy tentative decision with the evidence at hand. In that case he may put one or other or both alternatives into execution for a time in order to get more evidence based on experiential data, on living experience, before drawing a tentative conclusion. Clearly, the results of such experiments have nothing to do with confirming a tentative decision already reached; they are data from which evidence for a decision to be made is derived. So also, after a tentative decision, it may seem wise to experiment before finalizing it. In that case the results of the living experience could be seen as confirming or disconfirming the tentative decision. But such confirmation or disconfirmation is not to the point here. The question under consideration concerns confirmation by results in living experience after the decision has been finalized for choice and put into execution.

With these clarifications in mind, let us look for an answer to the question asked above. Nowhere to my knowledge is there evidence that Ignatius himself looked for confirmation or disconfirmation of any decision finalized for choice by the results of executing the chosen act. Neither is there evidence that he instructed others to do so. A reader may think to find such evidence if he does not distinguish it from evidence of Ignatius' concern for changing circumstances which call for a new discernment. What is learned by experience after a finalized decision has been acted on is of value to Ignatius for making future decisions and for reevaluating the *present* worth of decisions made in the past, but *not* for confirming or disconfirming the *past* decision as truly conforming to God's will for the discerner *at that time*.

This distinction between disconfirming the prior decision and being alerted to the need for a new discernment may seem at first

---

[8] See above, pp. 173–175; see also pp. 29–30.

glance to have no practical importance; for, in either case, discernment is now called for. But, as we shall now see, accepting or rejecting the principle which asserts that results can disconfirm a decision has great significance for our understanding and practice of discerning God's will.

If there is no explicit evidence that Ignatius thought an already-finalized decision needed further confirmation or might be disconfirmed by the results in execution, neither is there any explicit evidence to the contrary. Did he, then, intend to leave the question open? I do not think so; for, if we examine the matter more closely and keep in mind the limits of discernment, we find implicit evidence against confirmation or disconfirmation by good or bad results of executing a decision reached by discernment.

Ignatius proposes his way of seeking God's will for the sake of finding it *before* choosing and acting; and he firmly believes that we can find it (within limits and under certain conditions).[9] All his instructions and all we know of his own practice plainly show this to be so. If results were needed to confirm or disconfirm the decision, then what Ignatius intends through discernment would be impossible. The reason for saying so seems inescapable. If results of acting on a decision were necessary data for finding God's will, would it not be arbitrary and unreasonable to make a judgment on the basis of immediate results only? Would not the discerner have to wait until all the results were in? What is indicated by the immediate results might be contradicted by later results; and these later results, in turn, might be contradicted by still later results; and these later results, in turn, might be contradicted by further ones; and so on to the end of history. Consequently, before the end of history, no one could ever believe with any justifiable conviction that he or she had found God's will. This conclusion may be entirely acceptable to some, but certainly not to Ignatius.[10]

Further, even on the basis of immediate actual consequences only, no confirmation or disconfirmation of a decision and choice is possible. All there is to go on is the actual consequences of choosing and executing *one* of the alternatives for choice. If these

---

[9] See chapters 5–6 and 15–16.

[10] See below, pp. 281–286.

225

consequences are good, those of executing a different decision and choice might have been better; if they are bad, those which would follow from executing a different decision and choice might have been worse.

An illustration will bring out the point of the preceding argument. Suppose a young woman makes a discernment regarding marriage to a man whom she loves. She faithfully fulfills to the very best of her ability all the requisites for a good discernment and concludes that God wills for her to marry and to marry the man whom she loves. The first year of marriage is joyful. All goes well between her and her husband. She experiences God's presence and peace and is full of loving gratitude to him. All this she sees as a confirmation of her decision which led her to this marriage as truly being what God willed.

But then troubles begin. She and her husband begin to grate on each other. "What has become of the loving, understanding, generous one I married?" each one asks the other. The woman no longer experiences the presence and peace of God. She is in desolation, full of tension, full of resentment toward her husband. She finds it very difficult to pray or to have confidence in divine providence. All this, she thinks, throws doubt upon the discernment she had made concerning her marriage; in fact she feels quite sure now that she did not find what God willed. She begins to have guilt feelings about that discernment, thinking that, after all, she had merely deceived herself to get the decision that she wanted at the time. Now, so she thinks, God is punishing her.

Both she and her husband have enough sense and goodwill to talk things over and try to do better. They get help from attending a marriage encounter; finally, their relationship grows into a deeper and more beautiful one than before. Surely, she now thinks, the discernment she made about her marriage did, after all, lead to finding God's will. She is again at peace.

Later, a child is born and turns out to be retarded. Then her husband loses his job and takes to drink. She finds herself deeply involved emotionally with a man other than her husband. Although she remains faithful, she still feels frustrated. Again the thought: Her discernment had been a failure.

Her husband, through the help of AA and a profound religious conversion, is transformed personally and finds steady work; they are drawn together in special love and care for their retarded child. Another altogether-healthy child is born. They feel enfolded by God's love and each other's love and grow in prayer and do much good for others. Now, looking back, the woman has no doubt that, in the discernment she made, the Holy Spirit had led her to marry this good man. Here in marriage is the true meaning of her life.

And so on and so on until the end of her life and the lives of the children she and her husband had influenced and of their children's children, and eventually to the end of all history. If results in living out the decision are needed to confirm a discernment of God's will or if they can disconfirm it, then there is no way before eternity this woman could ever have any justified assurance of having found God's will. Even if she had knowledge of all the results of her choice through all history, in her life and the lives of all others, these results could not confirm or disconfirm her decision. If the results were, all in all, very bad, the results of a different decision and choice might have been even worse. If the results were, all in all, very good, the results of a different decision and choice might have been even better, more for the glory of God. How could she know unless she also knew all the results that would have actually followed in her life and the lives of others from any alternative decision which she did not make?

A difficulty might be urged that, at least in some cases, actual results in executing the decision reached in discernment not only can confirm or disconfirm a decision but are necessary for that purpose. Take, for example, a decision to join a religious community with vows of celibacy, poverty, and obedience. Like others before him, Ignatius required that such a decision be tested and confirmed by experience over a period of time before final vows. This fact which might be thought to raise a difficulty is clear, but as a difficulty it misses the point. The reason it does so is that it overlooks what has been shown about the limits of discerning God's will. As was shown when we treated that topic, a person cannot find through discernment whether God wills for him or her to succeed in actually accomplishing some project, but only whether God wills for him or her to intend to try to do so. Whether or not God wills the success of this attempt, whether or not God wills even the actual attempt—

the answers to these questions are predictions and beyond the reach of human discernment.

Concluding Summary

The results of this prolonged analysis (in Chapters 11–12) of Ignatius' teaching on seeking confirmation before and after finalizing the conclusion of the discernment process can now be briefly summed up. First, the confirmation sought at this step is primarily confirmation of the truth of the judgment to which a sound discernment has led and only secondarily a strengthening of the will to carry out the chosen course of action. Second, Ignatius' understanding of what constitutes confirmation (or disconfirmation) of the tentative judgment reached by sound discernment is, in one way, broader and more inclusive than is commonly thought. It is not limited to experience of spiritual consolation (or desolation), as many say it is; rather, it includes any and every kind of evidence that could help to reach the tentative decision for which confirmation should now be sought. Third, Ignatius' understanding of what constitutes such confirmation (or disconfirmation) is, in another way, narrower and more exclusive than is commonly thought. It excludes any need for confirmation by consequent events, even by those events which result from executing what is judged to be God's will. If confirmation by these results were possible and needed, then obviously God's will could not be found before seeing all the results through history. Neither could it be found after knowing all these results unless one also knew all the results that would follow through history if each of the other alternatives had been chosen.

The idea that a decision already finalized for choice after a sound discernment needs confirmation by consequent events is largely the consequence of failing to understand and remember the limits of discerning God's will or of confusing intellectual confirmation with confirmation of the discerner's will to execute the judgment. Such volitional confirmation may be needed and is possible at any time before or after finalizing a sound discernment.

Finally, it should be evident how important these findings about confirmation and disconfirmation are for the practice of discerning God's will, not only because they guard us against mistakes in the process of seeking confirmation, but also because, like accuracy

228

about the limits of discerning God's will, they can prevent many painful misunderstandings, much confusion, or unfounded doubts about having found God's will, which may lead to consequent hesitation to begin good works or consequent easy disengagement from them when the going gets rough.

John Futrell on Confirmation and Disconfirmation

Before concluding this analysis of confirmation in Ignatian discernment, I would like to say something about one of the rare treatments of the topic which take it with the seriousness it deserves and deal with it at any length, that of John Futrell, S.J. His thoughtful analysis, showing notable familiarity with the relevant texts, deserves more attention than that provided in a brief footnote or two.

Futrell distinguishes the continuing confirmation which is to be sought all through the discernment process from the confirmation sought for the final judgment at the end of the process. Regarding the former, he writes:

> Ordinarily, however, in both individual and communal discernment confirmation is experienced interiorly as profound peace, contentment, satisfaction, recognition in tranquility that the way has been found to respond to the word of God here and now. This interior confirmation is operative throughout the whole process of discernment, "testing the Spirit" at every step until the moment of judgment for action and the experience of final confirmation.[11]

However, he does immediately point out that this use of "confirmation" is not found in Ignatius' own writing. "Strictly speaking," Futrell adds, "Ignatius' own use of the word *confirmation* refers to the final, interior confirmation of the decision made at the end of the process of discernment."[12]

The confirmation sought for the decision made at the end of the process is said to be twofold, penultimate and ultimate. The penultimate confirmation is that received after that judgment is

---

[11] John Futrell, "Ignatian Discernment," p. 63.
[12] Ibid.

reached but before it is put into execution. Like the ongoing confirmation during the process, it is interior, an experience of profound peace, contentment, and so on, at that time. The ultimate confirmation comes after that, "given by God's active love in history"; it comes from authority or from experience of living out the decision and seeing the consequences.[13]

Confirmation may come from external authority as from the pope, as is exemplified in the constant effort of Ignatius to have papal approbation of the Company and its constitution through bulls and briefs. The hierarchical structure of the Company gives to local superiors the means of confirmation of their decision by the General. The confirmation of the subjective discernment of a companion is found in his conformity and obedience, after representation, to the final judgment of the Company through the superior. The principal means of confirmation of the decisions of the superior, however, are the mutual contentment of himself and his companions and the proof of living experience.[14]

Because of the context within which Futrell develops his interpretation,[15] the consequence on which he centers his attention is the mutual contentment or the contrary between the religious superior and the members of the community and among the members.[16] "The proof of experience," the ultimate confirmation, says Futrell, is "the *only sure* confirmation of the decisions of the superior for the life and action of the companions of Jesus."[17] I see no logical reason why he would not extend this statement to mean that the consequences in living experience, that is, continued contentment, peace, satisfaction, and so on, following on execution of the decisions, constitute the ultimate and only sure confirmation or disconfirmation of any decision made by Ignatian discernment.

If this is so, then it follows that no discernment is complete

---

[13] Ibid., pp. 64–65.
[14] MACL, p. 143.
[15] See above, note 4 of chapter 3.
[16] MACL, pp. 143–144.
[17] Ibid., p. 149 (emphasis mine).

until the evidence derived from living experience is in. If this experience is not good, the judgment arrived at was mistaken. Then further discernment is called for.

> At the end of this process the decision is made, but it is still open to verification through living experience and, if proved mistaken, subject to further discernment. This study has revealed repeatedly the central position of the teaching of living experience in the mental structure of Ignatius. It was in actual life-situations and through natural and supernatural experiences that he sought to discern the concrete will of God, rather than in some system of a priori principles from which he deduced practical conclusions.[18]

As remarked above, Futrell's analysis is admirably thought through and honestly in touch with what Ignatius says. There are, however, in light of my own efforts to understand what Ignatius says, a few comments to be made. First, Futrell ordinarily speaks of interior confirmation as constituted solely by experience of peace, contentment, and so on, whereas I think to find a wide range of interior confirmatiòn. However, in comment on Ignatius' diary, Futrell does note a confirmation by thought without consolation. How far he would want to go with this remark is not clear.

Further, to say that any interior confirmation by contentment, peace, and so on, consequent on the tentative decision, is necessary for finalizing the decision has, as I have thought to show, implications in discord with Ignatius' thought. Much more is this so when it is said that any such confirmation after finalizing the decision for choice and execution is necessary. But here also Futrell says something that would suggest there is less difference between his interpretation and mine than there seems to be. I refer to his remarks on the case in which it seems that, because some vital information was overlooked or a new situation has arisen, a decision by discernment appears to be mistaken.

> The *response* here and now is the important thing, and interior confirmation can occur because the decision

---

[18] Ibid., pp. 124–125.

231

reached is a truly free response to what is discerned as the word of God here and now. In this sense it is true to say that on the deepest level one has found and is doing "the will of God": the actual living of love. When it appears later on through experience that some necessary evidence has been inadvertently overlooked or unavailable, the necessary modification of decision is made in peace, and in trust that from the very "mistake" the Father will work a transforming good, a Paschal creation of "new life."[19]

Finally, in conflict with Futrell's understanding of Ignatius' thought, I have shown why I think that, whatever else approbation or disapprobation by authority may confirm or disconfirm, it can never confirm or disconfirm the decision of a sound discernment made within the proper limits of discernment. It may open or close the way to carrying out the decision, or it may so change circumstances as to make a new discernment necessary; but these consequences are neither confirmations nor disconfirmations of the preceding decision.

---

[19] "Ignatian Discernment," p. 65.

Chapter 13
The Relationship of the
Three Modes

*H*ow Ignatius understood each mode of seeking God's will has been worked through in the preceding chapters; now the three modes can be considered together in order to see how he understood their relationship in theory and in practice.[1] Before trying to do so, it will be advisable to note and describe the common structure which in those modes underlies all differences in the data, and the norms for evaluation and interpretation of data. Keeping this structure in mind will enable us to understand more readily the questions that have to be asked about the relationship of these modes and more

---

[1] One of the best studies to be found on how Ignatius himself understood the relationship of the three modes of seeking God's will is chapter 4, ''The Discernment of Spirits,'' in Hugo Rahner's *Ignatius the Theologian*. With perhaps one or two exceptions, his conclusions are all soundly based on the text of Ignatius rather than on theological speculation.

clearly to answer them. In describing this common structure of the several modes and in dealing with the questions about their relationship, we need to recall that we allowed for two possible ways of understanding the first mode of election, only one of them involving anything resembling an active search for God's will. In what follows, the first mode of discernment will be understood in this latter way. The reader who understands it the other way—namely, without any active search whatever—can simply leave out of consideration what is said about the first mode in this chapter.

The Common Structure: Three Moments

Each mode of discerning God's will begins from some first moment or moments in which data for the discernment process are either given by God in transient spiritual experiences (the first and second modes) or tranquilly searched out and organized by reason under the guidance of the Holy Spirit (the third mode).[2]

The second moment in each mode of election is a time of tranquil reflection on the data given or gathered in the first moment. During this time the data are critically examined and tested by norms appropriate to each kind of data, in order to see whether we have genuine data for that mode of discernment. The data which survive such testing are interpreted by norms appropriate for the purpose of determining to which alternative God is moving the discerner (in the first and second modes), or which alternative is more advantageous, that alternative which is more for the service and glory of God (in the third mode). If the interpreted data yield opposing sets of evidence, these are comparatively weighed to find which is weightier. The weightier evidence (or, if all evidence is for one side, that evidence) is itself weighed to see whether it is enough to justify a decision on the basis of it.

When time is reasonably available, this decision is to be only a tentative one; there is a following moment when divine confirmation is sought before finalizing the decision for choice. How that is done has already been described.

---

[2] See below, pp. 271–273.

The Main Questions

Does this common structure allow for a real and full distinction between the three modes, no one of them including any factor which specifies either of the other two? If so, can each one be autonomous, that is, adequate apart from the other two for reaching a trustworthy decision regarding God's will? If so, is there ever any need for more than one mode? These three main questions about the relationship of the three modes of discernment will be answered in the order just given; for the second and third presuppose an affirmative answer to the preceding one if it is to be a real question. Only if a mode is really and fully distinct from the others can it possibly be autonomous (although it might conceivably be distinct without being autonomous); and only if a mode is autonomous is there any point in asking whether more than one mode can sometimes be needed.

The second and third questions are obviously of great practical significance. The first question, that about the distinction of the several modes, may appear to be of merely speculative interest— and would be so in isolation. But, since a negative answer to it entails a negative answer to the second question and an affirmative to the third, it takes on all the practical importance of these other questions.

The answers to these questions given by interpreters of St. Ignatius are far from unanimous. In order to present my answers in relationship to the current discusssions, I shall first present a spectrum of diverse interpretations.

Further, for the sake of simplifying the problem, I shall narrow it somewhat. As we shall see, among recent writers there are those who deny any real distinction between the modes. Most authors, however, do not seem to question the full distinction of the first mode from the other two; it is only the second and the third that they see as lacking full distinction from each other. A notable group sees the third mode as ultimately entirely dependent on the second for arriving at a trustworthy conclusion. A few see the second as dependent on the third. Consequently, the main focus of this chapter will be on the distinction and autonomy of these two modes, largely leaving aside the first.

235

A Spectrum of Interpretations

In a spectrum of interpretations, the extreme position at one end is that proposed by Karl Rahner. The three modes, in his opinion, constitute "one identical kind of election"; they "have one and the same nature and are distinguished only by the different degrees to which they realize that nature."[3] That nature, Rahner says, appears "in its pure and fully developed form" in the first two modes of election, principally in the second, for the first is "the ideal limiting case of the second,"[4] "an extraordinary phenomenon which Ignatius mentions more out of a certain liking for system than for its practical importance."[5] The third mode is, in Rahner's view, only "a deficient form"[6] or a "deficient modality"[7] of the second. On the other hand, he says (with questionable consistency) that the third mode is related to the second as part to whole,[8] its rationality included in the second "as one of its own intrinsic elements."[9]

Harvey Egan, who for the most part follows Rahner very closely, admits that Ignatius does propose three distinct times for election; but, he adds, Ignatius does so only for the sake of clarifying one core experience and one election. Actually, he says, the three times "are not distinct ways of finding God's will," for there are elements of each way in the other two and all three interpenetrate or fuse. Egan even goes so far as to say that the three times are only "aspects" of the one core experience and election, "present in varying degrees of intensity," one or the other predominantly.[10] This way of speaking about the three times as merely aspects of one election might be thought to go beyond what Karl Rahner is saying. For, if taken at face value, it goes beyond and is not compatible

---

[3] Karl Rahner, *Dynamic Element*, p. 105.

[4] Ibid., p. 106.

[5] Ibid., p. 128, note 25.

[6] Ibid., p. 103.

[7] Ibid., p. 105.

[8] Ibid., p. 103.

[9] Ibid., p. 106. There is reason for thinking that Rahner and others say that third–time discernment or some elements of it are contained in the second because they fail to distinguish between the kind of reasons and reasoning which are peculiar to the third, those which are peculiar to the second, and those which are common to both. See below, pp. 242–243. They seem to think that any reason or reasoning which functions in second–time discernment is an element of third–time discernment.

[10] *Mystical Horizon*, p. 152.

with speaking of the third mode as a deficient form or modality of the second or as an intrinsic element of it. An aspect of a whole is not a deficient form of it or a part of it. Nevertheless, Rahner himself goes along with this way of speaking.[11]

The interpretation of the three modes as interpenetrating and, however one expresses it, in ultimate analysis constituting one mode of discernment, is given a more-developed and better-organized statement by Harvey Egan than can be found in the writing of Karl Rahner or anyone else I have read;[12] and, in a foreword to Egan's book, Karl Rahner has expressed his agreement with him.[13] In his statement Egan shows clearly how he thinks elements of each mode are constitutive elements of each of the other two.[14]

Rahner's and Egan's understanding of the three modes of election as one mode logically excludes attributing autonomy to any mode, even the first; this is so obvious as to eliminate need for discussion. One may, as Rahner and Egan do, devalue the third aspect (the third mode) and give total predominance to the second over the third. In such a conceptual framework, every sound and trustworthy election is a second-time election; but the second-time election is still only the predominant aspect of the one mode of election, which includes the third.

Although Thomas Green does understand the three modes of Ignatian election as three distinct ways of seeking God's will, he is, nevertheless, in agreement with Rahner and Egan that the third mode is not autonomous. Unless it ends up in the second mode, he says, it is "incomplete" and untrustworthy.[15]

While John Futrell never explicitly addresses the question of autonomy, his principal statements on the structure of Ignatian discernment easily lead to the conclusion that he sees Ignatius' second and third modes as inextricably interdependent, essential parts of one process, neither mode, therefore, able to function autonomously.

---

[11] See "Comments by Karl Rahner on Questions Raised by Avery Dulles, S.J.," *Ignatius of Loyola: His Personality and Spiritual Heritage, 1556–1956*, ed. Friedrich Wulf and trans. James M. Quigley, S.J., p. 193. p. 193.

[12] Harvey Egan, *Mystical Horizon*, p. 152–155.

[13] Ibid., xvi.

[14] See above, note 9.

[15] Thomas Green, *Weeds Among the Wheat* (Notre Dame, Indiana: Ave Maria Press, 1984), pp. 87–88.

The Ignatian discernment process, Futrell says, has three steps.[16] The first he calls prayer for light. Such prayer involves much more than that phrase would ordinarily be taken to mean, involving as it does the following elements: coming to see everything in the light of Christ as the model of response to the Father; becoming aware of one's own deep motivation; coming to an attitude of Ignatian "indifference"; praying over the evidence in order to find what is for the greater glory—the evidence gathered in the second step.

For that is the second step, gathering by observation, consultation, and dialogue all the evidence one can from the concrete situation.[17] This concrete situation is what Futrell calls the "existential word of God," which must be prophetically interpreted in the light of God's revealed word in order to find what is his call.[18] In Futrell's vocabulary, "evidence" has a more restricted meaning than I have been giving it. Evidence for him is limited to what is gotten through study of the actual concrete situation. In short, it is what I have referred to as third-time evidence. In Futrell's structure of Ignatian discernment, there seems to be no place for another kind of evidence, that obtained by second-time experiences, fully distinct from and independent of that reached by reflection on the concrete situation. Or, as Futrell sometimes puts it, the only source of "content" for a decision by Ignatian discernment is reflection on and interpretation of the concrete situation. Spiritual consolation or desolation, interpreted by the rules for discernment of spirits, does not function as evidence in his interpretation and does not provide content for a decision. Its function is solely to help a discerner to be liberated from the deceptions of egoism by testing and confirming or disconfirming judgments reached on the basis of third-time evidence.[19]

This use of consolation Futrell sees as the third step of Ignatian discernment. This step is "the continuing effort to find 'confirmation' during every step of the discernment process as well as for

---

[16] John Futrell, MACL, pp. 124–125 and "Ignatian Discernment," p. 59.

[17] "Ignatian Discernment," pp. 59–61; MACL, pp. 126–131.

[18] "Ignatian Discernment," pp. 49–50, 59, 61–62; MACL, pp. 124, 131–142.

[19] MACL, pp. 127–128.

the final judgment by the experience of deep interior peace."[20] This confirmation "is experienced interiorly as profound peace, contentment, satisfaction, recognition in tranquility that the way had been found to respond to the word of God here and now."[21]

From what has been said of these three steps, it is clear that Futrell does not think each one is to be completed before moving to the next one. For the first both precedes and succeeds the second; while the third occurs all through the process of gathering evidence in the second. "In practice," Futrell says, "they are intermingled and progress together toward the final determination."[22]

Perhaps Futrell wants to allow for a discernment in the second or third mode being made independently of the other. Perhaps he only intends to mean that ordinarily the two modes function together, that it would be quite exceptional not to do so. If that is his meaning, what he says in describing the structure of Ignatian discernment does not do justice to his thought; for it does not lead the reader to think that the Ignatian third mode can be a genuine discernment without the second, or the second without the third.[23]

---

[20] "Ignatian Discernment," p. 59.

[21] Ibid., p. 63.

[22] Ibid., p. 59; MACL, p. 125.

[23] After reading the presentation of his thought on "confirmation" (see pp. 229–231) and the foregoing presentation of his thought on the relation and distinction of the three Ignatian modes of seeking God's will, Futrell gave me the following statement regarding his present way of *expressing* his thought (no significant change of thought intended). All the emphases are his.

You have read my texts with great accuracy. The way I *now* distinguish first and second times of election from third time is thus:

(1) First and second time both reach a decision by way of *discernment*, since both terminate in the confirmation experience: "It is the Lord present in *this* choice." Finding God, one finds His will here and now. The only difference is *duration*: immediate confirmation (perhaps, though, after much time given to collecting evidence) vs. prolonged alternation of interior experiences (movements) until confirmation is at last experienced.

(2) In the third time the decision is reached by *Christian prudence*. Since a decision must be made *now* (external clarity of God's will about the time limit), and the Spirit's free gift of confirmation is not experienced, God wills that one make the decision by Christian reasoning. The process—gathering evidence, prayerful reflection, noticing movements, etc.—is identical with the second time. The *termination* is what distinguishes them: In the first and second times, we find *God* and so His will; in the third time, we find by reason that this choice is *best*, and so, trust that it is God's will. In the tradition, as well as in Ignatius, there seems a lack of satisfaction with this, so that one should continue praying to eventually experience confirmation *while* carrying out the decision made in the third time.

Influenced by Karl Rahner, it seems, but giving no evidence of fully adopting his extreme view, are many others who deny autonomy to the third-time discernment but do not seem to see all the modes as parts or aspects of one election. Second-time discernment, they say, can be adequate by itself; but the third cannot. Unless the latter receives confirmation by second-time evidence of consolation, it cannot yield a trustworthy conclusion. In this view, the decisive ground for assenting to the conclusion of a third-time discernment as truly expressing God's will is not the reason proper to that mode, but rather the second-time evidence given by God in the final step of seeking confirmation. Without the latter, no kind of evidence, no trustworthy decision can be made. For some of those who think this way, that second-time evidence is, in ultimate analysis, the whole ground for assent to the conclusion. The third-time discernment process of gathering reasons is of value only insofar as it leads to and prepares for reception of divine signs by spiritual consolations. In this view, it is clear "that this third moment [time] is not really a moment of choice at all; it only becomes so when we experience consolation proper to the second moment."[24] The second time is not only declared to have unqualified priority over the third, but the latter, it is said, "*requires* confirmation in the form of heaven-sent consolations and desolations."[25]

Such a way of interpreting the Ignatian modes of election seems to be clearly saying that the third mode not only cannot be autonomous from the second but cannot even be fully distinct from it— although the second can be distinct from the third and is autonomous. Not all of those who follow this interpretation, however, are willing to accept the implications in regard to distinction and autonomy. Thus, Pousset declares that the third mode of election is "permeated by the second."[26] Further, in discussing the search for confirmation in the third mode, he assumes that confirmation means second-time

[24] James Walsh, "The Discernment of Spirits," *The Way*, Supplement no. 16 (1972), p. 64 (emphasis mine). As support for his assertion, Walsh quotes without comment the main lines from Ignatius' letter to Borgia (see above, pp. 260–263) about his discernment regarding the question of creating Borgia a cardinal. Below I shall show why I think this letter supports just the opposite view.

[25] Nicholas King, S. J., "Ignatius Loyola and Decision–Making," *The Way*, Supplement 24 (Spring, 1975), p. 59 (emphasis mine).

[26] Edouard Pousset, *Life in Faith and Freedom*, p. 119. See also pp. 120, 122, 126.

evidence of consolation and sees such confirmation as necessary for a trustworthy conclusion of a third-time election. Certitude is there *only* because of the weight of my affectivity dragging along the weight of reasoning.[27] In such discernment "the choice cannot be concluded without God's felt response."[28] All this seems to deny that the third mode is fully distinct from the second and that it can be autonomous from the second. Nevertheless, Pousset, on the other hand, asserts that each of the three Ignatian modes can function in separation, or autonomously, from the other two. The relations between them are, he says, isolated by our analysis but do not imply any necessary dependence of one on the other.[29]

Finally, at the other end of the spectrum, there is the position of those who interpret Ignatius to mean that each of the three modes of election is fully distinct from the other two and can be autonomous, even though they should sometimes be combined. This opinion, I think, is clearly assumed in the directories[30] and appears in recent writing, but not at all as prominently as the other opinions already presented.

These conflicting interpretations make clear why we need to deal seriously with the questions regarding the relationship of the three modes of election which were set down at the beginning of this chapter. As noted there, these questions will be taken in their logical order: their distinction, their individual autonomy, their combination in practice.

In my treatment of these questions, it would be easy but unprofitable to become entangled in detailed controversy with those who espouse the opinions given above. For my reading of those who see in each mode of Ignatian discernment elements of the other two or, at the very least, elements of the second mode in the third reveals why my analysis of the Ignatian texts forces me to see these opinions as understandable but serious errors. Rather than becoming entangled in endlessly detailed controversy over the many statements

---

[27] Ibid., p. 124 (emphasis mine). Pousset here assumes that certitude is possible by reason of evidence from second–time experiences. For a criticism of this view, see below, pp. 277–280.

[28] Ibid., p. 126.

[29] Ibid., pp. 119–120, note 14 and p. 122. How these views can be logically reconciled is hard to see.

[30] See below, pp. 249–250.

to which I would have to take exception, I think it will be easier on the reader as well as myself, clearer, and, I hope, more convincing, if I simply present in a positive way my own interpretation of what Ignatius says.

Are the Three Modes Fully Distinct?

Does the common structure which we have found[31] allow for the three modes being fully distinct, no one of them including either of the other two as an essential element? If the analysis already made of each time for and mode of discerning God's will is accurate, then convincing evidence for holding a full distinction between them can readily be shown.

A good way of beginning to do this is to note the different questions which are immediately and directly answered in the different modes. All the modes ultimately answer the same question: What is God's will for my choice in this concrete situation? However, they do so by answering different, more immediate questions which imply what God wills. The third mode answers the question: Which real alternative for choice in this situation is more for the glory of God in us? (Or, if the alternatives appear to the discerner as equally for God's glory, which will make him more like the poor and humiliated Christ?)[32] Since in every concrete situation for choice, God always wills that I choose what is for the greater glory, that alternative which is more for the glory is what he wills. The first and second modes immediately and directly answer the question: To which alternative does God move my will? Again, since in every concrete situation for choice God always wills me to choose what is for the greater glory, that to which God moves me is for the greater glory and is what God wills.

The answers to these different questions rest on different kinds of evidence; and, although the first and second modes answer the same question, the evidence for that answer in each case is different. Each of the three kinds of evidence is peculiar to, and is found exclusively in, one mode of election. Thus, evidence in the third

---

[31] See above, p. 234.
[32] See above, pp. 177–178.

mode is without spiritual movement of consolation or desolation[33] and without any impulse which brings an experience of indubitable conviction regarding God's will. Evidence in the second mode lacks that experience of indubitable conviction and perceived advantages and disadvantages for God's glory; for it is not under the aspect of what leads to God's glory that the alternatives are judged in that mode.[34] Even if the second or third mode of discernment leads to a certain judgment, that judgment is the conclusion of the discernment process; unlike the first-time experience, it does not consist in data from which the discernment begins. Further, the evidence in the first mode of discernment does not include consolations as an essential factor[35] nor desolation nor weighed advantages and disadvantages for the glory of God.

If genuine third-time reasons (projected advantages or disadvantages for the greater glory) do occur to the discerner during the first or second modes of discerning, these reasons are not factors in either of those modes. Or if consolations and desolations with specified volitional impulses do occur during the first or third modes of discerning, these are merely concurrent events, not essential factors in either of those modes of discerning. More than one mode can be going on concomitantly;[36] nevertheless, one is not included in the other—no more than seeing and hearing are included in each other, although they are concurrent sense apprehensions joined in perceptions.

To say that the three modes of election are different by reason of the kind of evidence on which the conclusion rests is to say that they also differ both by reason of the kind of data needed for such evidence and by the norms or principles appropriate for critically evaluating and interpreting the data in order to arrive at each kind of evidence. Such striking and pervasive differences seem to show that the several modes are fully distinct.

---

[33] See above, pp. 163–167.

[34] See above, p. 140.

[35] See above, pp. 114–118.

[36] For illustration, see the election recounted in Ignatius' *Diario Espiritual*.

Can Each of the Fully Distinct Modes Function Autonomously?

The question remains: Did Ignatius think that each mode could be autonomous, that is, a trustworthy way of seeking and finding God's will independently of the other modes? (Obviously there can be no question of autonomy if the word is understood to mean a denial of dependence on the Holy Spirit in discernment.) For, while autonomy of one mode is impossible unless it is distinct from others, a distinct mode might still be inadequate by itself. On the other hand, since autonomy presupposes distinction, if Ignatius did think that each mode can function autonomously, then he thought that each is fully distinct from the other two.

In the discussions about autonomy of the three modes, no one seriously questions whether Ignatius thinks the first mode can be autonomous except those who think all three modes are only aspects of one single mode, in which now one aspect and now another is predominant. Reasons for rejecting that opinion have already been given. Neither does anyone other than those just mentioned propose a serious reason for doubting that Ignatius saw the second and third modes as entirely independent of the first. As we have seen, however, a notable number sees the third as dependent on the second and useless apart from it; some write in a way that suggests a mutual dependence of the second and third modes—not just on occasion, but always. In terms of the literature on Ignatian discernment, then, there are two principal questions to be answered: Whether the third mode of discernment can be independent of the second and whether the second can be independent of the third.

In presenting the evidence for Ignatius' thought on these questions, I shall first present evidence that he takes for granted the autonomy of every mode, then particular evidence that he considered the third mode autonomous from the second and, finally, the second from the third. All that will be said regarding the independence of these two modes from each other shows also their independence from the first mode.

Before presenting the evidence, several sources of confusion should be cleared away and the issue made precise. First, although Ignatius does, in fact, combine the third with the second mode during the election described in his diary, this fact by itself does not show any dependence of the former on the latter or the other way around. In a very important and difficult election, one may want every kind of evidence available. Using more than one mode to get two kinds of evidence in no way implies a denial of autonomy to either mode. Further, the question of autonomy is not whether in second-time discernment reason must function in some way or whether in third-time discernment affective feelings may function in some ways. As has been shown, reasoning is necessary in every mode of discernment, and affections may function in the third mode. The difference between the two modes lies in the different kind of data reasoned on and the different kind of evidence which is reasoned to. Finally, the question is not whether the second mode is superior to the third or the third to the second or whether one is as good as the other. The question of relative value is distinct from the question of autonomy. So also is the question whether Ignatius places much value on the third mode. He could see it as autonomous and yet value it very little, at least for important questions. (As will appear, the evidence for autonomy will say something about how Ignatius valued the third mode of election.) There has been such a concerted effort in recent writing on Ignatian discernment to denigrate the third mode that an extensive separate treatment will be needed in order to present adequately the evidence for Ignatius' valuation of that mode.[37]

What then is the real point of the question regarding the autonomy of the second and third modes of discernment? It is whether a trustworthy decision can be based solely on the kind of evidence found in either one of these modes.

General Statement regarding the Autonomy of Each Mode

When Ignatius begins his description of the three times, the heading reads, "Three Times, Each One of Them Opportune for Making a Sound and Trustworthy Election."[38] This heading is as plain an indication as could be wished that each of the three modes is autonomous. It is so clear that, in order to think that Ignatius did not see them that way, there would have to be evidence strong and

---

[37] See chapter 14.
[38] *SpEx*, [175] (emphasis mine). *Tres tiempos para hacer sana y buena elección en cada uno de ellos.*

clear enough to override the heading and show that what we find there is contrary to his true intent.

Rather than conflicting with that heading, what follows in the *Spiritual Exercises* and what Ignatius says in his autograph directory confirm its obvious meaning. In the latter document, Ignatius says that, if the discerner does not find God's will by the first mode, he should persevere by seeking it in the second;[39] and when that mode does not bring success, the third mode should be undertaken.[40] Contrary to the opinion of some, there is nothing here to suggest that the third mode is to be considered merely a preliminary exercise for returning to the second or that the second mode is merely a preliminary exercise for returning to the first.

Autonomy of the Third Mode in Particular

As said above, the question of the third mode's autonomy from the second calls for special attention because of the relatively recent and presently widespread denial of it by reputable Ignatian scholars.[41] Fortunately, besides what Ignatius says by way of instruction on the election in the *Spiritual Exercises* and in his autograph directory, we have his advice to an individual who brought to him this very question. Ramírez de Vergara, an eminent professor during Ignatius' life, was thinking of asking admittance to the Society of Jesus. He held back because, while faith-enlightened reason assured him it was the better way for him and more for God's glory, he did not experience a decision by the second mode of election, by consolations. His problem was presented to Ignatius, and Ignatius responded.

> Better than anyone else, the Holy Spirit will teach you how to taste with affection and carry out with sweetness what reason dictates as being for God's greater service and glory. It is true that for seeking what is the better and more perfect, the activity of reason is enough. Still, even though the other activity, that of will [volitional impulse in consolation], does not precede decision and

---

[39] *DirAutog*, [18].
[40] Ibid., [19]. See also *SpEx*, [178].
[41] See above, pp. 236–241.

execution, it can easily follow. In this way God our Lord rewards the trust put in his providence, the abandonment of self, the letting go of self-centered consolation; he rewards with great contentment and relish and with spiritual consolation all the greater in abundance as one seeks it less and intends more purely his glory and praise.[42]

If Ignatius had not seen the third mode of discernment as entirely trustworthy independently of the second, he would have had to tell de Vergara to continue waiting and praying until God gave sufficiently abundant second-time evidence. He does, in fact, tell him to act now on his third-time decision. Reason, without any second-time evidence, Ignatius says, is enough. Afterwards, he adds, while carrying out the decision, de Vergara may hope to be given spiritual consolation, provided he does not seek it for his own satisfaction. There even seems to be an insinuation that to demand consolations before deciding would show a lack of trust in divine providence.[43]

If the foregoing evidence needed any strengthening, we could find it in the document entitled *The Deliberation of the First Fathers*, an account of a group discernment in which, as we saw, Ignatius took part. We have already drawn heavily on this document for help in understanding Ignatius' teaching. What is relevant to our present question is that the document, which is mainly an account of developing a method of discerning God's will for a group, never speaks of any other mode of discernment than the third. Their way of proceeding is stated briefly and simply.

> We began, therefore, to expend every human effort. We proposed to ourselves some questions worthy of careful *consideration* and *forethought* at this opportune time. Throughout the day we were accustomed to *ponder* and *meditate* on these and prayerfully to *search into* them. At night each one shared with the group what he judged to be more appropriate and helpful, with the intention that

---

[42] *Obras Completas*, p. 945.

[43] The full significance of this last point will come out when Ignatius' ultimate ground for conviction about the conclusion of a sound discernment is brought to light. See below, chapters 15–16.

247

all with one mind would embrace the truer way of thinking tested and commended by the *more powerful reasons* and by majority vote.[44]

That the "reasons" spoken of are the advantages and disadvantages for the greater service and glory of God, which are sought for in the third mode of the election, can be seen in a later passage which takes up the main deliberation after the friends had taken some time to improve their dispositions for discernment.

> With the foregoing spiritual dispositions, we arranged to assemble all prepared the following day. Each one was to declare all those disadvantages which could be brought against obedience [by a vow to one of our group], all the reasons which presented themselves and which anyone of us had found in his own private reflection, meditation, and prayer. What he had gathered, each in his turn was to make known.[45]

> On the next day we argued for the opposite side of the question, each one putting before the group all the advantages and good consequences of such obedience which he had drawn from prayer and meditation.[46]

Examples of these reasons are given,[47] and the main reasons for their conclusion are all plainly third-time evidence.[48]

We may reasonably think that these men experienced spiritual consolation and desolation during this time, and the document states that their work was "completed and terminated in a spirit of gladness and harmony."[49] There is not a single hint that any consolations or desolations which they may have experienced were such as to pro-

---

[44] Jules Toner, "The Deliberation," p. 187.

[45] Ibid., p. 201.

[46] Ibid., p. 203.

[47] Ibid., pp. 202–205.

[48] Ibid., p. 205.

[49] Ibid., p. 208. The most that could be attributed with any reasonableness whatever to the expression "gladness and harmony" in this context would be that it was some helpful but altogether unnecessary confirmation for a decision which rested on third–time evidence. There is, however, really no good reason for thinking the experience was a spiritual consolation rather than merely a good feeling over having carried out together a very difficult and wearing undertaking.

vide a second-time kind of evidence or even any needed confirmation of a tentative third-time decision. Much less is there any indication that their conclusion rested mainly on such second-time evidence, not even in combination with third-time evidence. An account such as that given in this document, which is so attentive to method,[50] would hardly omit mention of the role that second-time evidence played if it were significant in their search for God's will.

If this third mode of discerning God's will can suffice for a group faced with making a decision of supreme importance to them all, then surely it can suffice for an individual.

There are other instances of important decisions by Ignatius for which there is no evidence that he used any mode of discernment other than the third: his discernment on whether to undertake studies; his discernment, during the years of study, on whether to move from Barcelona to Salamanca and from there to Paris; his discernments regarding Jesuits in general and Francis Borgia in particular accepting ecclesiastical dignities; his discernment about offering his resignation as general of the Society of Jesus. All these will be considered in the next chapter, where the value Ignatius put on the third mode of discerning God's will is discussed at length.[51] Besides the indications of the autonomy of the third mode which are found in Ignatius' own discernments, there are indications to be found in the Constitutions of the Society of Jesus, wherever he instructs superiors on how to make the decisions that are the responsibility of their office. These instructions will also be discussed in the next chapter.[52]

The foregoing evidence, drawn from Ignatius' own writing and *The Deliberation of the First Fathers* to establish his thought on the autonomy of the third mode, receives powerful confirmation from the early directories of Polanco, Miró, Dávila, Cordeses, and the Official Directory of 1599. Dávila and the Official Directory both explicitly declare in a general way that the third mode is more secure than the second.[53] If it is, then it must also be independent of the

---

[50] Ibid., p. vi.

[51] See below, pp. 258–265.

[52] See below, pp. 266–269.

[53] Dávila's directory, [129, 140] in *DirSpEx*MHSJ, pp. 518, 521; Official Directory of 1599, [190, 203–204], (ibid., pp. 701, 707–709).

second—unless the two modes are to be thought of as always mutually dependent, which is certainly not the case according to these directories. Polanco takes a particular case, when the conclusions of the second and third modes of discerning are in conflict and the second-time movements are uncertainly from God while the third-time reasons are clearly sound ones. In that case, Polanco says that the conclusion from the third mode is to be preferred and followed as more secure.[54] The clear implication is that the third mode can be trustworthy independently of the second. The same opinion is to be found in Miró, Dávila, Cordeses, and the Official Directory. All of these give the same direction as Polanco.[55]

Autonomy of the Second Mode

What about the second mode of seeking God's will? Can it serve to find God's will independently, without any support from the third mode? Some recent authors think not.[56] The Ignatian tradition from earliest times onward favors the autonomy of this mode. The passages noted above to show the autonomy of every mode of Ignatian election[57] are enough to reveal the mind of Ignatius on this question. The clear and certain belief in the autonomy of the second mode found in the directories supports this conclusion.[58] But it must be said that, compared with the evidence in the writings of Ignatius for the autonomy of the third mode, the evidence for the autonomy of the second is very slight.[59] It is difficult to find any account of

---

[54] Polanco's directory, no. 88, in *DirSpEx*MHSJ, p. 316.

[55] Miró, no. 87, in *DirSpEx*MHSJ, pp. 401–402; Dávila, [142], ibid., p. 522; Cordeses [139], ibid., pp. 557–558, and see [138], p. 557; Official Directory [207], ibid., pp. 709–711 and see [223], p. 719.

[56] John Futrell does not seem to allow for discernment by consolations alone; the function of these in his description of the structure of discernment is to confirm reasons, third–time evidence. (See above, pp. 238–239.) Ladislas Orsy, in *Probing the Spirit* (Denville, N.J.: Dimension Books, 1976), pp. 54–57 and 64–68, clearly and with reasons forcefully stated rejects discernment based on second–time experiences alone. Whether Orsy thinks this is Ignatius' view as well as his own he does not indicate; his arguments are presented without any reference to what Ignatius said. Those who think that doing the kind of reasoning done in the second mode of discernment is to include the third mode in the second logically imply that the second is not autonomous. It is not clear that all of them recognize this.

[57] See above, pp. 245–246.

[58] Polanco, no. 85 in *DirSpEx*MHSJ, p. 315; no. 88, ibid., p. 316. Miró, 87, ibid., p. 402; Dávila, [129], ibid., p. 518; Cordeses, [132], ibid., p. 556.

[59] This is a surprising fact and ironical to anyone who has read much of the more recent literature on Ignatian discernment, especially since Karl Rahner's *Dynamic Element*, in 1958.

Ignatius in his spiritual maturity, alone or with others, making a second-time election of any importance with which he did not combine the third-time—nothing comparable with the account in the *Deliberation of the First Fathers*, nothing comparable with the series of third-time discernments noted above and to be discussed further on. There is no statement in which he explicitly says in so many words that the second mode alone is enough, as he does say of the third mode in his letter to de Vergara.

Should the Autonomous Modes Be Combined?

Does the fact that each fully distinct Ignatian mode of seeking God's will can function autonomously imply that, when the person has sound and sufficient evidence for a decision by one mode, there is no reason to seek evidence by another mode? Or is it advisable, even required, for a well-made discernment to seek other evidence to be obtained by another autonomous mode of discernment? The question is not merely whether one can or may, if one so desires, seek further evidence by another mode. The question is whether one is well-advised to do so or even ought to do so. The question is not merely whether, in the process of seeking confirmation of a tentative decision already made by one mode, the discerner ought to look for some confirming (or disconfirming) evidence of a kind proper to another mode. That we should do so has already been shown in the chapter on confirmation. The question now is whether, when it is reasonably possible, it is better to carry out both the second and the third modes of the discernment process completely, testing each by the other and hoping to find their conclusions in agreement.

If it turns out that, whenever it is reasonably possible, one ought to combine the distinct second and third modes, will that call into question their mutual autonomy? Not at all. For there will be times when combining them is not reasonably possible, times when one does combine them but only one leads to a conclusion by evidence that can be seriously considered, or times when they will come to conflicting conclusions.[60] In all these situations, it may be possible to reach a trustworthy conclusion by one mode only.

The evidence for Ignatius' thought on combining the two

---

[60] See above, p. 250.

251

modes is somewhat ambiguous. The texts from the *Spiritual Exercises*[61] and his autograph directory[62] which provide clear evidence for the autonomy of each mode of election seem also to indicate that there is never any need for combining the modes if, by one of them, the discerner has reached what seems to be a sound and trustworthy decision. If a first-time experience, Ignatius says, is not given, God's will should be sought by the second mode. If by that mode a trustworthy conclusion is not reached, the third should be tried. Does not this way of speaking, at least at first glance, imply that the second mode of election is to be used only when a satisfactory decision is not reached by the first and, in a parallel way, the third is to be used only when a satisfactory decision is not reached by the second? If so, is Ignatius not implying that no combination of these modes is needed or even recommended?

On closer consideration, that certainly does not seem to be what he means. His fundamental teaching on the conditions for sound discernment of God's will and his own practice as seen in his spiritual diary forbid thinking so, unless we are to think that Ignatius was inconsistent on this point. Even if he was, the evidence on the side of combining the two modes is so much stronger and so much more coherent with the rest of his thought that it must be taken as more authentic.[63]

In his *Spiritual Diary*, both before the tentative decision (on February 9) and then while seeking confirmation of it, Ignatius time and again goes from the second to the third mode of discernment and from the third to the second.[64] The two kinds of distinct but converging evidence show that one same alternative, perfect poverty, is that to which God is moving Ignatius' will and that which appears to be more for the service and glory of God or more like the poor and humiliated Jesus.

---

[61] *SpEx*, [175–178].

[62] *DirAutog*, [18–20].

[63] Maurice Giuliani says that the second and third modes of discernment "call for each other and complement each other. St.Ignatius himself gives us a luminous example in his *Journal*" ("Movements of the Spirit," *Finding God in All Things*, p. 273, note 15).

[64] See the entries for Feb. 6, 8, 10, 11, 16, 22 (especially 16; here he speaks three times of going over the reasons of his third-time election). The two modes even come together so that he experiences spiritual consolation while considering the reasons (advantages and disadvantages) for complete poverty.

What is critically significant to notice is that Ignatius was not using the third mode because the evidence in the second was not by itself abundant or clear enough. It was extraordinarily powerful evidence. Why, then, did he make such a careful and thorough third mode of discernment and keep coming back to it time and again during his second-time discernment? On the other hand, one could hardly expect to have the balance in a third-time discernment more heavily weighted on one side than was the case in his third-time "election on poverty." Why then does he bother with a complete second-time election?[65]

Neither of the above questions can be fully answered until we have studied how firm an assent Ignatius thought could be given to the conclusion of a sound discernment and, especially, on what grounds he thought that assent ultimately rested.[66] At present, however, a satisfactory answer can be offered, based on what has been found about our relationship with God in discernment and the conditions for sound discernment. We have seen that Ignatius held no hope of finding God's will unless we could justifiably believe the Holy Spirit had led us. To believe that the Holy Spirit has led us, Ignatius thought, we must do our very best not only to become open to the Spirit but also to carry out the search for God's will in the discernment process.[67] It seems evident that for Ignatius, especially in what he considered a critically important decision, doing his best meant seeking God's will not only energetically and perseveringly but also in all the ways he reasonably could—therefore, by both the second and third modes when these were reasonably possible. Even if we allow for the case in which the evidence by one mode is such that it cannot be reasonably doubted, still as a general rule Ignatius seemed to think that an effort to combine the second and third modes is called for. Otherwise, his procedure recounted in his diary makes no sense.

What of his third-time discernments noted above in which we

---

[65] Some will surely want to answer this second question by saying, "Because he did not trust a third-time decision." But then it seems that consistency requires that a parallel reason be given in answer to the previous question; namely, he made also a third mode of discernment despite the powerful second–time evidence because he did not trust the second mode of discernment. Neither answer fits within the context of all that Ignatius has written.

[66] See below, chapter 15.

[67] See above, chapters 4 and 6. See also Jules Toner, A Commentary, pp. 157–160.

have no indication of any second-time discernment combined with them? Perhaps God did not give him second-time experiences during those discernments or not such clear and certain experiences that he was willing to base a decision on them. One can always try the third mode after the second; but one cannot undertake the second unless God gives the spiritual experiences which are data for that mode. Even Ignatius, who in his later years had the grace to find God at any time he desired, could not find second-time experiences whenever he would. Finding God present in himself and in all things does not necessarily include experiencing the volitional impulse toward one or another alternative for choice; and without that impulse no consoling experience of God is a second-time experience.[68]

Summary

What has been found in this chapter can be summed up in four main points. (1) The three Ignatian modes of discerning God's will have a common basic structure, one which is found in any intelligent human deliberation. (2) Each mode is clearly and fully distinct from the others by reason of its distinct kind of data, principles, or norms for critical evaluation and interpretation of the data, and the kind of evidence for the conclusion which it provides. (3) Each mode is also autonomous, that is, it can lead to a trustworthy conclusion without dependence on either of the other modes; it is, of course, not autonomous in the sense that it can do so without dependence on the Holy Spirit. (4) Whenever it is reasonably possible, however, a combination of the second and third modes is desirable for greater security and is even requisite, it seems, if the discerner is to fulfill the second essential condition for sound discernment, namely, doing one's best in seeking to find God's will.

---

[68] See above, pp. 134–138.

Chapter 14
A Special Question: What Is the Value of the Third Mode?

*E*ven if it is clear that Ignatius did understand each mode of election to be distinct and autonomous from the other two, there are several closely related questions which are discussed in recent writing on Ignatian discernment. The first of these concerns the value which Ignatius placed on the third mode. "Ignatius," writes one distinguished Ignatian scholar, "never at any time had great confidence in a choice made in the third time."[1] Another declares in favor of "the thesis that every individually important question [regarding God's will] can be clarified only by this method of the

---

[1] William Peters, *The Spiritual Exercises of St. Ignatius*, p. 126.

Second Mode of Election.''[2] These statements are representative of what is found in much of the most respected recent literature on Ignatian discernment.

One may reasonably wonder whether this recent trend is not an equally extreme reaction to a previous extreme which put the whole emphasis on the third mode and paid scant attention to the second. What was found in the preceding chapter on the autonomy which Ignatius (and the directories) gave to each mode and on the desirability of combining the second and third when reasonably possible, along with what will be shown in this chapter, will, I hope, help to restore Ignatius' more inclusive and balanced teaching.

In recent writing two other questions are closely bound up with the above question and given much attention. One is the question whether Ignatius gave a preferential status to the second mode of election. This second question is not the same as the first; for, even if Ignatius did value the third mode very much, he could still have valued the second even more. Leo Bakker sees a development in Ignatius' thought. Ignatius, he argues, at an early period (until 1539) gave priority to the first mode. Later (1539-1541) he transferred that priority to the second mode. Finally, in his most mature years, he valued the third most of all.[3] Others see the second mode as unquestionably the mode which Ignatius always emphasized and preferred for himself and others. They hold that, during the years after Ignatius' death, there was a regrettable development away from his authentic teaching, one that gave priority to the third mode.[4] One could hold either of these theses or neither of them and still admit that Ignatius greatly valued the third-time election as an autonomous mode. A third question commonly dealt with in relation to the preceding two is this: Which mode did Ignatius consider to be the normal one?

Each of the three questions does suggest the other two, but each is entirely distinct from the others. Assuming that the answer to one includes the answer to one or both of the others has led to some confused writing and to unjustifiable conclusions.

---

[2] Karl Rahner, *Dynamic Element*, p. 167.

[3] Leo Bakker, *Freiheit und Erfahrung* (Wurzburg: Echter, 1970), pp. 279–285.

[4] Jacques Roi, S.J., develops this thesis in "L'election d'apres Saint Ignace," RAM, 38 (1962), pp. 305–322.

It is only the first question with which I intend to deal, namely, whether Ignatius set much value on the third mode of seeking God's will. It is theoretically more fundamental than the other two and practically far more urgent. Asking which mode is to be preferred is, at least from a practical point of view, a question of no great significance. The better way for each one is whichever way the Holy Spirit makes possible; and, as has been shown, whenever it is reasonably possible to combine the second and third modes, that is a better way than to trust one of these modes alone. As for which mode Ignatius thought the normal or usual one among good Christians, it must be said that he never declared his mind on the matter; and any attempt to answer the question on the basis of his own practice is no more valid than trying to judge by his own mystical prayer life[5] what he thought to be the normal mode of prayer among good Christians.

Reasons Given for Devaluing the Third Mode

Several reasons for asserting that Ignatius had slight regard for the third mode are stated over and over again: (1) Ignatius in his own discernment did not make much use of it; (2) in his instructions for others, he set little store by it because he did not see it as reliable; (3) in particular, he would not trust a discernment of a state of life made by the third mode. Behind these reasons there appears to be the idea that Ignatius thinks the discerner in the second mode is under the influence of the Holy Spirit, whereas in the third mode the discerner is "on his own," is "left to fend for himself by the modest self-help of rational reflections."[6] Let us call each of these reasons into question and examine the evidence for and against them.

1. Did Ignatius Himself Make Much Use of the Third Mode in His Own Discernment?

A study of the accounts we have shows that the third mode

---

[5] Leaving aside the question of what Ignatius thought, if any assertion of what is in fact the normal mode of discerning God's will among good Christians is to be taken seriously, it would have to be based on careful investigation by investigators deeply knowlegeable about the several modes of discerning and highly skilled in questioning and statistical projections. Who has ever done any such work?

[6] Karl Rahner, *Dynamic Element*, p. 105; see all of pp. 103–108. A more moderate interpretation along the same lines is that of Thomas Green. (See below, Appendix B, pp. 324–325.)

played a major role in Ignatius' own discernments. At least in the accounts of the discernments he made after arriving at some mature judgment in spiritual matters, he rarely, if ever, came to a decision about God's will on any significant question without using the third mode either alone or in combination with the second—and then not merely as a preparation for the second but as a coordinate mode. The evidence for his use of it is at least equally as abundant as that for his use of the second mode, in fact even more abundant than for the latter. Let us look at some of the key discernments in Ignatius' life after his return from his frustrated attempt to live and serve God in the Holy Land.

Decision to Study

When Ignatius went to the Holy Land, he had every intention of remaining there, visiting the holy places and doing what he could to "help souls."[7] His way of life seemed clear to him. In obedience to the Franciscan provincial, however, he had to return to Europe. (The provincial held authority from the Holy See over pilgrims and had very sound reasons for sending Ignatius back home.) Now, Ignatius understood, "it was not the will of God that he remain in Jersualem" as he had intended.[8] Interestingly and perhaps significantly, this is the first time in the autobiography that Ignatius uses the phrase "the will of God."[9]

What was God's will for him in this new situation? Ignatius tells us that he "continually pondered within himself what he should do and finally was more inclined to study for some time in order to be able to help souls."[10] The question for discernment at this juncture of his life was crucial. The consequences of his decision turned out to be momentous. But all the record we have of how he arrived at his decision is contained in that one sentence. That sentence points to a discernment by the third mode: posing the question; pondering on it to see what will be more for the help of souls, more for God's glory in them; coming to a decision that studies more than any other

---

[7] *Autobiog*, [45].

[8] Ibid., [50].

[9] Nicholas King, "Ignatius Loyola and Decision Making," pp. 51–52. King's remarks on this whole incident are enlightening.

[10] *Autobiog*, [50].

real alternative which he could see would enable him to be of help to souls. That a man of his years and temperament should choose to begin studies for the sake of a more effective apostolate is a sure sign of his indifference to all but God's will, of his freedom to undertake anything with trust in God.[11] There is no mention of anything which suggests discernment by consolation and desolation as in the second mode; nor is there any suggestion of a first-time experience.

Consequent to the decision to study, there were two similar decisions: the first was to go from Barcelona to Salamanca to continue studies there;[12] the second was to leave Salmanca for Paris to study there.[13] In each case, more clearly in the second than the first, the decision rests on evidence of the kind found in the third mode of discernment: he could escape the limitations put by ecclesiastical officials on his efforts to help souls for God's glory while continuing his studies. If there was any second-time evidence (and, for all we know, there may have been), Ignatius does not mention it.

Decisions about Founding the Society of Jesus

What might, from the apostolic point of view, be considered the most important discernment in which Ignatius was ever involved was that of his companions and himself on the question whether God willed for them to take a vow of obedience to one of their number and so constitute a religious community. The result of this discernment, they saw, would be decisive for each and for the group as a whole, determining their state of life in the Church, provided that the pope ratified their decision. All the evidence we have shows without any doubt an election purely in the third mode, as we have seen.[14]

After finding God's will regarding that question, they sought

---

[11] Nicholas King, "Ignatius Loyola and Decision Making," p. 51. To see Ignatius' freedom of spirit based on trust in God when carrying out his decisions which he saw as God's will, see *Autobiog,* chapters 6–8, especially [63] and [71].

[12] *Autobiog*, [63].

[13] Ibid., [70–71].

[14] See above, pp. 247–249.

and found by the same method God's will on a number of further important questions regarding their life and work together.[15]

Decision about Poverty in the Society of Jesus

Later on, Ignatius was elected superior general and assigned to draw up constitutions for the approval of the whole group. During this work he wrote that part of his *Spiritual Diary* on his election regarding poverty, from which we have already drawn so much of our understanding of Ignatian discernment. Among other things, we saw what an important part the third mode of election played in combination with (not merely in subordination to) the second mode.[16]

Decision about the Cardinalate for Borgia

Another discernment about which we have some account in one of his letters (June 5, 1552) is the one he made when he heard that Emperor Charles V wished to have Francis Borgia made a cardinal.[17] This letter, so it seems to me, is quite facilely interpreted by some as if it gave evidence of a second-time discernment. Put in context and carefully studied, however, it seems rather to be an account of another third-time discernment.

When Ignatius heard of the emperor's intention, he says, "Immediately I had the idea or inclination to prevent it in any way I could." To understand this immediate reaction and to understand the discernment which follows, both must be seen in continuity with earlier events. In 1546 Ferdinand, king of the Romans, wanted to have Claude Jay, one of Ignatius' first companions, made bishop of Trieste. Ignatius wrote to Ferdinand telling him that one of the best means that could be imagined for ruining the Society of Jesus would be accepting a bishopric. Doing so would be "the undoing of the spirit of the Society" and so be its destruction. Then also, there was the very practical reason that there were only nine professed members of the Society, four or five of whom had already been presented for bishoprics, which they refused. If Jay were to accept, how could others be refused and where then would be the

---

[15] *Deliberatio Primorum Patrum,* [9] in *Cons*MHSJ, I, p. 7 and *Conclusiones Septem Sociorum,* ibid., pp. 9–14.

[16] See above, pp. 252–253.

[17] For a translation of this letter, see above, pp. 47–49.

Society of Jesus? Besides, the acceptance of even one would set tongues wagging and all would be suspect of ambition—with immense harm to their apostolate.

These and added reasons which Ignatius had are detailed in a letter from Bartolomeu Ferrão to Michael de Torres.[18] This letter gives a full account of the intense and long struggle that went on in Rome after Ferdinand wrote to the pope in an effort to persuade him to command Jay to accept the bishopric of Trieste. It tells how Ignatius tirelessly sought the help of cardinals and other influential persons in Rome, and finally the influence of Margaret of Austria, daughter of Emperor Charles V and wife of Ottavio Farnese. In this letter the attempt to impose a bishopric on Jay is spoken of as "a trial and scourge,"[19] and as "a secret persecution which the enemy of human nature [Satan] has these days been waging against the Society [of Jesus]."[20]

In light of Ignatius' response to the proposal of making Jay a bishop, it is understandable why his immediate response to the proposal of making Borgia a cardinal was to do all he could to prevent it. On the other hand, he also says that "many reasons on one side and on the other occurred to me"; therefore, he was uncertain of God's will.[21] Should he follow his immediate response and oppose as much as he could the plan of the emperor and pope? If he did, he might be in opposition to God's will. In this painful state of tension, he set about praying and discerning.

"Pondering on the matter and discussing it from time to time" during three days, Ignatius at times felt the fear of going against God's will and at other times was free of such fears. Such pondering and discussing were surely concerned with "the many reasons on the one side and on the other" of which he wrote a few lines earlier, that is, the advantages and disadvantages for the greater service and glory of God.[22] Everything points to the conclusion that he is de-

---

[18] *LettersIgn*, pp. 115–120. Bartolomeu Ferrão was Ignatius' secretary at the time and wrote the letter at Ignatius' order.

[19] Ibid., p. 120.

[20] Ibid., p. 115.

[21] See above, p. 48.

[22] The reader would do well to read the whole letter, given above on pp. 48–49. By referring to it, my argument can be followed more easily and checked against the actual text.

scribing a discernment by the third mode of seeking God's will. Finally, he tells Borgia, on the third day he came to "a fully settled judgment" with a tranquil will.

Those who want to find a second-time discernment here appeal to this tranquil will at the end of the discernment as a sign of such a discernment. They also appeal to the earlier passage where Ignatius speaks of sometimes experiencing fear during his praying and pondering, experiencing no liberty of spirit to speak against and prevent the emperor's project, and of sometimes experiencing the contrary, freedom from fear and freedom to oppose the emperor. Such an interpretation is at the very best highly dubious. The tranquil will at the end of the discernment appears to be the affective accompaniment or consequence of reaching a settled judgment rather than evidence on which the judgment is based. As for his earlier experience of fear to oppose the project lest he oppose God's will, this does not at all appear to be a spiritual desolation, but only the consequence of seeing good reasons on the side of making Borgia a cardinal. Likewise, the experience of being relieved of this fear does not seem to be a spiritual consolation at all, but only the consequence of seeing stronger reasons on the side of opposing the emperor's project.

In any case, even if there should be signs of a second-time discernment, the third-time mode is still clearly involved and even seems clearly to be the dominant mode. The foregoing interpretation is supported by what Ignatius adds when explaining how his conclusion would still be sound even if it should turn out that God was leading others to think differently than himself and led them actually to make Borgia a cardinal: "The same Divine Spirit is able to move me toward that action for certain reasons and for other reasons to move others toward the contrary action."[23] To be led by the Holy

---

[23] See above, pp. 50–53.

Spirit through reasons is proper to the third mode; as we saw, the second mode is *sine ratiociniis*.[24]

Decision to Offer Resignation

Another election to which Ignatius must have attached the greatest importance was the one regarding the question of his resignation as superior general of the Society of Jesus. In January 1551, at a gathering in Rome of the professed Jesuits, Ignatius presented an account of his discernment, along with his petition to have his resignation accepted. There is no detailed description of the discernment process such as is found in his *Spiritual Diary*, but what he does say in this brief document indicates a third-time election. While the second mode of election may have played a part in the process, nothing he says suggests it.[25]

In fact, so clearly is this the case that, in order to show it, all that has to be done is to present the document and insert references to paragraphs in the *Spiritual Exercises* where Ignatius describes the third-time mode of election. (The emphases found in the following quotation are in every case my own, given to call attention to significant phrases.)

> 1. On various occasions over months and years while *free from any interior or exterior perturbation,* [177, 179] I have *thoughtfully considered* [180] this matter and as far as I can perceive and understand, *before my Creator and Lord, who has to judge me always* [187], I shall, to the greater praise and glory of his divine majesty

---

[24] See above, p. 141. A reader might understand the "reasons" of which Ignatius speaks in this passage as reasons which the divine Spirit has for moving Ignatius one way and others another way rather than the reasons which Ignatius and the others have for their decisions. However, the fact that Ignatius says that he saw sets of reasons for both sides and that he shows himself to be at first troubled and hesitant because of the good reasons he sees against his own spontaneous inclination—all this argues for understanding the "reasons" spoken of as reasons in his mind and in the minds of those whom he is opposing.

[25] It might be said that second-time evidence, spiritual consolations with volitional drawing, would not be in place in such a document and, therefore, Ignatius omitted it. Given the relationship between Ignatius and this group, the close bond and their understanding of his teaching on discernment, that is a suggestion not easily granted. Even if granted for the sake of the discussion, it is clear that the third-time evidence played a major role in his coming to his decision; there is no reason to think that second-time evidence was either necessary or of greater importance.

declare what I have perceived about the matter in question.

2. Examining honestly and *without any strong emotion* [177, 179] what I perceived in myself, I have at many different times *come to the realistic judgment that, as a consequence of my numerous sins, numerous imperfections, and numerous infirmities of mind and body, I lack to an almost measureless degree the endowments required for bearing the burden of governing the Company [of Jesus]* [181], a burden I bear at present because I was persuaded to yield to the imposition of it.

3. I desire in our Lord that this matter be very seriously looked into and that another be elected who will *fulfill better or not as badly* [181] the office which I hold of governing the Company [of Jesus].

4. When such a person is elected, I likewise desire that the office be given to him.

5. Not only does my desire hold firm, but also my *judgment based on manifold reasons* [182] that this office should be given not only to one who would do better than or not as badly as I, but [even] to one who would do [only] equally as well.

6. With full consideration, in the name of the Father, of the Son, and of the Holy Spirit, my one and only God and Creator, I lay down and renounce simply and absolutely the office which I hold, petitioning and imploring in the Lord with all my soul the professed as also those who wish to join them to please accept my offered resignation which is *so greatly justified* [181, 182] before His Divine Majesty.

7. If any disagreement should be found among those who have to admit and judge this petition, I beg that for love and reverence of God our Savior, they would please commend the matter very much to His Divine Majesty in order that his most holy will be done entirely, to his greater glory and to the greater universal good of souls and of the Company [of Jesus]. Let all be undertaken in

view of His Divine Majesty's greater praise and glory forever.[26]

2. Did Ignatius Recommend and Teach the Third Mode of Discernment to Others as a Trustworthy Mode of Seeking God's Will?

Even if the facts were otherwise than we have seen them to be, even if it were true that Ignatius did not make much use of the third mode of discerning God's will, that would in no way justify the conclusion that he thought it to be of little use for anyone else— as some writers think. Ignatius was not one who thought that his own way of doing things should be normative for all others. In fact, he denounced that kind of thinking as one of the worst mistakes that can be made in spiritual matters.[27] On the other hand, the fact that in his own discernment Ignatius did greatly value the third mode of seeking God's will does not itself justify concluding that he thought it to be equally valuable for others. But it does justify thinking he would see it as at least one possible trustworthy mode for discernment for anyone.

To show more than that we will have to go to his instructions for others. There the same esteem for this mode is evident. In fact, the great concern which Ignatius shows for teaching and encouraging the use of the third mode of discerning God's will appears to be such that readers of his writing on discernment who have not been affected by the trend in recent Ignatian scholarship to devaluate the third mode might well wonder why the question of its value has been raised at all. Let us look at some of the evidence for saying this.

The Spiritual Exercises on the Third Mode of Discernment

The heading given to the section in the *Spiritual Exercises* where Ignatius explains the three times for making a sound election and gives instruction on how to carry out the third-time election reads, "Three Times in Any One of Which a Sound and Trustworthy

---

[26] *Obras Completas*, p. 757.
[27] FN, I, 676. See also *EppIgn* V, 714.

265

Election Can Be Made.''[28] The key phrase for our present discussion is ''in any one of which'' (*en cada uno de ellos*). If taken at face value, this phrase leaves no ambiguity: each and every one of the three ways of making an election, the third as well as the first and second, is said to be a sound and trustworthy way.

That Ignatius meant this phrase to be taken at face value and applied to the third mode of election as well as to the first and second is given significant support by the relative amount of space given to the instruction on the third mode and the detail into which he goes.[29] Why should Ignatius, in such a compressed little book, devote so much space to something of little or no importance?

The Constitutions on the Third Mode

The most abundant and clear evidence of how Ignatius valued the third mode of discerning God's will for others is in the Constitutions of the Society of Jesus, where he instructs superiors in the Society on when and how to discern God's will in matters of critical importance for the Society and its work, and where he sets down procedures for the general congregation.

Those who have to make the decision to accept or reject a candidate for probation in the Society of Jesus are warned by Ignatius about the need for freedom from any motive for their decision save the service and glory of God in accord with the Society's Institute. They are told to be familiar with the norms by which the candidate's aptitude can be evaluated [142–145],[30] and a long list of such norms is given [147–160]. Ignatius sees the difficulty in the concrete case of balancing out the positive and negative qualifications of a can-

---

[28] *SpEx*, [175].

[29] See *SpEx*, [175–188]. The many paragraphs devoted to the third-time election are in striking contrast to the one brief sentence devoted to each of the other two times and, in any case, surprising in such a compressed little book. One might be tempted to draw more far-reaching conclusions from this fact; all I wish to point out is the minimal conclusion that seems demanded, the incompatibility of this fact with the idea that Ignatius set no great value on the third-time election and did not trust it for making any important decision. The fact under consideration is made more significant and the conclusion from it given greater force when we see in the *Spiritual Exercises*, [337–344] that Ignatius devotes more pages in his rules for almsgiving to instruction on third-time discernment; for these rules are clearly concerned with a third-time discernment. (See above, pp. 188–189.)

[30] The references to the Constitutions of the Society of Jesus in this section are so numerous that it would be more convenient to insert the paragraph numbers in the body of the text rather than in the footnotes.

didate who may be highly qualified in some respects and lacking in others [161–162]. "But the Holy Unction of the divine wisdom" he says, "will teach [1 John 2:20, 27] the mean which should be retained in all this . . . "[161], that is, will enlighten the discerner's reason so as to evaluate reasonably the positive and negative qualifications of the candidate, giving neither too much nor too little weight to any of them and judging correctly the case as a whole.[31] Impulses in consolation are not given to help one judge correctly in the matter but only to judge to what God is drawing him.

When it is a question of dismissing one who is unsuitable for life in the Society of Jesus, Ignatius makes clear the motive and fundamental norm which should govern the discernment about it, that is, "the service of God our Lord by helping souls who are his" [204]—a norm for third-time discernment. The one who has the authority and responsibility to make the decision should ponder before God the *reasons* which suffice for dismissal [209], which Ignatius discusses under four headings [210–217]. He should pray that God will make his will known [220] and should seek out and listen to the opinion of others who can make good judgments [221]. Ridding himself of all affections except for the divine glory and the common good, "he should *weigh the reasons on both sides*, and make his decision to dismiss or not" [222] (emphasis mine). Without doubt, these are directives for a third-time discernment.

The superior also has authority and responsibility to try to find God's will regarding where to send those subject to his authority [621–622], what works to undertake [623], how many and whom to send [624]. Ignatius' instructions to the superior when seeking to find God's will in these matters are, if anything, even more clearly instructions for third-time discernment. The fundamental norm in all these discernments is the norm proper to the third mode, the

---

[31] In the context, it would not be reasonable to take the phrase "holy unction of divine wisdom" as signifying second-time experiences of consolation; to do so would constitute a sudden break from the line of thought about finding and weighing positive and negative qualifications. See also [414], where the unction of the Holy Spirit seems even more clearly a gift of the Spirit to help reason to evaluate advantages and disadvantages for the greater service of God in concrete situations. Even if the phrase "holy unction of divine wisdom" should be taken to mean second-time experiences of consolation with volitional drawing, it certainly does not do so exclusively; in context it would mean also the Spirit's enlightenment and guidance of reason in finding and weighing reasons.

greater service of God and the more universal good [622].[32] For each question, Ignatius develops this fundamental norm into more specific norms [622–624]. The whole section deals exclusively or almost exclusively with a rational search for and weighing of projected advantages and disadvantages for the greater service of God as judged by use of these specific norms.[33]

When Ignatius adds some counsel regarding the manner in which the superior is to send his men (with or without funds, with or without letters of recommendation, and so on), he tells the superior to "deliberate" on these matters in relation to "the greater edification of the neighbor and service of God our Lord and then decide what should be done"[625].[34]

When we look at Ignatius' directives for the supreme authority in the Society of Jesus, the general congregation, when making decisions of supreme importance to the whole Society, whether about electing a new superior general for the Society or about other decisions, we find the same emphasis on the third mode of discerning God's will.

When electing a general, the members are to keep a firm hold on the primary norm, "the greater service of God"[694, 698]. They are to pray for God's help and become well informed about those qualified for the office [694]. After some days for such prayer and gathering information, each one privately, without conferring with any other, is prayerfully to come to a decision *"by means of the information he has"* [701], that is, by reasons based on information, projected advantages or disadvantages for the greater service of God (emphasis mine). Each is to vote accordingly [701]. No mention is made of experiencing drawing in spiritual consolation. Allowance is made for the improbable but possible event of a "common inspiration" from the Holy Spirit "without waiting for methodical voting" [700].[35] For the rest, nothing Ignatius says suggests anything

---

[32] See above, pp. 173–175.

[33] Only once does Ignatius say anything that might suggest discernment in the second mode. In [624k] he uses the phrase "unction of the Holy Spirit." In this passage, the phrase cannot as surely be freed of ambiguity by the context as it is in [161] and [414]. (See above, note 31.) If Ignatius is thinking of second-time discernment in this passage, it is merely a passing reference to that mode embedded in a prolonged instruction on using the third mode.

[34] See also Ignatius' instructions to those who are sent, [633–634].

[35] For the meaning of this passage, see above, pp. 125–126.

other than the ordinary third mode of discernment by each member which issues in his vote.

On the way of reaching decisions about important matters other than the election of a superior general, Ignatius says very little; but again, what he says looks to the third mode of discerning God's will [711, 712, 715].[36]

In the overall picture, even if we can find a hint or two recommending second-time discernment when seeking God's will on administrative questions, Ignatius in the Constitutions puts heavy emphasis on the third mode and even seems to give it primacy.

More instances could be gathered of his recommendation of the third mode of discernment in preference to others as a trustworthy way of finding God's will. What has been already presented seems quite adequate.

3. Did Ignatius Trust the Third Mode when Discerning One's Vocation to a State of Life?

Even if Ignatius did set much store on the third mode, even if for some discernments he considered it preferable to the second mode, it might still be that, for at least one kind of discernment, that concerning one's call from God to a state of life, he considered the third mode inappropriate and untrustworthy. This opinion is presently rather widespread.[37]

The evidence, however, clearly and strongly supports the opposite view. In the *Spiritual Exercises*, the election which Ignatius

---

[36] Some, I have found, want to interpret a sentence in [711] as calling for a second-time discernment because Ignatius' reason for Masses and prayers to be offered is that "the light to perceive what can best be decided upon must come from the First and Supreme Wisdom." Such an interpretation can only be justified by an assumption, which I shall show to be untenable, namely, that in the third mode of discernment we are left on our own without divine guidance. (See below, pp. 271–273, and chapter 16.) Otherwise the sentence must be read without any conclusion as yet about what mode or modes of discernment Ignatius has in mind through which the First and Supreme Wisdom will give light. What follows in [711] and in [715] suggests a third mode of discernment.

[37] Karl Rahner denies any positive value to the third mode except as a way of returning to the second (*Dynamic Element*, pp. 97–100) and especially so when one is discerning a vocation from God (ibid., p. 167). William Peters even goes so far as to say the third mode does not belong in the Spiritual Exercises properly speaking (*The Spiritual Exercises of St. Ignatius*, pp. 126–127). Piet Penning De Vries does not exclude all positive value from the third mode but does exclude it as a way of making a vocation decision (*Discernment of Spirits*, pp. 63–64). John English also follows this line of interpretation (*Spiritual Freedom*, chapter 13, pp. 210–230).

has primarily in mind is an election of a state of life. No one, to my knowledge, denies this. Yet he speaks of three times "in any one of which a trustworthy election can be made."[38] He even speaks explicitly in one passage in the *Spiritual Exercises* of a third time of election as concerned with choosing a state of life.[39] He does the same in his autograph directory.[40] If all this is not enough, recall that Ignatius and his companions used the third mode to discern God's will regarding their own vocation, whether or not to vow obedience to one of their number and thus begin the Society of Jesus.[41] Recall too, that Ignatius plainly told Ramírez de Vergara that his third-time election to become a Jesuit was sufficient without second-time evidence, and that he should act on it. In fact, Ignatius implies in that letter that not acting after the third-time discernment would show a lack of trust in God.[42]

Add to the evidence from Ignatius' own writings the testimony of the early directories, especially that of his close associate, Polanco. These directories understand the instruction for the election in the *Spiritual Exercises* to be primarily for electing a state of life. Unless they say otherwise, their comments on the third, just as on the first and second, mode of election are concerned with a choice of vocation. That they have no doubt about the value of such a decision in the third mode appears with great clarity in what they say on two questions.

The first question involves what to do in an election regarding one's state of life when the second- and third-time elections reach contrary conclusions. Here they allow that, if the director has doubts about the movements in the second-time election, whereas the reasons in the third-time election seem sound, the decision should be

---

[38] *SpEx*, [175].

[39] Ibid., [177].

[40] In *DirAutog*, [18] Ignatius says that, if God does not move the person in the first time, he should insistently seek "to know his vocation" in the second. Then, in [19–20] Ignatius continues, if he does not come to a decision in the second, he should go to the third. In context there can be no reasonable doubt that the decision to be sought in the third mode is also a decision about his vocation from God. The objection might be raised that Ignatius would require the discerner to return to the second mode and would trust only the latter. That objection has been fully dealt with in chapters 11 and 13.

[41] See above, pp. 247–249, 259–260.

[42] See above, pp. 246–247.

made according to this latter mode.[43] Nothing is said or, given the conflict between the conclusions of the two modes, could reasonably be said in this situation about having to go back to the second mode, although many commentators say just that.[44] The advice given in the directories is simply to act on the decision by the third mode, even though it is in contradiction to the uncertain conclusion reached by the second mode.

In fact, even in a situation which allows for seeking consolations to confirm a decision reached in third-time discernment, both Polanco and the Official Directory explicitly reject the necessity of actually receiving such confirmation. This comes out clearly where they deal with the second question, what to do when nothing notable confirms or disconfirms the decision reached in the third mode. The decision, says Polanco, should be held to and "one should judge that God wishes his will to be found through the discourse of reason [*per discursum rationis*]."[45] Elsewhere, he writes that the director of the Exercises should beware of leading a discerner to one alternative or the other; rather, he should understand that his work is "to dispose the creature so that he may be instructed by his Creator either through inspiration and affective movement or through the discursive operation of the intellect."[46] How could he state more plainly that God teaches us his will by influencing our discursive reason in the third mode of discernment just as well as by influencing our will and affective acts and feelings in the second?

Did Ignatius Think the Holy Spirit Guides Our Reasoning in Third-Time Discernment?

As said above, behind all the reasons given for thinking that

[43] Polanco, no. 88, *DirSpEx* MHSJ, p. 316; Miró, no. 87, ibid., p. 402; Dávila, [142], ibid., p. 522; Cordeses, [139], ibid., pp. 557–558; Official Directory of 1599, [207], ibid., pp. 709–711.

[44] Polanco (no. 85, *DirSpEx*MHSJ, p. 314) does note that the exercise of the natural powers in the third mode of election disposes one for second-time experiences. To conclude from that remark, however, that he thought the third mode must lead to the second in order to arrive at a trustworthy decision would not only be logically illicit but also in conflict with what he is saying in this context and with what he says elsewhere, for example, in nos. 88 (p. 316) and 90 (p. 317).

[45] Polanco, no. 90, *DirSpEx*MHSJ, p. 317. The Official Directory, [232], ibid., p. 723 repeats Polanco's statement.

[46] Ibid., 84, 314.

271

Ignatius did not trust the third mode seems to be the idea that in the second God himself leads us to know his will, while in the third we are on our own, with nothing to count on but our natural reason using principles given us by faith.[47] But, in the light of what was said when we considered the meaning of using our natural powers freely and tranquilly in the third mode,[48] and in the light of what has been said in this chapter on how Ignatius himself used, trusted, and recommended the third mode in seeking God's will—in the light of all this, there can be no doubt that Ignatius believed the Holy Spirit to be actively directing us through the third mode of discernment just as well as through the second.

What is true is that ordinarily (not always) the influence of the Holy Spirit in the third mode of discerning God's will is not apparent as it is in the second. There is some parallel here with what Ignatius says about spiritual consolation and desolation. During spiritual consolation the loving presence and action of God is felt. But of the person in spiritual desolation, Ignatius says, "The divine aid . . . always remains with him even though he does not clearly perceive it." This divine aid is not a lesser aid than spiritual consolation; it is only a different kind of aid. So, also, the consolations given in the second time for an election, whatever else may be said about them as more excellent experiences of God, are not necessarily on that account greater aids to finding God's will than the Spirit's guidance in the third mode of discerning. This point will receive fuller development in our study of Ignatius' reason for conviction that God's will is found through sound discernment.

Another argument should be considered. If it were true that a conclusion of a third-time discernment is not trustworthy because during it the Holy Spirit leaves us to fend for ourselves, would there be any ground for trusting a second-time discernment either? Only recall how dependent the conclusion of a second-time discernment is on the use of natural reason after the initial data of consolation and drawing by the Holy Spirit are had. It is only by the use of natural reason to evaluate critically and interpret second-time experiences that we are able to get evidence and reach a decision. Is

---

[47] See above, p. 257.
[48] See above, pp. 169–171.

natural reason "on its own" in this reflective moment of second-time discernment of God's will? If so, the conclusion which is reached has no more value than the conclusion of reason on its own in third-time discernment. If, on the other hand, natural reason in second-time discernment is guided by the Holy Spirit, then why not in third-time discernment? In all logic we are forced to think that the Holy Spirit guides the natural working of faith-enlightened reason in both modes or in neither.

There are some who say that we can never be sure in either mode of discernment whether the Holy Spirit has guided us to our conclusion and, therefore, that we can never be sure of the conclusion reached by either of these modes. What was Ignatius' thought on this matter? Did he think we can find God's will and be justifiably confident that we have found it? That is a question of supreme importance in a study of Ignatian discernment. Drawing on all that has gone before, we can now try to answer it.

Chapter 15
What Kind of Assent Can Be Given to the Conclusion of a Sound Discernment?

*A*fter studying the meaning of God's will as object of discernment, the necessary conditions for sound discernment, and the modes of seeking God's will, we still have to ask in what sense Ignatius thinks we can find God's will.

The Question Clarified

That Ignatius was confident we can in some meaningful sense find God's will, there can be no reasonable doubt: all his writings and life testify to it. But in what sense? Does he mean that we can reach justifiably certain judgment or only a soundly probable one? If certain, with what kind of certainty? This is not the place to attempt any elaborate epistemological treatment of the modes of assent to a proposition. However, I shall try to clarify what I mean by the key terms to be used in posing the question and in attempting to answer it. This seems necessary for two reasons. The first is that, although my terms are traditional ones, I am not sure that all readers will understand them in the same way or grasp the precise meaning I have in mind. Second, although Ignatius did say enough for us to work out what his answer to the question would be if we could ask him, he did not take up the question thematically and gave us no set of terms for expounding his answer.

Assent to a proposition with certainty is, in general, assent without fear of error. If assent is without any fear of error because all possibility of error is thought to be excluded, the certainty is absolute. If assent is such as to allow for the possibility of error but is based on grounds that exclude any reasonable fear of error, the certainty is moral. Moral certainty can be more or less, as the grounds for assent more or less firmly exclude any reasonable fear of error. To say that certain assent (absolutely or morally certain) is given without fear of error is not to say that it is justifiably so given. There may or may not be grounds which actually justify the certainty with which assent is given. If there are such grounds, the person assenting may or may not be aware of them.

Whenever the person sees or thinks he sees grounds for reasonable fear of error, assent cannot be made with more than probability. Probability can be more or less as it approaches to or recedes from certainty and allows for contrary probability. It might be said with some reason that moral certitude, inasmuch as it still allows for the possibility of error, is really only extremely high probability, so high as to make fear of error unreasonable in the practical order. If so, the difference between it and probability in the ordinary meaning is still clear enough for our purposes. Two other key terms will be used: "practical certainty" and "faith conviction"; but these will be better explained in the contexts within which they are brought into use.

Can Evidence in Ignatian Discernment Justify Assenting with Certitude to the Conclusion?

When the evidence gathered in a sound discernment seems

sufficient for drawing a conclusion, that conclusion will follow from that evidence; and, of course, it will be a correct conclusion but will not necessarily be true. Our question is this: Did Ignatius think that a discerner can acquire a justifiable certainty, or at least a moral certainty, that the judgment about God's will which is reached at the conclusion of a sound discernment is *true*?

This question, for whatever reason, has rarely been seriously addressed in the literature on discernment.[1] With or without serious investigation to support it, the common view is that absolute certainty about God's will through discernment is not attainable, but only some kind of lesser certainty, which is variously labeled as moral, practical, spiritual, potential, reasonable, or subjective.[2] Others will speak only of a probably true conclusion.

The obvious way to go about answering our question seems to be by examining the kind of evidence in each of the three Ignatian modes of discernment to see what kind of assent each one can justify.

Certainty by Third-Time Evidence

Can projecting and weighing future advantages and disadvantages from different courses of action for the glory of God justify certainty, absolute or moral, of what is ultimately for the greater glory of God? Consider the limitation of my knowledge of the relevant information. There are always indefinitely more data of which I am unaware. Even supposing I had adequate information, think

---

[1] Few Ignatian scholars give evidence of seriously searching out Ignatius' own thought on this question; the answers they offer are usually their own rather than Ignatius' and are given without serious effort to justify them. Susan Rakoczy, in her study of the literature on discernment written in English between 1965 and 1978 (*The Structures of Discernment Processes*), finds that, apart from one exception, Karl Rahner, writers on discernment (Ignatian or other types) do not usually take up the question of certitude, and that those who do consider it treat it superficially, without clarity or systematic analysis, as if a matter of minor importance (pp. 193 and 205). Some seem to justify this attitude by saying that the important thing about discernment is not being sure of finding God's will but what goes on in the person seeking to find it. The latter benefit is without doubt a great one and sometimes of greater value than the decision reached; but, as I shall show, arriving at a justifiable conviction of having found God's will is also of greatest importance for living a Christian life. To the exception which Rakoczy makes of Karl Rahner as one who deals seriously with the question of what kind of assent can be given to the conclusion of a discernment, I must add one other, namely, Ladislas Orsy. See his essay "Toward a Theological Evaluation of Communal Discernment," *Studies in the Spirituality of Jesuits*, vol. 5, no. 5 (Oct. 1973) and his book *Probing the Spirit*. His understanding of discernment and his answer to the question we are discussing are very different from Rahner's, but both treat the question seriously and at some length.

[2] Susan Rokoczy, *The Structure of Discernment Processes*, pp. 193–206.

276

how much my temperament, my character, even my present mood, to say nothing of my assumptions and of unconscious forces at work in me, can affect my perception of the present, my memory of the past, and my projections of the future. Think how all these affect my way of sifting the data, projecting advantages and disadvantages, and comparatively weighing these.

Even leaving aside my limited information about the relevant facts and all the forces which affect my perception and interpretation of them, consider the impossibility of my knowing what will actually follow from any choice I make in a world shot through with contingency. Even if I could have a moral certainty that the immediate consequences of one alternative would be more for God's service, how could I know what would be better in the long run? To do so, I would have to know not merely all the actual consequences of my actual choice, even to the end of the world; I would have to know all the consequences that would follow through all time from each of the alternative choices if I had made it. In a world of interrelating forces beyond numbering, complex beyond all analyzing, and constantly changing not only by reason of natural evolution and chance but also by reason of multitudinous free choices, is it possible for me to make even a well-founded conjecture about which alternative for choice will turn out to be *ultimately* for the greater glory? All I can hope to reach is the well-founded opinion that the more or less immediate consequence of one alternative will be more for God's glory than the other. Even if I could have moral certitude regarding these consequences, I would still be altogether uncertain about what would be the consequences through the rest of history.

Could I, perhaps, at least in some cases, come to a moral certainty by looking at the past and seeing what God has been doing, where his providence has been leading me, and, by extension, where it will go now? Here again, my understanding of where the past has meant to lead me is not all that plain and sure. Even if it should be so, how do I know God has not planned some surprising change of direction, one of those crooked lines with which God is said to write straight?

Certainty by Second-Time Evidence

All the foregoing difficulties of projecting and weighing future advantages and disadvantages for God's glory are escaped in the first and second modes of discernment. The evidence in these modes answers a different question: To which choice is God moving me by interior impulses? Consider the second mode. Here the impulse itself carries no certitude that it is from God and toward what God wills. It is the matrix of spiritual consolation which indicates the source of the impulse.[3] Each such experience in which the impulse is marked by spiritual consolation as being from God gives some probability of what God wills. (Consolation without previous cause might be thought to be a special case. Whether it is or not can be taken up further on.) Plentiful evidence of this kind is called for in order to draw a trustworthy conclusion. Does this plentiful evidence justify certitude about the conclusion?

To answer that question affirmatively, many prior questions have to be answered affirmatively and with certainty. Was the consolation which I experienced prompted by the Holy Spirit? Was the volitional impulse, the drawing, integral with the spiritual consolation, not merely temporally related? In other words, can I be certain beyond all reasonable doubt that my experiences of consolation and volitional impulse do not arise from the influence of unconscious natural forces or from conscious but subtle and evasive self-centered desires and fears, or at least from the influence of these forces so closely and confusingly intermingled with living faith that I cannot with certainty discriminate one from the other? If I could be certain about the divine sources of the consolation and impulse, could I be certain that the object of the impulse to which I was moved was accurately understood at the moment of the experience and that I accurately remember it now? Even supposing I could give a certainly affirmative answer to all the foregoing questions, from weighing evidence could I judge with certainty when the evidence is enough to justify coming to a conclusion?

This much seems entirely clear: Ignatius did not think any single second-time experience can justify even a soundly probable conclusion. Does the amassing of such evidence come to the point of justifying certitude? If so, why? If it does, when is it enough to do so? What is the norm by which I can know with certainty it is

---

[3] *SpEx*, [315, 318, 335]

278

enough? Further, we have seen that Ignatius allows for different second-time experiences pointing in diverse directions.[4] When that is so, can the evidence on one side in a second-time discernment, even if much weightier, give me more than high probability?[5]

Given all the chances of error and all the possible reasons for uncertainty, it seems that anything more than a soundly probable assent to the conclusion of a second-time discernment is very rarely or never possible even on the basis of plentiful evidence.

What if the second-time experience involves a consolation which is "without previous cause"?[6] Such consolation, Ignatius says explicitly, is certainly from God and cannot be simulated by any created agent, human or diabolical.[7] In the *Spiritual Exercises*, where he says this, he clearly implies that God sometimes communicates his purpose during such consolation and that this communication, if it is certainly during the consolation, can be trusted without further testing. All this seems to mean that God's will can be known with at least moral certainty through even one such experience of consolation without previous cause.

Before accepting this implication and giving it practical significance, several reasons for hesitation must be considered. First, there is no certainty about what Ignatius meant by consolation without previous cause.[8] Second, even if it should be made certain what Ignatius meant by such consolation, can I (the subject of the consolation) be certain of having had that kind of consolation?[9] Further,

---

[4] See above, p. 157.

[5] Donald L. Gelpi, S.J., *Pentecostalism: A Theological Viewpoint* (New York: Paulist Press, 1971), pp. 192–193, 202.

[6] To avoid possible confusion at this point, the reader should keep in mind what has already been shown: that Ignatius did not identify consolation without preceding cause with the first-time experience and, in fact, did not see such consolation as necessarily present in a first-time experience (see above, pp. 114–118); that he did not see such consolation as necessary for a second-time experience (see above, pp. 140–141)—though, of course, some consolation (with or without preceding cause) is essential for that experience.

[7] *SpEx*, [336], and see Jules Toner, *A Commentary*, p. 219.

[8] Jules Toner, *A Commentary*, pp. 216–217, p. 291.

[9] Karl Rahner thinks that this consolation is self-justifying to the subject (*Dynamic Element*, pp. 143, 148). Harvey Egan disagrees with Rahner (*Mystical Horizon*, pp. 44–45). Daniel Gil, who understands this consolation very differently from Rahner and Egan, holds that the subject can have no more than a prudential certainty of having had it (*La Consolacion sin Causa Precedente*, pp. 31–36). I myself find nothing in Ignatius' description of this consolation which indicates that the subject is or is not justifiably certain of having it (*A Commentary*, p. 251).

can I be certain when the actual consolation ended and the afterglow began and, consequently, be certain whether the impulse came during or after the actual consolation? If I can be certain that the impulse came during and from the consolation, can I be certain that I then understood and now understand accurately to what the impulse was directed, taking nothing away, adding nothing? There is reason to think that one can never be sure of all that.[10] Yet, unless all these questions can be answered affirmatively and with certainty, no certitude about God's will based on consolation without previous cause is possible; and it is highly questionable whether Ignatius thought it to be so.

In fact, if we examine his own practice, there is strong evidence that he did not think so. During the discernment which he described in his *Spiritual Diary,* he had many sublime consolations joined with inclinations to one alternative; and it is hard to think that consolation without previous cause was not among them—no matter which of the several meanings we give it. It is, then, very significant that he never took any one of these spiritual experiences as certain evidence of God's will. If in Rule II, 8 of his rules for discernment of spirits he meant that an impulse during consolation without previous cause was unmistakably from God and known to be so by the subject, then any one such experience should have given him certainty regarding God's will.

There is, therefore, strong reason for thinking that, while Ignatius considered the experience of consolation without previous cause to be certainly from God, he did not think it could supply evidence on which a discerner could base a certitude about God's will.

Certainty from First-Time Evidence

There is one other kind of evidence which might justify certain assent to the conclusion of the sound discernment, the evidence found in a first-time experience. In this experience, Ignatius says, "God so moves and draws the will that without doubting or the power of doubting, the faithful person follows what is shown."[11]

---

[10] Ladislas Orsy, *Probing the Spirit,* pp. 59–60.
[11] *SpEx,* [175].

As we saw above,[12] there are two possible ways of understanding what Ignatius says about first-time experience. In the first way, a judgment of what God wills is given in the experience with such clarity and unshakable certainty of its meaning, truth, and origin that it does away with any need for, or real possibility of, reflective questioning and critical evaluation by the recipient. In the second way, although the judgment given in the experience arises with unshakable certainty at the moment of reception, nevertheless, the person who has such an experience can afterwards critically reflect on it, questioning its source and meaning and certainty, applying sound theological norms.

In the first way, the certain assent is not thought to be reached by any active discernment process; and there is no need for, or possibility of, providing directives and norms. It just happens or does not happen. The person has certitude, but not a certitude from discernment. In the second way, the first-time experience offers only data for discernment, either to be accepted after evaluation as evidence or rejected. If accepted, can a single such experience or a number of them ever yield a justifiable certainty regarding God's will? There are far too many questionable factors in the experience to let us easily think so. Was the original experience accurately understood at the time? Was it perhaps subtly but significantly other than the person now remembers it to be? Has something been added or subtracted? Are the norms by which it is judged certainly valid ones? If so, can we be certain they are applied correctly with no defective reasoning? Further, some of the subtle possibilities of error in the second mode of seeking God's will come into play here also.[13] The possibilities of error seem so large as to leave little or no possibility of any reflective, reasoned conclusion being more than a sound opinion.

Ignatius' Certainty of Finding God's Will

Despite the general inadequacy of evidence to justify giving certain assent to the conclusion of a discernment, throughout his whole body of writings, Ignatius gives the impression of having an

---

[12] See above, pp. 121–127.
[13] See above, pp. 277–281.

unquestioned belief that we can and do through discernment find God's will with justified certainty. For the moment all I want to do is to show evidence for the preceding statement. After that we can ask about Ignatius' reason for his belief, how he thought to justify it.

All through his writings Ignatius speaks without qualification about knowing God's will. Never, to my knowledge, neither in any of his instructions on how to seek God's will[14] nor in any exhortation to seek it nor in all the accounts of his own seeking and finding it— never does a single sentence suggest that what he or others conclude from a sound discernment is merely probable. He acts on what he finds and perseveres in doing so despite opposition or persecution, as if what he has found is without doubt God's will. He urges others to do the same.

What is more significant, he sometimes uses language which strongly implies, or even explicitly expresses, a certainty about the conclusion, a conviction which seems to exclude doubt. Thus, in treating the question of when to finalize a decision from discernment, we found that the sign on which Ignatius depended was a sense of "security."[15] This security does not seem to be merely a security in the conviction of having done his best to fulfill all the essential requirements and, consequently, being able to act with a good conscience even if a mistaken one. It seems to be also a security in the certainty of having reached a true judgment of what God wills, a freedom from fear of error.

On one occasion, in the course of his discernment recorded in the *Spiritual Diary*, he thought he had completed it, but wanted one last powerful confirmation. Despite great confirmation by intense spiritual consolation, he still did not at some moments experience the abundance of feelings and tears he had looked for. As a consequence, "some slight doubt remained." He would not conclude with this slight doubt. Although his devotion lasted all day, it was, he said, attacked in some little ways. Because of this slight disappointment, he was "afraid of making some *mistake*" and would not

---

[14] See *SpEx*, [1, 15, 23, 173, 180].
[15] See above, p. 214.

282

finalize his decision.[16] His insecurity about making a mistake regarding God's will was such that he would not conclude while he had these slight grounds for fear of error. When, later on, he did bring the discernment to an end, he says that he had "complete security about everything he had decided."[17] (Again, the complete security, absence of all uneasiness, was concerned with *what he had decided to be God's will,* not merely with having done all he could.)

At another time, in his discernment regarding what his response should be when the pope planned to make Borgia a cardinal, Ignatius said that, at the conclusion of the discernment, he found himself with a "complete judgment" and with a tranquil will, feeling entirely free to oppose as much as he could the plan of the emperor and pope to make Borgia a cardinal. He held "as a certainty" that if he did not do this he could not give a good account of himself to God.[18] One might want to interpret this message to mean that he was certain that God willed for him to act on his concluding judgment even though it might be erroneous. However, that is not the impression any reader would take from Ignatius' words unless he was looking for a way to save Ignatius from appearing to hold what he, the benevolent reader, considered a naive belief. Just reading the text as it stands, I think the reader would surely take Ignatius to be asserting that he was certain the conclusion he reached by his discernment truly expressed God's will for him.

It is true that a little further on in the letter Ignatius says that he had no certainty about what God willed for the pope to do or what God intended to be the outcome of his opposition. But that was beyond the scope of his discernment. All that he could and did discern was what God wanted him to choose to do in the situation— more exactly, what God wanted him to choose to effectively intend to do.[19] About that he was certain he had reached a true judgment.

Ignatius' Source of Certainty

There is other, and perhaps even stronger, evidence that Ignatius believed in reaching a justifiable certainty about God's will

---

[16] Entry for Feb. 18.
[17] Entry for March 12.
[18] See above, p. 49.
[19] See above, p. 66.

through spiritual discernment; it will be noted in a moment. Right now, a question presses for an answer. Am I contending that, despite all that was said above, Ignatius after all had a conviction that the kinds of evidence in his three modes of election are sufficient to justify assent with certainty? Or am I implying that, without ever reflecting on what could ground his certainty, Ignatius was swept along by his emotional personality, his mystical prayer life, and his enormous enthusiasm for doing God's will in everything, to the uncritical assumption that he and we could have valid certitude about what God wills regarding our choices for his greater glory? The answer is neither of these. There are signs that Ignatius did reflect on the question and saw an ultimately justifying source of certainty beyond the evidence found in any or all of the three modes of election. What that ultimate source is appears especially in two documents, *The Deliberation of the First Fathers* and the Constitutions of the Society of Jesus.

In *The Deliberation of the First Fathers*, before the discernment begins, there is a firm declaration of where Ignatius and his companions put their ultimate hope of finding God's will regarding the decisions they were undertaking to make. Recall what has already been shown,[20] namely, that the deliberation was in the third mode. Nevertheless, it was not to be the reasons which they would seek with long and prayerful thought and discusssion on which they would ultimately base their certainty of God's will. These reasons (or some other form of evidence) would be essential to finding God's will; through these God would lead them to their conclusions. But their certainty about the truth of the conclusion to which they were led would not rest on the reasons but on trust in God leading them.

> In full agreement we settled on this, that we would give ourselves to prayer, Masses, and meditations more fervently than usual and, after doing our very best [in seeking God's will], we would for the rest cast all our concerns on the Lord, hoping in him. He is so kind and generous that he never denies his good Spirit to any one who petitions him in humility and simplicity of heart;

---

[20] See above, pp. 247–249.

rather, he gives to all extravagantly, not holding back from anyone. In no way, then, would he who is kindness itself desert us; rather, he would be with us more generously than we asked or imagined.[21]

To read this passage in the context of their lives, their formation through the Spiritual Exercises, and their present situation[22] leaves no room for reasonably doubting that these men were convinced that God would lead them to know what would be more for his praise and service. That is what they had principally gathered for, not just to make some good human decisions nor to deepen their union and mutual understanding. When they said that God would not deny his Spirit to them, but give him beyond all they hoped or imagined, they meant that God would give his Spirit to them to help them find his will. So, after the account of their first decision, we read this emphatic declaration:

> We wanted it understood that nothing at all that has been or will be spoken of originated from our own spirit or our own thought; rather, whatever it was, it was solely what our Lord inspired.[23]

What they meant by saying our Lord inspired them is clear when this phrase is read in the context of the document. In that context the phrase means that the Holy Spirit has led them to one conclusion, and would lead them to others through their searching for and weighing advantages and disadvantages for the service and glory of God.[24]

In the Constitutions of the Society of Jesus, this confidence of finding what God wills, based on belief in the Holy Spirit's loving guidance, runs through all Ignatius' counsels to superiors and to the general congregation regarding their decision making. He speaks of the Holy Spirit leading us to know God's will,[25] teaching us what

---

[21] Jules Toner, "*The Deliberation*," p. 186. See Dávila, [110] in *DirSpEx*MHSJ, p. 514 and Official Directory, [173] (ibid., p. 693).

[22] Jules Toner, "*The Deliberation*,," pp. 185–186.

[23] Ibid., p. 193.

[24] See above, pp. 247–249.

[25] *Cons*, [583].

that will is,[26] inspiring those who seek it,[27] giving them light from above,[28] and efficaciously guiding their deliberations to a right conclusion.[29] The assumption throughout seems to be that, with such guidance, they will surely reach a true conclusion if they conscientiously do their part. Hence the conviction which Ignatius has regarding the conclusions of his own discernments and which he thinks others may rightly have regarding theirs.

To sum up what has been found, we can say that, so long as the ground for certain assent to the conclusion of a discernment is sought in the evidence on which the conclusion rests, there is no ground for absolute or even for moral certainty—or if there ever is, it is in very exceptional cases. Leaving aside the possibility of rare exceptions, probability is all that can be hoped for from evidence for what God wills. Nevertheless, Ignatius sees a ground for genuine certitude which I have not found taken in full seriousness by writers on Ignatian discernment except in the early directories.[30] For Ignatius, that on which certainty indubitably rests is not any experience of consolation or any reasons, but faith in God's gift of the Holy Spirit to guide those who do their utmost to be open to him and to seek his will.

If my interpretation of Ignatius on this question of certainty is accepted as accurate, it may seem to some readers that his answer to the question is simplistic. In the following chapter, I shall try to show the intelligibility and credibility within the faith of what I take to be Ignatius' thought. I will do so by recalling and developing the truths of Christian faith, to which he refers only very briefly and lightly as the justifying ground for his conviction, and by showing how the principal difficulties which can be raised against the possibility of reaching a justifiable conviction are resolved within his full teaching on discernment.

---

[26] Ibid., [161, 414].

[27] Ibid., [700].

[28] Ibid., [711].

[29] Ibid., [624a].

[30] "God will not allow the pure-hearted discerner to be deceived. The one who seeks him wholeheartedly will find. We cannot believe otherwise of the divine goodness." Thus Dávila, [110] (*DirSpEx*MHSJ, p. 514). The same conviction founded on faith in God's goodness is declared in the Official Directory, [173] (ibid., p. 692).

Chapter 16
A Reflection on Ignatius'
Certainty of Finding God's
Will

*S*o obviously and supremely important for understanding the value of Ignatian discernment in Christian life is the question regarding the trust we can put in the conclusion of it that we must now reflect on and develop the key factors found in Ignatius' answer to that question.

The Practical Consequences of Different Answers

If my free choice does make a difference for achieving divine glory in human life, then uncertainty about which alternative is truly for the greater glory leaves me in an uncomfortable situation—the more so the more I love God and neighbor and, consequently, desire the greater glory of God in my neighbor.

The discomfort from that uncertainty can be eased in some measure by the certainty that, when I do the best I can to find out what is for the greater glory, God is pleased with my choosing in accord with my merely probable conclusion; for doing so is an act of sincere and pure love for him and my neighbor and, therefore, is for his glory, even if *what* I choose is not for the greater glory.

But this certainty cannot suffice to release my full energy for carrying out what I have chosen, when to do so calls for courageous perseverance through opposition, danger, pain, ridicule, and apparent failure or threat of failure. Even a person fully dedicated to God's service may find it impossible to respond with vigor in the face of uncertainty whether the action decided on by spiritual discernment is really more for God's glory than another action (which might be very delightful and fulfilling), or whether, while good, it is not really a hindrance to the greater good. Who can leap to the struggle at the sound of an uncertain trumpet? (1 Cor. 14:18). Who can carry on the struggle with courage, energy, and enthusiasm when uncertain whether engaged in the right struggle?[1]

Further, to be realistic, most of us, even if for a brief time we reach a very pure heart while discerning God's will, have not reached in our ordinary lives or even during discernment a love for God which renders us totally and perfectly indifferent to all but God's greater glory. When, therefore, I am faced with a crucial decision in which my whole life in time is at stake, in which what seems to be God's will demands letting go of what would, apart from the greater glory, be supremely precious—when faced with such a decision and, even more so, with the long, hard living out of that decision, how can I not be seriously and often disturbed and weakened by the thought that I am making such a sacrifice as a result of a mistake and that I could have had what seems so precious in this life while also doing what is more for the glory of God?

Being able to live with uncertainty is a part of personal ma-

---

[1] On the results of not really trusting the conclusions of discernment, see the thought-provoking pages by Robert Ochs, S.J., *God Is More Present than You Think* (New York: Paulist Press, 1970), pp. 13–16.

turity. Nevertheless, uncertainty about the value of what one is doing and enduring is an impedient to wholehearted action and endurance. There is something splendid, even heroic, in risking all on an uncertainty. Nevertheless, uncertainty hinders a wholehearted dedication to, and an enthusiastic and persevering execution of, the chosen action.

This reason, offered to show our need for certainty about what God wills for the greater glory, does not, of course, show that we can be certain. What it is intended to show is, on the one hand, that the question whether we can be certain is a question worthy of serious, prolonged, and open-minded consideration before reaching a negative answer. On the other hand, awareness of our needs warns us against the possibility of being subtly impelled by that need to an affirmative answer, without open-minded consideration of how surprising it is to claim certainty about what God wills in situations for choice where all alternatives are either indifferent or good in themselves. Did Ignatius really believe what he seems to have believed? If he did so believe, was his reason for doing so a good one?

Main Steps in Discussing the Issue

Without all that has been already worked out in this study, one might not be ready to think that Ignatius really did so believe; it would probably seem to be far too great a claim. However, given what we have seen about the limits of Ignatian discernment of God's will and about his understanding of our relationship with God in doing it, to claim certainty for the conclusion of a sound discernment appears as a much more modest claim than it appears to be outside the context of his thought. Further, when the claim with the meaning which it has in his thought is seen within the context of Christian faith in God's love for us and his call to us to love as he does, it seems altogether justifiable.

In order to clarify my reasons for these assertions, I shall now try to do three things: (1) show that the difficulties commonly raised against finding God's will with certainty through sound Ignatian discernment overlook some important points of that teaching; (2) develop more fully the justifying ground for such certainty; (3) resolve a problem raised earlier and left unsolved at that time; namely,

the problem regarding the possibility of being sure that I have sufficiently fulfilled the essential conditions for a sound discernment
of God's will and, consequently, for believing that the Holy Spirit
has led my discernment. In all these steps, it must be strongly emphasized that only certainty from a sound and complete discernment
is under consideration.[2]

1. Solution of Common Objections

The difficulties commonly raised against any justifiably certain
assent to the conclusion of a sound discernment of God's will have
two main bases. The first is the impossibility of getting evidence
for such an assent. The data from which certain evidence could be
derived are not available to us and, even if they were, the defectibility
of our reasoning on them would prevent certitude in our assent to
the conclusion.[3] The second basis is the disappointing and frustrating
events which sometimes follow on sound discernment. The facts
which are thought to constitute these bases seem to me incontro-
vertible. What I think can be shown, however, is that these facts
cannot serve as bases for valid objections; their relevance for that
purpose is nullified by a correct understanding of what Ignatius
teaches.

Elimination of the First Basis for Difficulties against Certainty

The first basis is removed by a correct understanding of what
Ignatius sees as the ground for certainty. For that ground is *not* the
evidence which justifies drawing the conclusion; the evidence which
enables us to draw a conclusion cannot justify holding the conclusion
with certainty, whether absolute or moral. The ground which justifies
the certainty with which the assent is given is faith in God's love
for us and his fundamental will regarding every situation in human
life, that is, his will for our greater good, his greater glory in us.[4]

---

[2] *SpEx*, [172–174].

[3] In Susan Rakoczy's account of the reasons given for denying unqualified certainty of
finding God's will (*The Structures of Discernment Processes*, pp. 193–206), all the reasons
seem to flow from the assumption, expressed or unexpressed, that if there could be any such
certainty, it would have to rest ultimately on the evidence for the conclusion. Making that
assumption, those reasons are unanswerable—as I have argued as strongly as any other. (See
above, pp. 276–281.) But can the assumption stand?

[4] See above, chapter 2 and pp. 284–286.

Because he believes God loves us so much as to give us his Son and make us his sons and daughters in him and, consequently, wills in every situation our greater good (or lesser harm)—because he believes this, Ignatius logically believes that, if we freely do our utmost to find and choose God's will for the greater good, we can be certain that he will lead us to the true conclusion.

The certitude grounded in this way is a conviction of faith. For Ignatius spiritual discernment of God's will begins from Christian faith, is carried on in faith, and is concluded in faith. His confidence when undertaking to seek God's will, his unstinting and persevering efforts during discernment, and his unshakable resolution in executing difficult enterprises when once discerned to be for the greater glory of God are all equally the fruit of his invincible faith. This faith is the foundation on which his practice of discernment and his theology of discernment are founded.

His faith-conviction regarding the conclusion of a spiritual discernment of God's will is, however, not altogether independent of the evidence for that conclusion. On the one hand, in his way of seeking God's will, only finding sound and sufficient evidence can justify a person's assent to a conclusion; on the other hand, only faith in having been led by the Holy Spirit to that conclusion through the evidence can justify (within the realm of faith) assenting to it with a conviction that excludes fear of error. Faith without that evidence cannot justify drawing a conclusion, and that evidence without faith in divine guidance cannot justify assenting with certainty.

There is, then, this important difference between a faith conviction regarding the conclusion from Ignatian discernment and justifiable absolute or moral certitudes in the purely rational realm. The latter certitudes are based solely on the evidence which justifies the conclusion. Therefore, they necessarily involve certainty regarding the evidence on which the conclusion rests and certainty regarding the correctness of reason in drawing a conclusion from that evidence. Ignatius' faith-conviction, on the contrary, does not imply a faith-conviction regarding the validity of the evidence for the conclusion nor, therefore, regarding the accuracy of observation.

291

Nor does it imply the truth of judgments and correctness of reasoning in the process by which the evidence is established.[5]

What happens in the discernment process may in some respects be compared to making a journey. A traveler may mistakenly leave the right road, wander around in the wrong directions, and still end up by a winding and crooked way at the desired destination. It may even be that the erroneous route had advantages other than getting to the journey's end. On the winding route one may have met certain people who were and are an enrichment of life or may have seen certain beautiful sights or have gotten some needed exercise.[6] Like-wise, in discernment God can lead us by true and false premises through correct or incorrect reasoning to the true conclusion. Mistakes made in the process could be, in the providence of God, the occasion for side benefits—or, perhaps, only allowed by the Holy Spirit as consequences of certain factors in one's personality which he sees are not to be changed just yet without loss to the person.

It must be emphasized that to believe the Holy Spirit can and under certain conditions will lead one, even through errors, to find God's will in no way excuses laziness and negligence in the discernment process. Such an attitude would be a failure to fulfill the essential conditions for sound spiritual discernment and leave no grounds for believing that the Spirit had guided one.

If the preceding clarification of Ignatius' justifying ground for his faith-conviction regarding the conclusion of a sound and complete discernment of God's will is acceptable, it should remove any objection based on the limitations of our knowledge and the defectibility of our reasoning. Such an objection simply misses his point. The only objection which engages his thought is one which calls into question his belief in God's fundamental will in our regard or his illation from that belief to the belief that God will surely guide to a true conclusion one who fulfills the essential conditions for sound discernment.

---

[5] There is a further difference between Ignatius' faith-conviction and absolute certainty. The latter excludes even the *possibility* of doubt by anyone who really sees the evidence, whereas the Christian act of faith is a free act, for which there is no evidence that removes the *possibility* of doubt. Therefore, when a conviction about the truth of a conclusion from discernment is based on Christian faith, it leaves open that possibility.

[6] For an interesting parallel with making errors when reading Sacred Scripture and yet arriving through them at charity, see St. Augustine, *De Doctrina Christiana*, I, 36.

Is the assent given in the faith conviction to the conclusion of a sound and complete discernment of God's will given with more or less certainty than an assent in the purely rational order, an assent based solely on the evidence for the conclusion? The answer to that question depends on the answers to several other questions: What does the discerner believe about God's love, power, wisdom, and providence? What relationship does he see between this belief and his efforts to find God's will? How strong or weak is his belief?

Finally, some comments on the practical value of this solution. Obviously, it not only gives confidence in the decision but also gives courage in carrying it out when it is a difficult one. Very important also is its value after a decision is carried out when we may need assurance that we have not carried out a wrong decision. For it can happen that we look back with new data, with more developed powers of critically evaluating and interpreting the data, and we then think that we would now not reach the conclusion we did at an earlier time, even though the earlier conclusion was reached through a process that fulfilled all the required conditions. Should we call the conclusion into doubt now and have regrets about having trusted it? After doing our best there is no reason at all within the Ignatian framework for us to do so. Within that framework the conviction with which we assented to that conclusion was not based *ultimately* on the evidence for it but on trust in God's guidance through whatever evidence we were able to reach. The ground for our conviction is unchanged. There may or may not be reason to initiate a new discernment. Even if there is and if a different course of action is determined as being God's will, we can still have confident trust that what we arrived at earlier was what God willed then and until now. So also, when presently discerning, we need not be upset and doubtful of a decision because some data are unavailable now, and the decision cannot reasonably be delayed in order to search for such data.

Elimination of the Second Basis for Objections against Certitude

The second main basis for objections against certain assent to the conclusion of a sound discernment is the occurrence of some events consequent on concluding. Thus, by sound discernment two persons arrive at decisions which, they find, put them in conflict,

293

each one thinking to have found what God wills. Again, someone makes a sound discernment and then finds it is impossible to carry out what appeared to be God's will or is commanded to do otherwise by another person with just authority. Or it may happen that the decision to do some action is carried out but fails to achieve the goal which gave meaning to the action. Or again, the goal may be achieved but have consequences that do not seem to be for the glory of God.

Just as the difficulties against certainty which are raised on the basis of the limitation of human knowledge and the defectibility of human reasoning overlook the source of certainty in Ignatius' thought, so likewise the difficulties raised on the basis of events consequent to the finalized conclusion of discerning God's will overlook Ignatius' understanding of the limits of such discerning. All the difficulties from this second base have been brought up and resolved already in the chapters on the limits of discerning God's will and on the question of finalizing a decision which comes from sound discernment.[7]

2. A Fuller Development of Ignatius' Ground for Certainty

Hopefully the preceding solution of difficulties has removed, at least to a large extent, the uneasiness with what at first might have seemed an irrationally exaggerated claim. If so, a positive clarification of Ignatius' reason for certainty from spiritual discernment may make it fully acceptable.

By developing what Ignatius indicates briefly and in passing (as something that seemed to him too obvious to delay over), I think I can show more convincingly why his certainty is reasonable within the context of Christian faith, even demanded by it. For it not only coheres with a number of New Testament teachings but even seems to be called for by them.

Despite all the limits and qualifications already explained, some may still balk at the assertion that we can with certainty find God's will for the kind of situation with which Ignatius is concerned. It has a ring of presumption for a creature to make such a claim. At first glance, given God's infinite transcendence, this attitude

---

[7] See above, chapters 5 and 12.

strikes one as a fittingly humble and reverent one, as well as the only reasonable one. Here, as in so many other things, however, Christian revelation has surprising consequences, which Ignatius with strong faith and logical mind did not hesitate to draw and to live by. His belief in God's love revealed in Jesus Christ led him, as we saw, to believe also that whatever God wills regarding human life is for our greater glory, his greater glory in us. These two beliefs seemed to him to justify a further belief, that we could find God's will of the greater glory in concrete situations for choice. The reason is simple enough, so simple as to seem naive and dangerous—as, indeed, it would be without all the limitations that Ignatius' teaching puts on the belief in order to exclude rash claims. Keeping those limits in mind, let us try to see with greater force and clarity the reasonableness of Ignatius' belief within the context of Christian faith.[8]

Think of someone who loves God and neighbor so much that he or she desires intensely to find and to choose to do whatever is more for the kingdom of God. To fail to find it, when every alternative is in some measure conducive to the kingdom and to the glory, may not be a disaster; but it will be some loss for the one seeking God's will, for others directly involved, and ultimately for all of us. Now, according to Christian faith the following statements are true: God loves each and every one of us personally; calls each into being by name; gives us his only-begotten Son to be our brother; delivers his beloved Jesus to shame and death for each of us; calls each of us into his own life in Christ, as closely one with Christ as vine and branches, head and members; reveals the truth about himself as far as we can understand; gives his Holy Spirit to each one as a gift of love; makes his home in each of us and wants us to make our home in him; destines each and all together to inherit the fullness of his own life and joy—in short, loves each as he loves Jesus. So we must believe that God looks with such love on the one we are thinking of, who is lovingly and trustingly seeking to know the Father's will so as to choose in this situation what will be for the greater glory in all God's children. Can any reason consistent

---

[8] Those of other religious faiths may find that what is said fits, with some necessary changes, their beliefs too.

with the love God has revealed be found for thinking that we cannot be certain of God, by means of a sound discernment, leading his truly loving child in Christ to a true judgment about his will, about what is for the greater glory?

The answer I find in Ignatius seems to be an unqualified and strong no. Any other answer would imply a deistic God, who has no providence over our lives, or a provident God with power so limited that we could not be sure of his leading us to the true conclusion even if he wanted to, or a provident God of limited love who could so lead us but might not care enough to do so—who, therefore, might love us in some or all instances less than we love each other.

An Objection Based on a False Parallel with Discerning Morally Good from Morally Evil Alternatives

An objection might be urged which, at least at first glance, not only undercuts the reasons presented above but seems to call for a critical reconsideration of the theological reasons just given. It is an obvious fact that, in making judgments whether an act is for God's glory (or at least not opposed to it) or is opposed to it, even very good and intelligent people, who love God and neighbor, do make mistakes or have to act as best they can with uncertainty. But the kind of moral discernment we are here considering is more fundamental to our vocation to do God's will than is discernment among alternatives which are all for God's glory. If we cannot argue from God's infinite benevolence toward us to the certain truth of our judgments in the more fundamental discernment of God's will, does it not seem strange to suggest that we can do so in the less fundamental and less important kind of discernment? In discernment on matters of primary importance, we believe that God in his loving providence will make up for our errors made in good conscience and will ultimately turn all to our good. Why is such belief not enough when discerning about secondary matters is concerned? Why do we have to believe that we can actually exclude grounds for reasonable fear of error?

This objection appears to be insuperable until a crucial weakness in the parallel between the two types of discerning God's will is noted and taken into account. When in all sincerity I make a mistake and judge that some act is morally good although it is in fact morally evil, I can count on God to take care of the consequences, turning all to good, perhaps even to a greater good. Therefore, allowing me to make a mistake is compatible with God's all-powerful, all-wise, and boundless benevolence toward me. When, however, I make a mistake about what is for the greater glory, the case is not the same. To try to resolve the problem in the same way runs into a contradiction. If God can turn my mistake to good, intends to do so, and does so, is that good not equal to or greater than the different good that would have followed on my choice if I had not made a mistake? If it is, then I did not, in fact, make a mistake at all; for I did not choose what was less for the glory of God. I chose what was in fact more or, at least equally, for the glory. The likelihood or even possibility of two consequences being perfectly equal for God's glory is highly dubious, almost incredible. But if the two alternatives were, in fact, such as to be perfectly equal for God's glory, then the situation was not one for Ignatian discernment and is irrelevant to our discussion. As far as Ignatius is concerned, it would not make the least difference which alternative was chosen.

Other Starting Points for Ignatius' Argument

The theological argument thus far has been based on the revelation of God's love for us and, consequently, his will for our sharing in his glory. Several other lines of thought, beginning from other starting points in Christian faith, converge with the foregoing reasoning. They may perhaps help the reader to consider more sympathetically Ignatius' belief in God's guiding our sound discernment so that we do find his will and can have a justifiable faith-conviction that we have found it.

We can, for instance, instead of beginning from God's love, begin from our love, the Christlike love God calls us to have for him and for each other and wishes us to express in deed and in truth. This love above all constitutes the glory of God in us for which God wills all that he wills in human history. God's command to love in this way contains virtually all that he commands us to do in order to achieve the intended glory. So, in every concrete situation for human choice, God wills us to choose what in the long run will be more for building up the life of Christian love in his people. This love finds its essential expression in doing God's will as the subject sees it and doing it just because it is God's will. But a truthful expression of love requires that we find what really is God's will and be sure it is found. When we do our part fully, our very best, will God withhold from us the help we need in order to fulfill our vocation as Christians to love in deed and in truth? Can we believe in his love and fidelity and believe that?

Another starting point: Jesus tells us to seek first the kingdom of God and all else will be added to us. The kingdom of God is the kingdom of Christlike love, of truthful love,[9] flowing from faith in Jesus Christ and truthfully expressed in action. Since what God wills us to choose in every situation for choice is that act which is truly more for the kingdom, what could those who do seek first the kingdom of God more reasonably expect to be added to them when they have to make a choice than the truth about what God's will is?

A third starting point is Christ's teaching on prayer of petition. Jesus assures us over and over that God will give us anything we ask, even his own Spirit. In one of his characteristic *a fortiori* arguments, he tells us that when we pray we should believe we already have what we ask for[10] and chides our lack of simple faith in God's love and power.

> For everyone who asks receives, and he who seeks finds, and to him who knocks it will be opened. What father among you, if his son asks for a fish, will instead of a fish give him a serpent; or if he asks for an egg, will give him a scorpion? If you then, who are evil, know how to give good gifts to your children, how much more will the heavenly Father give the Holy Spirit to those who ask him![11]

Now, if God will grant us anything we ask for, then above all and more surely than all else, he will grant our prayer for what is necessary in order to choose freely what is for his greater glory in us, namely, a true judgment of what is for his greater glory.

Although scriptural teaching on prayer puts conditions on this

---

[9] See Jules Toner, *The Experience of Love*, pp. 155–162.

[10] *Mk*. 11:24, and see 1 *Jo*. 5:14–15.

[11] *Lk*. 11:10–13, and see *Mt*. 7:9–11.

assurance of having prayers answered, these conditions only strengthen rather than weaken the point being made here. Consider some of these. We are told that our petitions must be in accordance with God's will.[12] What could be more in accord with God's will than the request, springing from obedient love, that I may know what his will is so as lovingly and freely to subject my will to his and bring his greater glory to his children? We are told that our requests should be in Jesus' name,[13] and that they will be answered if we remain in him and his word remains in us.[14] What request could be more in Jesus' name, what request could more express our union with him, than asking to know what the Father wills so as to do it for his greater glory?

Time and again faith in God's love and power is stressed as a condition for effective prayer.[15] Granted that we can and often do ask to find God's will with little real faith of finding it, with less faith sometimes than we have in God healing our physical ills or solving our economic problems, nevertheless, once we consider the reasons already given, it should be easy to believe that God will lead us in seeking what is for the greater glory. If he leads us, how could we not find?

3. A Final Problem regarding Certainty

Even if the reader accepts as accurate all the foregoing explanation of Ignatius' ground for giving certain assent to the finalized conclusion of a sound discernment process, there is one serious difficulty still to be met. It is the one that was noted at the end of the chapter on the essential conditions of sound discernment of God's will but deferred till now.[16] Recall those essential conditions: The discerner must be open to the Holy Spirit and must sincerely and intelligently seek to find God's will. Inevitably, these conditions are fulfilled in varying degrees by different persons and by the same person under varying circumstances. This fact raises a problem.

---

[12] 1 *Jo*. 5:14–15.

[13] *Jo*. 14:13–14; 16:23–24.

[14] *Jo*. 15:7, 16.

[15] *Mt*. 21:22; *James* 1:5–8. Recall the many times mentioned in the Gospels when Jesus made faith the condition for working miracles.

[16] See above, pp. 100–101.

299

What degree of openness to the Spirit and how great and prolonged and proficient an effort at discernment is necessary in order that it be sound and the conclusion trustworthy? Two extreme answers were noted. One of them appears to be the result of presumption or ignorance. The other depicts sound discernment of God's will for the greater glory as something only a relatively minuscule group, even among good Christians, could hope to do. Neither of these views can fit into Ignatian thought. What did Ignatius think to be the necessary and sufficient degree of the essential conditions for discerning God's will?

Ignatius' Solution of the Problem.

The answer to that question is implicit in Ignatius' understanding of God's fundamental will regarding human life,[17] our relationship with God in discerning his will[18] (from which the conditions flow),[19] and the ultimate reason for believing that God will lead and guide our search for his will, namely, his boundless, faithful, and utterly gratuitous love. All these elements in Ignatius' theology of discernment are presupposed in the *Deliberation of the First Fathers*, where an answer to our question appears expressly, even though only in passing, as if something too obvious to him and his companions to delay over: "After doing our very best we would for the rest cast all our concerns on the Lord. We began, therefore, to expend every human effort."[20] The necessary and sufficient degree of the conditions for being guided by the Holy Spirit appears to be "our very best." The required degree is neither high nor low nor in the middle on an objective scale that is the same for all. It is relative to the capability of each discerner in the concrete situation. If that person is as open to the Holy Spirit as he is reasonably capable of being after his sincerest striving to be so for as long as reasonably possible, and if he has carried on the search for God's will as best

---

[17] See above, chapter 2.

[18] See above, chapter 4.

[19] See above, pp. 70–71.

[20] Jules Toner, "*The Deliberation*," pp. 186 and 187.

300

he knows how with all reasonable human effort and time devoted to it, then he has fulfilled these essential conditions.[21]

In the Ignatian view, to find God's will for the greater glory is not only a reward to those who have merited it by becoming pure of heart and living extraordinarily virtuous lives. Much less is it only the prerogative of those who are gifted with high intelligence, abounding energy, and ample leisure. It is rather a necessity for every human person in order to respond to the universal human vocation from God to choose freely in every situation for choice what God wills for the greater glory. Therefore, it will be given by God to anyone who here and now does the very best he or she can to yield to God's influence and actively to seek the truth.

There is, to be sure, a degree of openness which, until we are confident of having reached it, we must keep striving for as long as it is reasonably possible to delay making the decision. It is such a dominant love for God and neighbor and such a dominant desire for the greater glory of God as to assure us of already choosing in principle whatever will be found to be God's will, no matter the cost, and to assure us of being able to carry through the discernment process free from the adverse influence on our judgment of disordered desires and fears. So also, sufficient time and effort must be devoted to seeking God's will; enough, that is, to reach evidence which justifies drawing a conclusion and to experience a sense of security in having done all we reasonably could and in having found God's will.[22] But to say this is only another way of saying that we must do our very best. When we have done all we reasonably can without reaching those goals and when it would be unreasonable to continue our striving or to put off the choice to another time, then we have adequately fulfilled the conditions for a sound discernment.

What "Doing Our Very Best" Does and Does Not Mean

The phrase "doing our very best" could easily be interpreted so as to understand Ignatius' view as one or the other of the extreme

---

[21] Support for this interpretation can be found in the directories, which in a number of contexts stress the necessity of our strenuous efforts in order to do our best, while putting trust in God for all the rest. See, for example: Polanco, nos. 5–8 (*DirSpEx*MHSJ, pp. 277–279); Miró, nos. 86, 87 (ibid., p. 401); Dávila, [111, 140] (ibid., pp. 514, 521); Official Directory of 1599, [204] (ibid., p. 709).

[22] See above, pp. 158–159, 214–215.

views described above. It could be used to justify a halfhearted, careless discernment, as if that were one's best, or it could lead to making demands on oneself and others which would render discerning God's will impossible except for those who have reached heroic virtue, and even for them only when they could put forth great energy over a long time. To avoid either of these extremes, what the phrase means must be made as exact as may be.

Our Best in Becoming Open to the Spirit's Guidance

What Ignatius thought could be required for doing one's best in ideal circumstances can be seen in the *Spiritual Exercises*. Before undertaking the election the exercitant is required as a minimum to have come to the attitude of "the second mode of humility."[23] This attitude presupposes a love for God in Jesus Christ so intense that one is free of any preference for riches, honors, health, long life, "and so of all other things" and desires only whatever is for the greater glory of God. Coming to this attitude is expected to take many hours, and to involve many days of meditation, contemplation, prayer, penance, and self-examination.

Outside the Spiritual Exercises and especially for ordinary, everyday choices, there seems to be no necessity to strive for indifference extending to all possible choices; it is highly desirable, but indifference to the alternatives involved in the present choice and decision seems entirely sufficient. To expect in all discernments outside the Spiritual Exercises the same intensity of faith, hope, love, and indifference to all but God's will would make discernment of God's will an impossibility for most good people most of their lives—something that could not fit into Ignatius' thought. The *Spiritual Exercises* present to those discerning under ordinary circumstances the ideal attitude to work toward, and some ways of working toward it insofar as they reasonably can; but the prerequisites for entering the election in those Exercises are by no means the same as those needed for every sound and trustworthy discernment of God's will.

On the other hand, whoever does not do all that can be reasonably done in the actual situation in order to come as near as

---

[23] *DirAutog*, [17], and see *SpEx*, [166, 179].

possible to the second mode of humility before discerning has not done his or her best. What can reasonably be done in the actual situation may vary from a long and patient preparation to a momentary preparation for discernment on a decision that simply must be made now or is of such slight importance as not to merit a long delay. All depends on the importance of the alternatives and the difficulty of becoming indifferent to them, on the discerner's present stage of spiritual development, on the time that can be reasonably taken from one's duties, and on the energy one can reasonably spare.

Our Best in Seeking God's Will through the Discernment Process

Even with entire indifference to all but God's will, lazy, careless, or impatient discernment would leave us with no grounds for believing that the Holy Spirit has led us to find it—any more than adequate, energetic, and persevering discernment without indifference would. Doing our best in seeking God's will through a discernment process involves at least the following four factors: (1) learning how to do it as far as our abilities and circumstances make reasonably possible, (2) preparing for and carrying out the discernment in the most favorable external circumstances that are available, (3) getting whatever help from others is needed and available, (4) persevering in the search as long as is reasonable, never concluding quickly merely out of impatience. Each of these factors needs some comment.

1. It is unreasonable and altogether opposed to Ignatian teaching to think that one may undertake discernment of God's will without trying as much as possible to learn the principles governing discernment and the way of applying them in practice. The great value Ignatius puts on sound method in discerning God's will is clearly evident in the instructions he gives[24] and in the accounts of his own practice.[25] Learning and following sound method saves us from impetuous decisions or endless muddling. It helps preserve indifference. It saves us from a biased selection and interpretation

---

[24] See above, chapters 9–11. It can be said with justification that the election is the most difficult and dangerous part of the Spiritual Exercises, requiring from the side of the exercitant more intense concentration of attention and more intense prayer for light and, from the side of the director, more skill than any other part of the Exercises (Hugo Rahner, *Ignatius the Theologian*, pp. 139–140).

[25] See Ignatius' *Diario Espiritual* and the *Deliberatio Primorum Patrum*.

of data in the third mode of discerning and from judgments based on shallow discernment of spirits or on deceptions of the evil spirit in the first and second modes. Good method is truly part of using our God-given intelligence to the utmost in seeking God's will. To muddle along with no concern for learning how to go about the search can spring from ignorance or from laziness and presumption.

On the other hand, to think that those who are open to the Holy Spirit but have little or no learning about how to discern God's will, who do, however, want and generously try to learn, and who use whatever they have learned when they have to make decisions— to think that such discernment by such persons cannot be trusted also seems contrary to Ignatius' understanding of our relationship to God in discerning his will[26] and contrary to the ground on which he bases his trust in the conclusion of discernment.[27]

2. Ignatius was keenly aware of the way external circumstances help or hinder our reception of divine movements and our capacity to reflect and deliberate calmly and clearly. Solitude, especially, being apart from friends and acquaintances and having leisure from all distracting occupations, seemed to him the best circumstance for making the Spiritual Exercises and especially for making the election. In these circumstances one can concentrate fully on the one concern of finding God's will in the question for discernment and can seek for it tranquilly.[28] The ideal external circumstances for discernment are not usually possible, but Ignatius' strong counsel indicates that approaching them as far as possible is part of doing our best.

The importance for discernment that Ignatius and his companions put on these external circumstances and the difficulty in deciding what was reasonably possible in their situation stand out prominently in the *Deliberation of the First Fathers*. They experienced a tension between their need to make the best discernment they could and the needs of others to whom they were ministering.

---

[26] See above, pp. 34–38.

[27] See above, pp. 284–286, 294–296.

[28] *SpEx*, [20]; *DirAutog*, [6] (*DirSpEx*MHSJ, p. 71); *Directorium Patri Vitoria Dictatum* [4–8] (ibid., pp. 92– 95). See also Polanco, no. 79 (ibid., p. 310); Miró, no. 84 (ibid., p. 400); Dávila, [110] (ibid., p. 514); Official Directory, [173] (ibid., pp. 691–693); Jules Toner, "The Deliberation," pp. 196–197.

This tension shows up especially when their discernment came to an impasse and they had to consider what to do about it. They did reflect on their indifference and on their method; but the first thing they considered was the setting in which they were discerning and their division of time between discernment and apostolic work. They even seriously considered withdrawing from all such work and going off to some hermitage. This proposal was finally rejected in favor of continuing their needed and fruitful ministry, but it shows the importance they put on solitude and leisure as circumstances favorable for discerning God's will.[29]

3. In addition to learning method and seeking favorable circumstances, doing our best in the discernment process requires consultation with others insofar as this is needed and available. Consultation and discussion with others was something that Ignatius practiced in his own attempts to find God's will[30] and something he recommended to others. In fact, he required it of superiors in the Society of Jesus.[31] The value, sometimes necessity, of such consultation is so obvious that there is no need to delay on the point but only to note and emphasize it as an essential of doing our best.

4. Finally, for some the factor in doing our best which most needs emphasis is patient perseverance in carrying on the search or, sometimes, willingness to end it temporarily without a decision and to wait in uncertainty for a more opportune time to take it up again. We cannot predict when the Holy Spirit will bring our search to an end; much less can we schedule his action to fit our pleasure in the matter and expect him to follow our schedule.

In some situations the discernment process will be brief, because the conclusion is easily reached or because the decision cannot be delayed. In other situations the process will be prolonged and painfully wearing. In the third mode of discernment, the necessary information may be hard to acquire or hard to interpret, or the reasons based on the interpreted information hard to weigh. In the second mode of discernment, God may delay giving sufficient second-time experience to ground any secure judgment. Doing our best at the

---

[29] Jules Toner, "The Deliberation," pp. 195–197.
[30] See above, p. 48, Ignatius' letter to Borgia,
[31] *Cons.* [211, 221, 431, 667, 804, 810].

process, therefore, will often require patient endurance of prayerful labor, tension, and uncertainty. Ignatius' own experience described in his diary is a model of what I am talking about;[32] so also the *Deliberation of the First Fathers*. In the former we saw how even Ignatius broke momentarily under the strain and, in his own words, became "impatient with the Holy Trinity"[33] when he did not receive at Mass and prayer the final assurance from God that he was expecting and thought he needed.

Sometimes it will happen that after a prolonged discernment in which the discerner has done all that could reasonably be expected, no trustworthy conclusion has been reached and, for some reason or another, the discernment process has to be discontinued. It may be that the discerner cannot take any more time or has run out of psychic energy. There may be some time left but not enough; so continuing under the circumstances with hope of reaching a conclusion would likely issue in hurried and pressured discernment. Or it may be that necessary information for a third-time discernment is not now available or clarity about the comparative weight of reasons on each side is not sufficient—a case of six of one and half dozen of the other and no new evidence in sight.

Rather than try to force a conclusion before the time available for discerning runs out, the discerner who wants to do his or her best will simply believe that God is saying that there is at present no need to know the answer. When the answer is needed, it will be given. For now, God's will is that the person wait and pray and later on, when the opportunity is present, take up the search. Waiting, praying, searching to know God's will *is* doing God's will. It can also be a special time of spiritual growth. That could be one main reason why God leaves a person without a decision, namely, to keep him or her doing what causes growth in faith, love, hope, patience, and so on.

To interpret this experience of seeming failure as necessarily meaning that the discernment has been unsound would be precipitous and perhaps quite unjust; on the other hand, the experience may well call for an examination of one's openness to the Spirit and one's

---

[32] See above, pp. 195–201.
[33] See above, p. 197.

306

way of going about discernment.[34] To interpret the experience as a sign that the choice to be made is of no significance for the greater glory of God would rest on one of two assumptions. The first would be that some choices of action with all their endless consequences have no relevance to God's glory and, therefore, have no significance in Christian life. The second possible assumption would be that the alternatives for choice with all their endless consequences have indeed relevance to God's glory in us but are exactly of the same value. Either assumption seems to be at least entirely arbitrary. What could be said to make either of them seem even plausible?

What I have been saying could lead the reader to think that no hurried or pressured discernment of God's will can ever be trusted. As already noted, such a conclusion would also be in discord with Ignatius' conviction that, when we have done our best, we can trust in God somehow to lead us to a true judgment about his will.

Suppose that, despite the discerner's best effort in the circumstances, he does not feel confident of having reached a degree of openness which assures that disordered desires and fears will not badly influence the discernment process. Or suppose that, even with sufficient openness to the Holy Spirit, he does not have sufficient time to gather evidence and reach a soundly justified conclusion. Suppose that, nevertheless, deferring the decision would in the concrete be equivalent to coming down on one side of the question or would cause disproportionate harm or hardship to someone. What does Ignatius' norm for fulfillment of the essential conditions mean then? Clearly, in such a situation, all that can be done is to turn to the Holy Spirit with as much openness as presently possible and, trusting in his aid, make the best judgment that can be made in these circumstances. Not to decide and act might even be sinful. Would this be a genuine and trustworthy discernment?

A negative answer to this question would imply the unexpressed supposition that finding God's will demands something further than doing the best we can to fulfill the conditions from our side or that we cannot be sure that the Holy Spirit will exercise his power and wisdom to lead us to the true judgment unless we come up to a certain objective and universally applicable standard, which

---

[34] Jules Toner, "The Deliberation," pp. 194–201.

is presently beyond our reach. Such a supposition is altogether un-acceptable within Ignatius' way of thinking—and, one might with reason suggest, unacceptable within a Christian understanding of God.

On the other hand, was it not asserted above that we cannot schedule the Holy Spirit and expect him to follow our schedule? Emphatically yes. Am I not then holding contradictory positions? If expecting the Holy Spirit to lead us to find God's will in the situations just described is truly scheduling him, then the objection is well-taken. The truth seems to be, however, that the discerner in these situations is not scheduling the Holy Spirit. Rather, historical circumstances under the rule of divine providence are scheduling the discerner.

A Warning

In contrast to the impetuosity of some in leaping to conclusions, there is the indecisiveness of others. This can result in delaying to conclude a discernment when there is every reason to do so, and thus in throwing the whole process into confusion. We saw how Ignatius on one occasion accused himself of this very mistake, and with good reason, it seems; when, that is, he set his heart on ending his discernment with intense, prolonged, and unbroken consolation, which he in no way needed.[35]

A Final Difficulty: Can We Be Certain We Have Done Our Best?

We have seen that justifiably certain assent to the conclusion of a discernment depends on being certain that the Holy Spirit has led us and that the latter certainty depends on being certain we have fulfilled the essential conditions for sound discernment. But the fact that these conditions have degrees raised a problem. What degree of fulfilling them is sufficient and necessary? We have found Ig-natius' answer: the degree which is one's reasonable best. What that means has been explained. Now another difficulty occurs: Can we ever be certain that we have done our very best? Unless we can, we are, for all practical purposes, back where we began; for, even if we have in fact done our very best, unless we are justifiably certain

---

[35] Ignatius' diary, entries for Feb. 18 and March 12. See above, pp. 199–200.

that we have done so, the Holy Spirit will have led us, but we will not be justifiably certain that he has done so. Consequently, we cannot be certain of the conclusion. Is there any way in which we can be justifiably certain of having done our best to be open to the Holy Spirit and to seek God's will?

At first glance, it seems impossible to reach that certainty. Our motivation is so complex, our self-awareness so superficial, our memory so unreliable, our disordered affections so powerful and subtle, our minds so capable not only of lying to themselves but even of lying to themselves about themselves.

Ignatius himself seems to reinforce this difficulty in what he writes in a letter to Francis Borgia about the difficulty or impossibility of judging the extent to which we obstruct God's work in us: " . . . there is no one who can fully ascertain or judge how much he impedes what God wishes to work in his soul and how much he opposes it."[36] If Ignatius thinks we cannot judge to what extent we impede God's work in us, it does not seem that he could consistently hold we are able to be certain of doing our best to fulfill the requisite conditions for finding God's will. How then can he consistently have a conviction that the Holy Spirit has led him or anyone through discernment to the truth about God's will?

Solution of the Difficulty

What at first appears as an insoluble difficulty can be solved by reflexively applying the norm of doing my reasonable best to my very judgment on my effort to do my best; that is, within the discernment process, not afterwards, at the very time of deciding whether or not I should conclude. If at that time I do my best honestly to judge my striving for openness to the Holy Spirit and my effort to carry out the discernment process, and if I reach the judgment that I have done my reasonable best in fulfilling these essential conditions, then, *in the concrete*, I have in fact done my best to fulfill them and can be justifiably sure that I have.

Let me clarify what I mean by what must surely seem to be a puzzling statement, one that is in thought, if not in words, really quite simple. Doing my best necessarily involves reflectively con-

---

[36] *Obras Completas*, p. 665, and *LettersIgn*, pp. 84–85.

sidering whether this is my best. If I think I could do better, then I either try to do so or else I am aware that I am not doing my best. But, if with all the care for honesty in the matter which I can summon, neither swallowing camels nor straining gnats, I judge that I have done my reasonable best in the circumstances and would surely do more, would try harder and longer, if I thought I reasonably could and should do so—in that case, how could I concretely do any better? To say that I may be mistaken, that it may still be reasonably possible for me to do better is to speak in the realm of abstract possibilities. Concretely, a reasonable better is not possible; for ultimately I have nothing to consult except my judgment; to try to do better, to strive longer and harder to fulfill the conditions for discernment would, in my judgment, be altogether unreasonable. Therefore, I may safely put my trust in God's love and power and believe he has led me to the conclusion my discernment has reached.

What about the uncertainty of how much I impede God's work in me, of which Ignatius spoke in the letter just quoted? All the impediments within me to seeing the truth regarding God's will are either in reflective awareness and subject to my free control or they are not. If they are and I do not do all I reasonably can to remove them, then I am not truly doing my best. If they are not in awareness and, therefore, not subject to my free control, so long as my attitude is such that I want to be aware of them and that I would want to remove them if I were aware of them, then I am doing the best I can in my present concrete circumstances, and can be certain that I am. That is why all the obstacles in himself of which Ignatius wrote in no way disheartened him. "For my part," he wrote, "I am persuaded that both before and after, I am only an obstacle [to what God wishes to work]; and seeing that I cannot attribute to myself anything which appears to be good brings increased contentment and spiritual joy."[37] All his confidence in finding God's will as well as in the value of his apostolic work rested ultimately on faith in God's love and power, not on trust in his own good dispositions and efforts and freedom from impediments. This is a cause of contentment and joy to him.

---

[37] Ibid.

An Appreciation of Ignatius' Thought on Conviction regarding God's Will

Ignatius' answer to the question whether we can find God's will with justifiable certainty might seem, at first hearing, to be pious but simplistic and unrealistic, an answer which does not take into account the real complexity and subtlety of the problem. But behind the apparently simplistic answer, we have found a subtle line of thought which is firmly founded on Gospel teaching and can meet all the objections raised against it by anyone with Christian faith. It is not only comprehensive of, and coherent with, all the other elements in his theology of discernment, but it also integrates them in admirable balance, without diminishing or exaggerating any of them. It stresses the universal call to discern God's will but does so within the limits of human elective discernment. It stresses the boundless trust we should have in God's guidance, while stressing also the necessity of doing our utmost to be open to his influence and to search for his will in all the ways we can. It takes account of the ideal which we must with utmost effort strive to approach in fulfilling the conditions of openness and searching, while also taking realistic and compassionate account of human actuality; of the concrete limitations beyond our present control which we all find in varying degrees in ourselves and in our situations; of our spiritual, rational, and emotional weakness at the present stage of growth; of the unavoidable distractions and demands on our time; of our physical weariness, and so on.

By giving these apparently conflicting factors their full value and yet holding them in fruitful tension, Ignatius' thought on the trustworthiness of discerning God's will remains at a great distance from either of the extreme positions described above. In his thought, reaching a justified conviction of God's will for the greater glory through sound discernment is not so demanding that any sincere Christian is excluded from doing it; but it is demanding of all that anyone in his present state of growth and present circumstances can give of faith, hope, charity, prayer, time, concentration, patience, energy, and willingness to consult others more learned and more experienced than self, willingness to learn more about how to discern God's will as opportunity offers, willingness to defer important de-

311

cisions which can and should reasonably be deferred until one has better dispositions or more knowledge or more time and energy. It gives grounds for carrying out the decision courageously, energetically, perseveringly, with a conviction of doing God's will for the greater glory while also remaining free to discern again and take a new, even opposite, direction whenever a new situation calls for doing so.

A Surprising Consequence: The Proportional Equality of All Discerners

This Ignatian way of thinking neither vulgarizes spiritual discernment of God's will nor reserves it to a psychological and spiritual elite. In fact, there seems to be a surprising logical implication of Ignatius' view (which I find no evidence that he ever drew explicitly); namely, the demands on all discerners of God's will are *proportionally* equal and the certainty of their conclusions is equally justifiable when each in his or her measure has done his or her best.[38] This means that you and I and the next person can have just as much confidence of finding God's will as Ignatius of Loyola, Teresa of Avila, Dominic, Catherine of Siena, and others who are less saintly than these but have very great practical intellects. All of us have the same ground for conviction, namely, belief that the Holy Spirit has led us. Justifiably to have that belief, we are all equally required to do the very best we reasonably can at the time to be open to the Spirit and to search. Although some have greater gifts of grace or nature, from those to whom more has been given more is required in order to have done their best. If someone with Ignatius' gifts did not have greater openness to the Spirit and carry out the process of discernment better than most others, he would not be doing his reasonable best. Consequently, there would be less reason to trust his conclusion than there would be to trust the conclusion reached by someone much less gifted who is doing his or her very best.

Lest what has just been said be misunderstood, several cautions

---

[38] This assertion will surely sound ridiculous unless the reader remembers that the conclusion of a discernment is limited to what God wills this individual freely to choose to intend at present (see above, p. 66) and that certainty about the truth of the conclusion does not imply certainty about the truth of the premises or about the correctness of the logical connection of the conclusion with the premises. (See above, pp. 290–294.)

are needed. First, our proportional equality does not mean that we should deny our need to choose gifted, learned, experienced, and saintly persons to hold positions in which discernments have to be made which have direct and serious consequences for others' lives, for instance, administrators, religious superiors, chapter members, and so on. Not to choose such persons would be a failure to do our best as a group. Second, part of doing one's best, even the greatest part for some, may mean seeking advice from those more learned, experienced, and gifted. Third, what has been said does not conflict with Ignatius' explicit advice not to accept many people for the Spiritual Exercises beyond the "first week."[39] To discern God's will is one thing; it is quite another to do so within the Spiritual Exercises, with their demands for intelligence, physical and mental endurance, emotional balance, time, and promise of great fruit for God's glory. Even those who are fit for, and have made, the Spiritual Exercises must make most of their discernments before and after that experience in a way that may not measure up to the ideal situation during the election in the Spiritual Exercises. In these other situations they can only do their best.

What about a person who loves God with a very pure heart, who wants to do his will always in everything, but to whom it does not even occur in many situations to wonder which alternative for choice is more for God's glory when every alternative is plainly for his glory? There are, it would seem, many such persons and many such situations. Should we believe that whatever they choose, God will see to it that their choices are for the greater glory even though they do not know it? Ignatius' teaching upon the fundamental will of God regarding human life seems to require an affirmative answer to that question. Such an opinion does not imply the uselessness of learning all one can about how to discern God's will and of giving the effort and time that discernment requires. To think it does would show a rather complete failure to understand most of what is in this book.

A Final Word: Concrete Practical Certainty

The foregoing answer to the question of what Ignatius thought

---

[39] *SpEx*, [18], and see also *Directorium Patri Vitoria Dictatum*, [1] (*DirSpEx*MHSJ, p. 90).

on the possibility of discerning God's will with certainty may fail to convince some students of Ignatius. Others may be willing to accept my answer but not be convinced that Ignatius' way of thinking is true. Either or both of these groups may find satisfaction in the answer to a somewhat-different question. This question does not ask whether I can have certainty or only probability regarding the truth of the conclusion reached by the discernment process. Rather, it asks whether, no matter how I answer that question, I can still be certain how I should choose. After making my best efforts to be open to God's spirit and to seek out what is for the greater glory, can I, even if I arrive only at what seems to be more probably God's will, still justifiably conclude with certainty that God wills for me to choose what seems more probably his will? Unless he is going to be inconsistent with the basic Christian principle which he sees as the controlling principle of discernment and choice, Ignatius' answer to this question clearly must be affirmative.

My choice, Ignatius says, must be motivated solely or at least predominantly by pure love of God and of my neighbor and myself in God, love "from above."[40] If my discernment reaches the conclusion that one alternative for choice is more probably God's will, more probably for his greater glory in us, a pure love could not move me to choose any other alternative. That I am careful to choose only among alternatives all of which are in themselves for God's glory (or at least indifferent) shows some love, in some cases even notable love for God and neighbor. But to choose among those alternatives one that I judge to be less probably for the greater glory shows some failure of pure charity; some other less compelling motive has to be operating and in conflict with pure charity. It follows then that, even though the evidence I have justifies only a probable conclusion about what is for the greater glory, nevertheless I can be certain that God wills for me to choose in accordance with what appears to me a greater probability. In other words, I have a practical certainty about what God wills for me to choose in this concrete situation of uncertainty about the truth of my conclusion to the discernment. To set this certainty apart from any certainty

---

[40] *SpEx*, [84], and see above, pp. 73–77.

about the truth of that conclusion, let us reserve for it the name "concrete practical certainty."

Even if one believes that such certitude of God's will is the best that can be hoped for in the kind of situations for choice with which Ignatius is concerned, all that he has said about openness to the Spirit and about the times for, and the mode of, seeking God's will retains its full value. For the probable judgment in accord with which I am certain God wills for me to choose draws its probability not only from the evidence but also and mainly from belief that the Holy Spirit has probably guided me to this judgment. That belief, in turn, presupposes believing with at least solid probability that I have fulfilled the essential conditions for sound discernment.

Appendix A
Karl Rahner's
Interpretation of Ignatian
Discernment of God's Will

*N*o one in the last quarter of a century has influenced thought on Ignatian discernment of God's will as much as Karl Rahner through his essay "The Logic of Concrete Individual Knowledge in Ignatius Loyola."[1] He has written some other pages on this topic, but nothing that adds anything of great importance to that essay. Although I have made copious references to Rahner's essay and briefly expounded some parts of it in this study, because of his importance it still seems fitting to give a brief ordered statement of the main elements in his interpretation of Ignatian discernment of

---

[1] *Dynamic Element*, pp. 84–170.

316

God's will. I do so for the sake of those who are not familiar with his essay or have not had time to work through an egregiously difficult piece of writing. Such a statement will provide a framework within which to place any particular element of Rahner's interpretation which comes up in relation to one or other issue discussed in this book. It will also provide an occasion to bring together briefly the main differences between my interpretation and Rahner's.

Before beginning, however, there is a problem that needs some comment: how to read Rahner's essay? The title of the essay as given above from the English translation is an abbreviation of the original German title, which in a precise literal translation would read: "The Ignatian Logic of Existential Knowledge: Some Theological Problems in the Rules for Making an Election in St. Ignatius' *Spiritual Exercises*."[2] This title indicates more accurately than the abbreviated one in the English translation what appears to have been Rahner's intention when he was writing the essay, namely, merely to propound some questions for theologians regarding Ignatius' teaching in the *Spiritual Exercises*. This limited intention Rahner insisted on at least three times in his essay, remarking that, if he seemed to make assertions more often than he propounded questions, he was doing so simply to avoid the monotony of repeatedly asking questions.[3]

Nevertheless, right from the start this express intention was ignored by readers, and his essay was universally taken to be proposing an impressive new interpretation of Ignatius, even a "major breakthrough in the theology of the *Spiritual Exercises*."[4] Rahner himself came to accept this way of reading his essay.[5] Consequently, throughout this book and now in this Appendix, I have accepted Rahner's essay as not merely propounding questions or even making a number of assertions but as presenting a carefully worked out,

---

[2] See the editor's note in *Ignatius Loyola: His Personality and Spiritual Heritage*, p. 280.

[3] *Dynamic Element*, pp. 89 (note 3), 169. See also Jules Toner, *A Commentary*, pp. 301–302.

[4] Avery Dulles, "Finding God's Will," *Woodstock Letters* 114 (Spring 1965), p. 152.

[5] Rahner's "Foreword" to Harvey Egan's *Mystical Horizon*, pp. xiii–xiv, and his way of responding to some criticisms by Avery Dulles (see *Ignatius Loyola: His Personality and Spiritual Heritage*, pp. 290–293) show that he accepts without demur the assumption of these authors that he has presented not merely some questions but a more or less complete and coherent interpretation of the main lines of Ignatian discernment of God's will.

interiorly coherent interpretation of St. Ignatius' teaching on discernment in the *Spiritual Exercises*.

Main Steps in Rahner's Interpretation

Here are what seem to me the main elements in Rahner's interpretation. In stating them, as also in noting the contrasts with my own interpretation, I shall not explain again what I have already explained in this volume or elsewhere. It will be enough to give references to where such explanations can be found.

1. Consolation without previous cause is the first principle, the *sine qua non*, of all discernment of spirits and discernment of God's will.[6]

2. Therefore, all Ignatian discernment of God's will is in ultimate analysis second-time discernment. The first-time election, says Rahner, is only the "limiting case" of the second mode of election[7] and is mentioned by Ignatius more for systematic completeness than for its practical importance.[8]

The third mode of election, he asserts, is subsidiary to, prepares for, tends to return to, and is an intrinsic element of, the second mode of election; apart from its relationship to the second mode, the third mode has no positive value for finding God's will.[9] In it, no positive assistance from the Holy Spirit is given;[10] rather, the discerner is left with only "the modest self-help of rational reflection,"[11] and must "fend for himself."[12]

3. The time for seeking God's will in the second mode of election is not the time of actual consolation without previous cause in its pure form. During such consolation, Rahner says, there can be no thought about a finite object of choice, no inclination to, or counsel regarding any act to be done;[13] and, therefore, no discernment process can be carried out during the consolation. The time

---

[6] *Dynamic Element*, pp. 130–131, 158, 160, 164, 167. See also Jules Toner, *A Commentary*, pp. 294–299.

[7] *Dynamic Element*, p. 106.

[8] Ibid., p. 128, note 25.

[9] Ibid., pp. 103, 105–106, 169.

[10] Ibid., p. 97.

[11] Ibid., p. 105.

[12] Ibid., p. 168.

[13] Ibid., pp. 158–160.

for that process is rather during "the time immediately following"[14] the pure consolation without previous cause. At that time, according to Rahner, the consolation is still actual but is no longer pure; it is now a consolation "of the second degree," mixed with thoughts and impulses which have finite objects.[15] Only in this time immediately after pure consolation without previous cause is it possible to carry on discernment of God's will.[16]

4. What is the discernment process which is carried out during this time?

> . . . in this election of the second mode what is in question must be that by frequently confronting the object of election with the fundamental consolation, the experimental test is made whether the two phenomena are in harmony, mutually cohere, whether the will to the object of election under scrutiny leaves intact that pure openness to God in the supernatural experience of transcendence and even supports and augments it or weakens or obscures it; whether a synthesis of these two attitudes, pure receptivity to God (as concretely achieved, not as a theoretical principle and proposition) and the will to this limited finite object of decision produces "peace," "tranquility," "quiet," so that true gladness and spiritual joy ensue, that is, the joy of pure, free, undistorted transcendence; or whether instead of smoothness, gentleness and sweetness, sharpness, tumult and disturbance arise (n. 335).[17]

In this passage "fundamental consolation" is the original consolation without previous cause which "is still operating even if no longer in its pure form."[18] In his transcendental theology Rahner conceives of such consolation as "pure openness to God in the

---

[14] *SpEx*, [336], and see *Dynamic Element*, pp. 158–160.
[15] *Dynamic Element*, p. 160.
[16] Ibid., pp. 160–162.
[17] Ibid., p. 158.
[18] Ibid., p. 160.

supernatural experience of transcendence.''[19] Note, then, that for Rahner it is neither the experience of pure consolation without previous cause nor even the immediately following consolation of second degree nor any volitional impulse toward a course of action which originates with and from within the consolation—it is none of these which constitutes evidence of God's will; it is, rather, the experience of harmony, the coherence of the consolation and the discerner's own proposal when these are brought into confrontation.

Contrast of Rahner's Interpretation with Mine

My study of Ignatius' writing has led me to conclusions which sharply contrast with each of the above main elements in Rahner's interpretation.

1. I am unable to find in Ignatius' writing any evidence that he thought consolation without previous cause is the first principle of all discernment of spirits and of God's will, and I find in Karl Rahner's essay no indication of any such evidence. Rather, I find that such an opinion conflicts with what Ignatius taught.[20]

2. In contrast with Rahner's opinion that all Ignatian discernment of God's will is ultimately reducible to second-time discernment, I have found: that Ignatius presented each mode as fully distinct from the other two and able to function autonomously, that is, as an adequate way in itself of seeking and finding God's will,[21] although his principles seem to call for using both the second and the third modes of discernment together whenever reasonably possible;[22] that the third mode, which Rahner denigrates and does not seem to understand,[23] was really highly valued by Ignatius as a way through which the Holy Spirit guides us to God's will even as he does by the first two modes;[24] that Ignatius himself used it as an

---

[19] See Jules Toner, *A Commentary*, pp. 295–298. See Harvey Egan's development of this experience of supernatural transcendence in *Mystical Horizon*, pp. 37–43.

[20] Jules Toner, *A Commentary*, pp. 303–313.

[21] See above, pp. 242–251.

[22] See above, pp. 251–254.

[23] See Avery Dulles' well-founded criticism of Rahner's understanding of third-time election as sketchy and almost rationalistic ("Finding God's Will," pp. 142, 144). In Rahner's response to Dulles' criticisms (see above, note 5 of this Appendix), he does not advert to this one. Rather he seems to continue speaking of third-time election as he did in the essay Dulles was criticising.

[24] See above, pp. 271–273.

320

autonomous way of finding God's will in many major decisions of his own life[25] and recommended it to be so used by others,[26] even for a vocation decision.[27]

3. It does not seem to me that what Rahner calls consolation of second degree is a spiritual consolation at all or has any value for discerning God's will.[28] Even making the supposition that the afterglow of consolation without previous cause is a genuine spiritual consolation, Rahner's understanding of it as *the* time for finding God's will in the second mode of discernment cannot stand. It does not fit with what Ignatius says about the second-time election.[29] His interpretation of paragraph [336] in the *Spiritual Exercises* as meaning that no communication from God regarding the object for choice is given during consolation without previous cause is in direct conflict with what Ignatius says there and elsewhere.[30]

4. Finally, even if we leave aside the questions whether the consolation for second-time election must be without previous cause and whether the election can take place only during the time immediately following pure consolation of this sort, it must still be said that the election process which Rahner describes does not correspond to what Ignatius says. Ignatius does not speak about bringing our own proposals to a consolation to see which one harmonizes with it and which causes discord. Rather, he tells us to observe to what God moves us when we are in consolation.[31] Rahner does not seem to see consolation as a matrix from within which the discerner experiences a volitional movement, a conative impulse, from God toward a proposed alternative. All Rahner seems to look for is harmony or disharmony between *our own* previously formed proposals and *our own* inclinations on the one hand and the afterglow of consolations (in second degree) on the others.

It is true that in his autograph directory Ignatius does recom-

---

[25] See above, pp. 257–265.

[26] See above, pp. 265–269.

[27] See above, pp. 269–271.

[28] Jules Toner, *A Commentary*, pp. 246–248.

[29] See above, chapter 9.

[30] Ibid., pp. 249–50, 298–299.

[31] See above, pp. 131–138; for the full meaning of Ignatius' directive, see the whole of chapter 9.

mend offering now one alternative and now another on different days to see what signs God will give.[32] But that is quite different from what Rahner proposes. Ignatius gives no indication that the offering must be made only in time of consolation, least of all in the time immediately following pure consolation without previous cause; and offering an alternative is not at all the same as bringing it into confrontation with an already-given consolation, least of all consolation without previous cause in second degree. Rather the offering is to be made with a hope of receiving some light through second-time experiences of consolation with impulse from God, that is, second-time experiences as described a few lines previously in this context.[33] In fact, in context, the greater sign of God's will of which Ignatius speaks could be not only second-time experience, but third-time reasons as well.[34]

---

[32] *DirAutog*, [21].

[33] Ibid., [18].

[34] See above, p. 154, note 77.

Appendix B
A Critical Evaluation of Thomas Green's Interpretation of Ignatian Discernment of God's Will

*T*homas Green's recent book on Ignatian discernment[1] is another work of the high quality we have come to expect from him as one of the premier spiritual writers of our time. It is a popular presentation, but based on serious scholarship and long experience. It is very broad in scope, treating as it does both discernment of spirits and discernment of God's will in the Old and New Testaments

---

[1] Thomas Green, S.J., *Weeds Among the Wheat* (Notre Dame, Indiana: Ave Maria Press, 1984).

and, more fully, in the writings of St. Ignatius of Loyola. Given the author's already soundly established reputation, this book will surely be widely read and will widely influence thought on Ignatian discernment.

For these reasons and the reason that the different interpretations of Ignatius' teaching in Green's work and in mine have very different consequences for practice, it seems advisable to present an account of these differences in some organized way for those who use or direct others in using Ignatian discernment of God's will. Let it be clear, however, that the differences between our interpretations and any consequent negative criticism by either of the other's view involve only a small portion of Green's book.

While Green rejects Karl Rahner's understanding of the role of consolation without previous cause in Ignatian discernment, it seems to me that, like many others, he gives consolation with previous cause much the same role that Rahner gave to consolation without previous cause.

Green's Interpretation of Ignatius' Three Modes of Election

The meaning Green gives to the term "discernment" is a key to his understanding of the three Ignatian modes of election. In the context of those modes, he gives that word an extremely narrow meaning. "It is the feelings we discern and not thoughts,"[2] Green says; "without the feelings, the whole process of discernment has no content."[3] Consequently, he denies that finding God's will in the first or third mode of Ignatian election is a discernment in the proper sense of the word. The first time, he says, is a "revelation time"; in it there is no reflective moment and nothing to discern.[4] The third, he says, is a "reasoning time," without any spiritual movements to be discerned.[5] The second time, therefore, "is the only one of the three times or occasions for making a good choice which Ignatius calls 'discernment' ";[6] for only in this time do we find feelings to be discerned.

---

[2] Ibid., p. 98.
[3] Ibid., p. 100.
[4] Ibid., pp. 83–84, 91.
[5] Ibid., p. 84.
[6] Ibid., p. 87.

Green does call decisions by the third mode of election "faith decisions,"[7] and says that "even though the presence of the Holy Spirit is not felt during them, we hope and trust that the Spirit is guiding our decision-making process." In Green's opinion, however, this trust is not very firm; for any decision reached by that process must be confirmed by second-time evidence (spiritual consolations); without that evidence "the direct, hoped-for guidance of the Spirit, should not suffice."[8]

Contrast and Evaluation

First of all, a comment on Green's use of the term "discernment." He is, I think, entirely correct in asserting that Ignatius never spoke of first-time or third-time discernment of God's will. But I think he is incorrect in asserting that Ignatius called the second time or the second-time election a discernment of God's will. At least I have not found any evidence of his doing so. Ignatius does, of course, say that the second mode of election includes feelings of consolation and desolation, as well as discernment of spirits. Discernment of spirits and discernment of God's will, however, are not the same thing; the former, as shown above, is only one step in the process of the second-time election.[9] If, then, we are going to use the word "discernment" in naming any Ignatian mode or modes of seeking and finding God's will, it is our word, not Ignatius'; and no argument about his thought can be based on this use of the word. In common current usage (and certainly in my own), "discernment" of God's will covers all that Ignatius means by "seeking God's will" or "making an election" and, in this current usage, can be applied correctly to any of the Ignatian ways of seeking God's will.

More important, beyond a mere difference in the use of a term but implied by that use, there are substantial disagreements between Green's interpretation and mine regarding Ignatius' teaching on the first-time and third-time ways of seeking and finding God's will.

Regarding the first-time election, whether it should or should not include a reflective moment after the first-time experience cannot

---

[7] Ibid.

[8] Ibid., p. 91.

[9] See above, chapter 9.

325

be satisfactorily decided on the basis of Ignatius' description in *Spiritual Exercises*, [175]. However, contrary to Green's understanding, I have given reasons based on what Ignatius says elsewhere for thinking that the first mode of election does need a reflective moment and is a discernment in the proper sense of the word.[10]

My major disagreement with Green is one regarding the third-time election. Green, like many others, thinks that this mode of election is to be used only if there are no consolations and desolations to interpret and that, when it is used, it is "incomplete" unless it ends up in the second mode.[11] His textual basis for saying this is the same as that given by Karl Rahner and others, namely, the final step in the third-time election.[12] There, Ignatius tells the person who has come to a tentative decision to seek divine confirmation for it. The argument based on this text makes two unfounded assumptions. First, this divine confirmation is assumed to be "the consolations and desolations of the second time."[13] This assumption is followed by another when Green (again like Karl Rahner and others) says that the step of seeking confirmation "can only mean . . . returning to the 'second time,' to discernment proper."[14] In other words, while we may sometimes have to make a decision by third-time reasoning alone, such a decision cannot have value as an independent mode of Ignatian election. In the thought of Ignatius, according to this interpretation, the third-time election is merely a way that leads to and depends on the second-time; the second-time election alone is said to be a true and trustworthy discernment. The difference between the third-time and the second-time elections, Green says, is the difference between listening to our own better judgment and listening to God's voice[15] or "the difference between guessing what my friend is thinking and hearing him *say* what he is thinking."[16]

In contrast with this way of understanding the third mode of election, I have pointed out above that Ignatius says nothing in step

---

[10] See above, pp. 121–127.
[11] *Weeds Among the Wheat*, pp. 88, 91, 98.
[12] Ibid., pp. 91, 98. See *SpEx*, [183] and above, pp. 236–241.
[13] Ibid., pp. 88, 98.
[14] Ibid., p. 91.
[15] Ibid., p. 87.
[16] Ibid., p. 88.

six of the third-time election[17] which would explicitly or even implicitly indicate that confirmation of the tentative decision is constituted always and only by experiences of spiritual consolation or desolation. Neither does he elsewhere; rather, he clearly indicates that there are several other forms of confirmation, including third-time reasons. What is more, Ignatius seeks confirmation of the second mode of election as well as the third, and there appears to be no necessity of actual confirmation in order justifiably to finalize the conclusion of an election in either of these modes. In short, the third-time election (even without confirmation by consolation and desolation or by anything else, for that matter) is just as autonomous as the second-time election.[18]

Regarding the second way of the third-time election (Ignatius does give two ways), it is not altogether clear to me how Green sees it; but his treatment gives me the impression that he sees the second as independent of the first.[19] If so, it should be noted that there is strong evidence that Ignatius saw the second way only as auxiliary to the first.[20]

As for the idea that the third-time election is merely a matter of natural reasoning reaching a guess about God's will, while the second-time election is more like hearing God say what he wills, there is some point to it, but also considerable misunderstanding. There is a point inasmuch as Ignatius considers genuine spiritual consolation a grace from God that serves to mark as also from God (at least with probability) an attraction to one of the alternatives for choice. However, this idea about the second-time and the third-time elections overlooks the fact that a second-time election is not merely a matter of experiencing spiritual consolations and, together with them, attraction to some alternative for choice. Such experiences are, as Green himself points out, merely data, the "raw material of discernment."[21]

Turning data into evidence involves a process of using natural reasoning: in applying the rules for discernment of spirits to the

---

[17] *SpEx* [183].

[18] The evidence for all these assertions can be found above, chapters 11 and 13.

[19] *Weeds Among the Wheat*, p. 86.

[20] See above, pp. 182–190.

[21] *Weeds Among the Wheat*, p. 88.

consolations in order to see if they are truly spiritual;[22] in recalling and examining the whole second-time experience to see if the volitional attraction came during the consolations and was integral with them; in weighing the evidence that withstands such critical reflection and judging when the weighed evidence justifies coming to a conclusion. In none of this reflective rational process is God saying to the person what his will is any more than in the faith-enlightened reasoning of the third mode. The reasoning in the second mode has different data and different principles for critical evaluation, but it is every bit as "natural" as the reasoning in the third mode and just as much subject to error.[23] On the basis of evidence, conclusions reached by both the second and third modes of election are only well-founded, intelligent guesses. If Ignatius has any certainty of finding God's will through discernment (and he does), that certainty rests ultimately, as I think to have shown, not on the evidence but on faith in God's guidance.[24]

The foregoing differences between the understanding of Ignatius' teaching on how to seek God's will which Thomas Green has proposed and the understanding I have proposed in this book have very great consequences for anyone practicing such discernment and, therefore, deserve very careful consideration by those who use or direct others in using the Ignatian method. On the other hand, I want to stress that my negative criticism applies to only a very small portion of Green's book.[25] There would be just cause for regret if anyone who agrees with my criticism should be thereby deterred from reading and recognizing the value of Green's book as a whole. (It may, of course, happen the other way around—which turn of events I might consider with more grievous regret!)

---

[22] Ibid., pp. 98–99. Green obviously sees the need for applying the rules for discernment of spirits, but does not see what seems to me to be the inescapable implication of that, namely, that the conclusion of a second-time election depends on natural reasoning just as much as the third-time election.

[23] Above, chapter 9 and pp. 272–273, 274–276, 277–280.

[24] Above, chapters 15–16.

[25] This is not to say that I have no other questions or difficulties (e.g., regarding Green's treatment of consolation without previous cause, his understanding of desolation in the dark night as described by John of the Cross). But even if my opinions on these matters should be right and Green's wrong (which I do not assume is so), these matters are immersed in a mass of wise writing which should not be missed by those interested in discernment.

BIBLIOGRAPHY

Primary Sources

Conclusiones Septem Sociorum. Series 3, vol. 1 of Monumenta Ignatiana, 9–14. Vol. 63 of Monumenta Historica Societatis Jesu. Rome: Historical Institute of the Society of Jesus, 1934.

Cons. See The Constitutions of the Society of Jesus, any edition.

ConsMHSJ. See Constitutiones Societatis Jesu.

ConsSJComm. See Ignatius of Loyola, Saint. *The Constitutions of the Society of Jesus.*

Constitutiones Societatis Jesu. 3rd series, vol. 1–3 of Monumenta Ignatiana. Vols. 63–65 of Monumenta Historica Societatis Jesu. Rome: Historical Institute of the Society of Jesus, 1934–1938.

Cordeses, Antonio. "Directorium." *DirSpExMHSJ,* 533–561.

Dávila, Gil González. "Annotationes." *DirSpExMHSJ,* 533–561.

"Deliberación sobre la pobreza." Ed. Iparraguirre, Ignacio, S.J. *Obras Completas de San Ignacio de Loyola.* Madrid: Biblioteca de Autores Cristianos, 1963, 297–299.

"Deliberatio Primorum Patrum." Series 3, vol. 1 of Monumenta Ignatiana, 1–7. Vol. 63 of Monumenta Historica Societatis Jesu. Rome: Historical Institute of the Society of Jesus, 1934.

DirAutog. See Directoria Ignatiana Autographa, in *DirSpExMHSJ.*

Directoria Exercitorum Spiritualium (1540–1599). Ed. Ignacio Iparraguirre, S.J. New ed., vol. 2 of Monumenta Ignatiana. Vol. 76 of Monumenta Historica Societatis Jesu. Rome: Historical Institute of the Society of Jesus, 1955.

Directoria Ignatiana Autographa. Directoria Exercitiorum Spiritualium (1540–1599). Ed. Ignacio Iparraguirre, S.J. 2nd series, new edition, vol. 2 of Monumenta Ignatiana, 70–79. Vol. 76 of Monumenta Historica Societatis Jesu. Rome: Historical Institute of the Society of Jesus, 1955.

"Directorium Patri Vitoria Dictatum." *DirSpExMHSJ,* 90–105.

Directory of the Spiritual Exercises of Our Holy Father Ignatius (Official Directory of 1599). London: The Manresa Press, 1925. *Also see Directoria Exercitiorum Spiritualium (1540–1599).*

DirSpExMHSJ. See Directoria Exercitiorum Spiritualium.

EppIgn. See Ignatius of Loyola, Saint. *Epistolæ et Instructiones.*

Fontes narrativi de S. Ignatio de Loyola et de Societatis Iesu initiis. Ed. Cándido de Dalmases, S.J., et al. 3 vols. Vols. 66, 73, and 85 of Monumenta Historica Societatis Jesu. Rome: Historical Institute of the Society of Jesus, 1943–1960.

Ignatius of Loyola, Saint. "Autobiografía." In Iparraguirre, *Obras Completas,* 89–159.

———. *The Constitutions of the Society of Jesus.* Trans. with introduction and commentary by George E. Ganss, S.J. St. Louis: The Institute of Jesuit Sources, 1970.

———. *Diario Espiritual (1544–1545).* In Iparraguirre, *Obras Completas,* 318–386.

———. *Epistolæ et Instructiones.* Ed. M. Lecina et al. 1st series, 12 vols. Monumenta Ignatiana. Monumenta Historica Societatis Jesu. Madrid: 1903–1911.

———. *Exercitia Spiritualia.* Ed. José Calveras, S.J., and Cándido de Dalmases, S.J. 2nd series, new edition, vol. 1 of Monumenta Ignatiana. Vol. 100 of Monumenta Historica Societatis Jesu. Rome: Historical Institute of the Society of Jesus, 1969.

———. *St. Ignatius' Own Story (Autobiografía).* Trans. William J. Young, S.J. Chicago: Loyola University Press, 1956.

———. *The Spiritual Journal of St. Ignatius Loyola (Diario Espiritual).* Trans. William J. Young, S.J. Woodstock, Md.: Woodstock College Press, 1958.

Iparraguirre, Ignacio, S.J., with Cándido de Dalmases, S.J., eds. *Obras Completas de San Ignacio de Loyola.* Madrid: Biblioteca de Autores Cristianos, 1963. A later edition of this work was published in 1977.

Letters of St. Ignatius of Loyola. Trans. William J. Young, S.J. Chicago: Loyola University Press, 1959.

LettersIgn. See Letters of St. Ignatius of Loyola.

MHSJ. *See* Monumenta Historica Societatis Jesu.

Miró, Diego. "Directoria." *DirSpExMHSJ,* 369–418.

Monumenta Historica Societatis Jesu. Madrid and Rome: Historical Institute of the Society of Jesus, 1894–.

Polanco, Juan Alonso de. "Directorium." *DirSpExMHSJ,* 274–328.

SpEx. See St. Ignatius of Loyola. *Exercitia Spiritualia,* any edition.

SpExMHSJTe. See Ignatius of Loyola, Saint. *Exercitia Spiritualia.*

Secondary Sources

Augustine, Saint. *Christian Instruction (De Doctrina Christiana)*. Trans. John Gavigan, O.S.A. Vol. 4 of The Writings of St. Augustine, 19–235. The Fathers of the Church. New York: Cima Publishing Co., 1947.

Bakker, Leo. *Freiheit und Erfahrung*. Wurzburg: Echter, 1970.

Bottereau, Georges, S.J. "La Confirmation divine d'apres le Journal Spirituel de Saint Ignace de Loyola." *Revue d'Ascétique et de Mystique* 43 (1967): 35–51.

Byron, William J., S.J. "Discernment and Poverty." *The Way*. Supplement no. 23 (Autumn 1974), 37–42.

Callahan, William R., S.J. "The Impact of Culture on Religious Values and Decision-Making." *Soundings*, 8–12. Washington, D.C.: Center of Concern, 1974.

Clancy, Thomas H., S.J. "Three Problems Concerning Obedience." *Review for Religious* 33, no. 3 (1974): 844–860.

Clémence, Jean. "Le discernment des esprits dans les Exercices spirituels de saint Ignace de Loyola." *Revue d'Ascétique et de Mystique* 27 (1951): 347–375; 28 (1952): 64–81.

Coathalem, Hervé, S.J. *Ignatian Insights*. Trans. Charles McCarthy, S.J. 2nd ed. Taichung, Taiwan: Kuanchi Press, 1971.

Delmage, Lewis, S.J. *Spiritual Exercises of St. Ignatius Loyola*. New York, 1968.

Dulles, Avery, S.J. "Finding God's Will." *Woodstock Letters* 94 (Spring 1965): 139–152.

———. "The Ignatian Experience as Reflected in the Spiritual Theology of Karl Rahner." *Philippine Studies* (1965), 471–491.

Dunne, Thomas A., S.J. "Models of Discernment." *The Way*. Supplement no. 23 (Autumn 1974), 18–26.

Egan, Harvey D., S.J. *The Spiritual Exercises and the Ignatian Mystical Horizon*. St. Louis: The Institute of Jesuit Sources, 1976.

English, John, S.J. *Spiritual Freedom*. Guelph, Ontario: Loyola House, 1973.

Fessard, Gaston, S.J. *La dialectique des Exercices de saint Ignace de Loyola*. Paris, 1956, 1966.

Fleming, David L., S.J. *The Spiritual Exercises of St. Ignatius: A Literal Translation and a Contemporary Reading*. St. Louis: The Institute of Jesuit Sources, 1978.

Fortman, Edmund J., S.J. *Everlasting Life after Death*. New York: Alba House, 1976.

Futrell, John C., S.J. "Ignatian Discernment." *Studies in the Spirituality of Jesuits* 2, no. 2 (April 1970).

———. *Making an Apostolic Community of Love*. St. Louis: The Institute of Jesuit Sources, 1970.

Gagliardi, Achille, S.J. *Commentarii seu Explanationes in Exercitia Spiritualia Sancti Patris Ignatii de Loyola*. Desclée de Brouwer et Soc., 1882.

Ganss, George E., ed. *Jesuit Religious Life Today*. St. Louis: The Institute of Jesuit Sources, 1977.

Gelpi, Donald L., S.J. *Pentecostalism: A Theological Viewpoint*. New York: Paulist Press, 1971.

Gil, Daniel, S.J. *La consolación sin causa precedente*. Rome: Centrum Ignatianum Spiritualitatis, 1971.

Giuliani, Maurice, S.J. "Movements of the Spirit." *Finding God in All Things*. Trans. William J. Young, S.J. Chicago: Henry Regnery Company, 1958.

Green, Thomas. *Weeds Among the Wheat*. Notre Dame, Indiana: Ave Maria Press, 1984.

Guillet, Jacques, S.J. *Discernment of Spirits*. Trans. Sr. Innocentia Richards. Collegeville, Minn.: The Liturgical Press, 1970. Originally published as "Discernment des esprits." *Dictionnaire de Spiritualité Ascétique et Mystique*. Vol. 3. Paris, 1957.

Haas, Adolf, S.J. "The Mysticism of St. Ignatius according to His *Spiritual Diary*." *Ignatius Loyola, His Personality and Spiritual Heritage, 1556–1596*. Ed. Friedrich Wulf, S.J., 164–199. St. Louis: The Institute of Jesuit Sources, 1977.

Hauser, Richard J., S.J. *Moving in the Spirit: Becoming a Contemplative in Action*. New York: Paulist Press, 1986.

King, Nicholas. "Ignatius Loyola and Decision-Making." *The Way*. Supplement no. 24 (Spring 1975), 46–57.

Kyne, Michael, S.J. "Discernment of Spirits and Christian Growth." *The Way*. Supplement no. 26 (May 1968), 20–26.

MACL. *See* Futrell, John C. *Making an Apostolic Community of Love*.

Margerie, Bertrand de, S.J. *Theological Retreat*. Chicago: Franciscan Herald Press, 1976.

McKenzie, John L. *Dictionary of the Bible*. Milwaukee: Bruce, 1965.

Murphy, Laurence J., S.J. "Psychological Problems of Christian Choice." *The Way*. Supplement no. 24 (Spring 1975), 26–35.

Nee, Watchman. *The Spiritual Man*. Trans. Stephen Kaung. New York: Christian Fellowship Publishers, 1968.

Newman, John Henry Cardinal. *Grammar of Assent*. Garden City, N.Y.: Image Books, 1955.

O'Brien, Elmer. *Varieties of Mystical Experience*. New York: Holt, Rinehart and Winston, 1964.

O'Leary, Brian. *The Discernment of Spirits in the "Memoriale" of Blessed Peter Favre*. *The Way*. Supplement no. 35 (Spring 1979).

———. "God and Evil Spirits." *The Way* 15, no. 3 (July 1975): 174–182.

Ochs, Robert, S.J. *God Is More Present Than You Think*. New York: Paulist Press, 1970.

Orsy, Ladislas, S.J. *Probing the Spirit*. Denville, New Jersey: Dimension Books, 1976.

———. "Toward a Theological Evaluation of Communal Discernment." *Studies in the Spirituality of Jesuits* 5, no. 5 (1973).

Osuna, Javier, S.J. *Friends in the Lord*. Trans. Nicholas King, S.J. *The Way*, series 3 (1974).

Peters, William, S.J. *The Spiritual Exercises of St. Ignatius: Exposition and Interpretation*. Jersey City, N.J.: Program to Adapt the Spiritual Exercises, 1967; reprint, Rome: Centrum Ignatianum Spiritualitatis, 1978.

Poulain, A., S.J. *The Graces of Interior Prayer*. Westminster, Vermont: Celtic Cross Books, 1978.

Pousset, Edouard, S.J. *Life in Faith and Freedom: An Essay Presenting Gaston Fessard's Analysis of the Dialectic of the Spiritual Exercises of St. Ignatius.* Trans. and ed. Eugene L. Donahue, S.J. St. Louis: The Institute of Jesuit Sources, 1980.

Puhl, Louis J., S.J. *The Spiritual Exercises of St. Ignatius.* Westminster, Md. 1951; reprint, Chicago: Loyola University Press, 1968.

Purcell, Mary. *The First Jesuit.* Westminster, Md.: Newman, 1957.

Quay, Paul, S.J. "God's Call and Man's Response." *Review for Religious* 33, no. 5 (1974): 1062–1099.

Rahner, Hugo, S.J. *Ignatius the Theologian.* Trans. Michael Barry. New York: Herder and Herder, 1968.

———. *The Vision of St. Ignatius in the Chapel of La Storta.* 2nd ed. Rome: Centrum Ignatianum Spiritualitatis, 1979.

Rahner, Karl, S.J. "Comments by Karl Rahner on Questions Raised by Avery Dulles, S.J." *Ignatius of Loyola: His Personality and Spiritual Heritage, 1556–1956.* Ed. Friedrich Wulf, S.J., trans. James M. Quigley, S.J., 290–293. St. Louis: The Institute of Jesuit Sources, 1977.

———. *The Dynamic Element in the Church.* New York: Herder and Herder, 1964.

———. "The Logic of the Concrete Individual Knowledge in Ignatius Loyola." *Dynamic Element in the Church.* New York: Herder and Herder, 1964.

Rakoczy, Susan. "The Structures of Discernment Processes and the Meaning of Discernment Language in Published U.S. Catholic Literature, 1965–1978: An Analysis." Unpublished dissertation, School of Religious Studies of the Catholic University of America, Washington, D.C., 1980.

Roi, Jacques, S.J. "L'election d'apres Saint Ignace." *Revue d'Ascétique et de Mystique* 38 (1962): 305–323.

Roustang, François, S.J. *Growth in the Spirit.* Trans. Kathleen Pond. New York: Sheed and Ward, 1966.

Stierli, Josef, S.J. "Ignatian Prayer: Seeking God in All Things." *Ignatius of Loyola, His Personality and Spiritual Heritage, 1556–1956.* Ed. Friedrich Wulf, S.J., 135–163. St. Louis: The Institute of Jesuit Sources, 1977.

Thomas Aquinas, Saint. *Summa Theologiæ.* 4 vols. Ottawa, Canada, 1951.

Toner, Jules, S.J. *A Commentary on St. Ignatius' Rules for the Discernment of Spirits.* St. Louis: The Institute of Jesuit Sources, 1982.

———. "The Deliberation That Started the Jesuits." *Studies in the Spirituality of Jesuits* 6, no. 4 (June 1974).

———. *The Experience of Love.* Washington, D.C.: Corpus Books, 1968.

———. "A Method for Communal Discernment of God's Will." *Studies in the Spirituality of Jesuits* 3, no. 4 (September 1971).

Vries, Piet Penning de, S.J. *Discernment of Spirits.* Trans. W. Dudok Van Heel. New York: Exposition Press, 1973.

Walsh, James, S.J. "Discernment of Spirits." *The Way.* Supplement no. 16 (Summer 1972), 54–66.

INDEX OF PERSONS

Detailed Table of Contents

337